Moms'
Ultimate Guide
to the
Tween Girl
World

Other Books by Nancy Rue

FOR TWEENS

On Authenticity

Everybody Tells Me to Be Myself, But I Don't Know Who I Am

Dear Nancy

The It's MY Life Book

The Creativity Book

The Uniquely Me Book

The Fun-Finder Book

The Sophie Series, fiction, Books 1–12

The Lily Series, fiction, Books 1–14

On Beauty

The Skin You're In

Dear Nancy

The Beauty Book

Here's Lily, fiction, Lily Series Book 1

The Lucy Novels, fiction, Books 1–4

On the Changing Body

Body Talk

Dear Nancy

The Body Book

Lily Robbins, M.D., fiction, Lily Series Book 2

Sophie's Secret, fiction, Sophie Series, Book 2

Lucy Out of Bounds, Lucy Novels, Book 2

On Relationships

Girl Politics: Friends, Cliques, and Really Mean Chicks

Dear Nancy

The Buddy Book

The Best Bash Book

The Blurry Rules Book

The Lily Series, fiction, Books 1–14

The Sophie Series, fiction, Books 1–12

The Lucy Novels, fiction, Books 1–4

On Spiritual Formation

The FaithGirlz Bible (edited by Nancy Rue)

That is SO Me: A One-Year FaithGirlz Devotional

The Year 'Round Holiday Book

The Values and Virtues Book

The Lily Series, fiction, Books 1–14

The Sophie Series, fiction, Books 1–12

The Lucy Series, fiction Books 1–4

For Teen Girls

Motorcycles, Sushi, and One Strange Book

Boyfriends, Burritos, and an Ocean of Trouble

Moms' Ultimate Guide
to the
Tween Girl World

Nancy Rue

ZONDERVAN®

ZONDERVAN.com/
AUTHORTRACKER
follow your favorite authors

We want to hear from you. Please send your comments about this book to us in care of zreview@zondervan.com. Thank you.

ZONDERVAN

Moms' Ultimate Guide to the Tween Girl World
Copyright © 2010 by Nancy Rue

This title is also available as a Zondervan ebook.
Visit www.zondervan.com/ebooks.

This title is also available in a Zondervan audio edition.
Visit www.zondervan.fm.

Requests for information should be addressed to:

Zondervan, *Grand Rapids, Michigan 49530*

Library of Congress Cataloging-in-Publication Data

Rue, Nancy N.
    Moms' ultimate guide to the tween girl world / by Nancy Rue.
       p.   cm.
    Includes bibliographical references and index.
    ISBN 978-0-310-28474-1 (softcover)
      1. Mothers and daughters—Religious aspects—Christianity. 2. Daughters—Religious life.
  3. Girls—Religious life. 4. Preteens—Religious life. I. Title.
    BV4529.18.R84   2010
    248.8'45—dc22   2010003117

All Scripture quotations, unless otherwise indicated, are taken from *The Message*. Copyright © by Eugene H. Peterson 1993, 1994, 1995, 1996, 2000, 2001, 2002. Used by permission of NavPress Publishing Group.

Any Internet addresses (websites, blogs, etc.) and telephone numbers printed in this book are offered as a resource. They are not intended in any way to be or imply an endorsement by Zondervan, nor does Zondervan vouch for the content of these sites and numbers for the life of this book.

Published in association with the literary agency of Alive Communications, Inc., 7680 Goddard Street, Suite 200, Colorado Springs, CO 80920. www.alivecommunications.com

Cover design: Merit Creative Design
Cover photography: Claire Artman / Veer
Butterfly illustrations: Andrea Venanzi
Interior design: Sherri L. Hoffman

Printed in the United States of America

10 11 12 13 14 15 /DCI/ 24 23 22 21 20 19 18 17 16 15 14 13 12 11 10 9 8 7 6 5 4 3 2 1

For all the mothers of mini-women . . .
and, of course, for Marijean

Contents

Why Do I Need an Ultimate Guide?

If you ask a seven-year-old girl what she would like to have on her pizza, she will undoubtedly tell you. In detail. Leaving nothing to chance lest she should be confronted with something gross and disgusting and icky. Ewww.

If you ask a twelve-year-old girl what she would like to have on her pizza, she will more than likely roll her eyes or stuff her hair behind her ears or make some other pubescently awkward gesture and say, "I don't know." Or, perhaps the more hip version: "Whatever."

If you ask a sixteen-year-old girl what she would like to have on her pizza, she will probably give you the now-polished version of that same gesture and say, "What would *you* like to have on our pizza?"[1]

What happens to girls between the ages of eight and twelve? Before they hit that pivotal period, they were so sure of who they were and what they wanted and didn't hesitate to tell you whether you wanted to hear it or not. What goes on in those five years? What makes sweet little baby girlfriends gradually lose their minds and become teenagers who, despite their show of independence, can't choose a pizza topping without taking a poll of their peers?

What happens is tween-hood. It isn't the innocent early childhood that, tantrums and potty training notwithstanding, was relatively easy to understand. And it isn't adolescence which nobody understands, though some misguided souls have tried.

This age eight-to-twelve period in our daughters' lives didn't even have a name until about ten years ago when the advertising world came up with the term *tween*. It's clever, but it implies that its members are merely sandwiched between two more important and infinitely more interesting stages of their lives. Freudian psychologists even used to call it "the latent period," and unfortunately a lot of people still see it that way. Tweens are old enough to take themselves to the restroom and, speaking of sandwiches, make their own, but we don't yet have to worry about them wrecking the family car or piercing their tongues. Nice. Let's take a rest period before your household turns into WWE.

If you were one of those people who thought that, you wouldn't have picked up this book. I'm betting that you're a mom who knows her daughter is not just "latent," or simply "between" one thing and another, or silently gearing up to drive you nuts the minute she turns thirteen. You know that she:

- may or may not brush her hair on a regular basis, but she already knows that what she looks like makes a difference in how people treat her.
- is in possession of a body that's changing right before her eyes, or is wondering why hers isn't changing when "everybody else's" is.
- would almost lay down her life, or at least her favorite hoodie, for that center of her universe, the BFF (for the uninitiated, that's Best Friend Forever).
- will probably roll her eyes right up into her head if you say to her, "Just be yourself and you'll be fine," because she's discovering that who she thought "herself" was is now in question.

That's your tween girl—a rapidly transforming mini-woman, if you will. And yet like all human beings in transition, she's not on a linear track. Have you noticed that:

- one day she wants no part of your advice, and the next she's in your lap begging for help?
- one hour she's playing dress-up with her little sister, and the next she has a sign on her door that reads NO SIBLINGS ALLOWED?
- one minute she wants to operate the stove or the ATV or the chain saw, and the next she's afraid to ask a waiter for a glass of water?

Out of the Mouths of
Mini-Women

"The only thing I want in my life is this: for Mom and me to be close. But I can't tell my mom how I feel, and I feel alone. Can you PLEASE help me?"

age 12

- one second she's asking you to drop her at the corner so her friends won't see what you're wearing (Mo-om!), and the next she wants to borrow that cool necklace you just bought?
- one nano-second she doesn't get why you won't let her stay alone in the house at night and the next she's climbing into your bed, convinced the boogeyman is alive and well and headed down the hall?

Her world is exciting and confusing, inside and out, and it's made more so by the society she lives in. That is probably one of the biggest reasons you've opened this book. You know that as a Millennial (born between 1982 and 2002) your mini-woman is growing up far differently than you did. The *average* tween girl today:

- enters puberty at age nine, eight if she's African-American (a full year earlier than in 1960).
- prefers the same television programming as most fourteen-year-olds,[2] not good news since 70 percent of what's available for viewing contains sexual content.[3]
- spends ten hours a week at her computer, with seven of those taken up with computer games, surfing the Web, and emailing friends[4] (not homework, as she claims!).
- has a 33 percent chance of having a cell phone by age eleven.[5]
- spends ten hours a week texting.[6]
- influences 30 percent of her family's purchases.[7]
- at age twelve is likely to have higher levels of aggressive fantasies than boys of the same age[8] (who admittedly don't have to have fantasies because they are out there actually duking it out).
- has a 25 percent chance of being physically bullied and a 45 percent chance of being cyber bullied by her peers.[9]
- can pick up a magazine designed for girls ages ten to fourteen and read:

"Can Your Crush Go the Distance?"
"Get Your Ultimate Bikini Belly"
"Boobology Basics"
"Love Your Butt"

- has a one in four chance of being sexually molested by the time she's 18.[10]
- is 75 percent more likely to commit suicide before she is fourteen than her counterparts in 2004.[11]
- refers to her childhood in the past tense. (And who wouldn't with those statistics?)

The world she has to navigate has been altered so drastically since you were her age, it's hardly recognizable as the same place. In this foreign-to-you land she is trying to navigate she is keenly aware of the breaking of public trust. Tweens on the upper end of the age range can remember 9/11, and all of them are living in the wake of it. Even those who can't tell you what insider trading or subprime lending is are aware that somebody messed up someplace and now people's moms and dads don't have jobs.

She is also likely to feel rather entitled. Many tweens are chauffeured everywhere, given every possible opportunity, and consistently entertained. That's what good parents do these days, and many kids expect it.

Her time is probably tightly structured. She may have to squeeze free play in between dance classes, soccer practice, and a Happy Meal in the back of the SUV on the way to Wednesday night church. When she does have down time, the increasing parental fear of predators makes playing outdoors with friends or (gasp) on her own completely out of the question. According to psychiatrist Stuart Brown (Baylor), who has studied the importance of play for forty-two years, "the lack of opportunities for unstructured, imaginative play can keep children from growing into happy, well-adjusted adults."[12] Free play—not a play date with a full agenda of activities planned by moms—is critical for developing problem-solving and stress-reducing skills.

Your daughter is no doubt a digital native. The computer, the cell phone, and the MP3 player, to name only a few, have become the constant companions of our tweens. Even if your daughter owns none of the above, she undoubtedly has acquaintances who do and may secretly covet these instruments of belonging.

Many of our tweens can't find their way to the grocery store, the church, or their BFF's house because their portable device keeps them glued to a tiny screen while their moms are driving them to those places. They think of the Internet as a neighborhood, and they have virtual friends there. Surreal to those of us not on Facebook — perfectly normal to them. And if your tween daughter isn't technically savvy — well, there's one more area where anxiety can soar and self-worth can plummet.

If she's like the majority of tweens, she lives with parents who may themselves be digitally focused. No judgment intended here — just some facts. Sixty-seven percent of moms check their email three to four times a day. The average dad spends nineteen hours a week playing video games or surfing the Net.[13] I personally seldom see a young mother without a cell phone on her person — not just in her purse, but inserted in her ear or clutched in her hand. I don't doubt that her thumbs go through the motions of texting while she sleeps.

Needless to say (but let's do), the tween girl lives in a world of accelerated change with few cultural or social traditions, norms, and support to help her feel secure. Nothing in the world is the same as it was last year or last month or sometimes last week, just when she needs for it to be. So she looks for a deeper emotional connection with her parents — and you're in the midst of dealing with that schedule overload and economic insecurity and post-modern iffiness yourself. How are you supposed to provide centering, connecting events for your family when it's all you can do to get them from school to softball practice to Awana to homework to bed before midnight without screaming, "Shut up — I'm sick of all of you!"

Now, before you toss this book in the trash (who needs this downer, right?), not all of the change that has happened in our culture since you were ten has been negative. As a society we have a much better understanding of mental health than we did twenty-five years ago (good news for those of us being driven crazy by parenthood!). Thanks to the Internet and social networking, we can find anything and anyone we want right at the computer terminals found in most of our households — everything from how to help our kids with ADHD to where there might be a G-rated movie playing this weekend (if indeed such a thing still exists). We know more about the benefits of nutrition, exercise ... even chocolate. We've elected an African-American president, which, no matter what your politics, is a sign that we are making progress in overcoming prejudice and bigotry. Even a fresh look at Christianity has transformed many pew potatoes into true disciples who are working to solve the problems Jesus cares about. Many Christians in the generation your tween will follow (those brought up in the eighties and nineties) are showing a greater awareness of the world, says Reverend Romal Tune, CEO of the Washington, DC-based Clergy Strategic Alliances. "They're connecting through Facebook and using scripture to support their causes on social issues ...The church will in 20 years not be defined by a building that people attend for worship on Sunday morning, but by how Christians treat people in the world.[14]

Yet still you worry. Old seems to be happening sooner, a phenomenon paraphrased by marketers as K.G.O.Y — Kids Growing Older Younger.[15] Ten, "they" say, is the new fifteen. You go shopping for clothes with your eight-year-old and find only smaller versions of what the teenagers are (barely) wearing. Your eleven-year-old, like 54 percent of her same-age peers, doesn't think she's too young to wear makeup.[16] Your nine-year-old is convinced she's grossly overweight. Your ten-year-old is in tears because her BFF stole the boy *she* was "going out with" (though no one knows where it is they were going or how they planned to get there).

Worrying because that's what mothers do is one thing. Just try and stop us, right? But the lie-awake-at-night kind of concern the tween world presents us with shouldn't rob us of the joy of raising daughters. And it doesn't have to.

Tween Positives

In my thirty-five years of teaching, writing for, hanging out with, and raising one of these, my favorite brand of kid, I have come to know many positive, joyous, soul-boosting things about the tween years.

For example, in the tween years, your daughter is still more likely to look to you for guidance, security, and all-out authority than she is to anyone else, including the all-knowing BFF (or group thereof). She wants you. She responds to you. She soaks you up like the proverbial sponge, especially when you aren't looking.[17]

Even while the continual movement toward adolescence teems beneath the surface, she is still a little girl in so many ways. She may roll her eyes and use "whatever" as every part of speech but a subordinate conjunction, but she will play at the slightest suggestion—and giggle and snuggle and dream and squeal over the Easter basket with every bit as much delight as she did when she was three years old.

She is, by the nature of her developmental stage, open to all that the Christian faith has to offer: forgiveness, hope, empowerment, a sense of belonging and acceptance, and the knowledge that she is loved unconditionally. Even secular sources, such as Dr. James Barbarino, author of *See Jane Hit*, say that nonpunitive, love-centered religion has been shown to create a buffer against a sick society.[18] He continues: "Children with a true belief that there is something beyond themselves that has power and who see a God-given purpose for themselves are far more likely to become confident, productive, empathetic and loving than those who don't." Since 90 percent of Christians make a commitment to follow Christ with their lives before age twenty—you can see where I'm going with that.[19]

In short, your tween daughter is in prime time. She can absorb all that you, the faith community, and her own unsullied instincts offer her, with far more wisdom than her early-childhood sisters, and with far less cynicism and confusion than her teenage ones. In other words, get her now, before she thinks she knows almost everything and thinks what she doesn't know she sure isn't going to get from you. It is never too late for our daughters, of course, but it sure can be too hard if we wait.

Pick Your Parenting Style

So who's waiting? Most moms I've talked with in workshops have chosen a parenting style and are running with it as fast as they can.

From my observation, they—you!—seem to embrace one of three ways to approach the awe-full task of raising a tween daughter.

- *The Greenhouse Approach.* Care for her like an orchid in a hot-house, sheltering her from absolutely everything "out there," beyond the glass walls, that might put anything negative or doubtful into her mind. The Greenhouse Mom's mantra: "If she doesn't know about it, she won't do it."
- *The Throw-Her-to-the-Wolves Method.* It's a tough world out there and she's got to learn to deal with it eventually, so bring it on. The Wolf Mother's mantra: "She's going to do it anyway, and she might as well be prepared."
- *The Open-Handed Philosophy.* She is still a young girl and should be protected, but not from herself. She needs careful guidance into the next appropriate thing so she can gradually go out into that tough world. The Open-Handed Mama's mantra: "She's going to decide what she's going to do someday, and I have to teach her how to do that now."

Do I need to point out which style I think gives a daughter her best chance of becoming the marvelous human being she was born to be? I'm all about Open-Handed Parenting, so I won't be giving you a list of things to keep your daughter away from. She isn't an orchid, but more like a tree, which needs to be exposed to the elements in order to grow. And I definitely won't be telling you how to "survive" parenting her as she goes out and does her own thing.

Instead, I would love to be your ally, encouraging you to be the most important influence in your mini-woman's life. I've brought together what I've learned from my work with tween girls and their moms, my training and experience as an educator, and my, shall we say, interesting journey as a mother, into a place you can turn for empathy, understanding, information, and suggestions. I would love to provide you with something like that instruction manual we all whined for when we got home from the hospital with our newborn baby girl and realized we didn't know what the Sam Hill we were doing. However, every make and model is different, so we'll have to rely on the truths that seem to apply to all of our tween girls and to us, and learn to know our daughters well enough to find the truths unique to each of them. In short, I want to help you open your hands, with confidence and joy.

Just So You Know Before You Read On

I am not a perfect mother. That's kind of like admitting I'm not a unicorn. Neither creature exists. Both are fantasies. As the mother of a tween girl, I was anxious, overcommitted, and anorexic. I spent what we used to call "quality time" with my daughter (a term I've come to hate), but on a daily basis I was often distracted and snarky and oblivious to the fact that my girl-child hadn't brushed her hair in a week. And yet, when I recently asked my now thirty-year-old daughter Marijean what she feels was messed up about her child-hood, she pondered far longer than she usually does (she is seldom at a loss for words) and finally said, "About the only thing was getting my body image issues from you. But, Mom, I always wanted to be like you, and if you'd been perfect, I would have had to kill you." I'm going to take that as a you-did-many-things-right. I want to share those things with you, as well as what I learned from doing some things wrong.

So it only follows that—well—you aren't a perfect mom either. Maybe you play the role of peacemaker and never let your kids fight their own battles. Maybe you're basically the maid, and have the oc-casional bout of furious resentment that sends everybody to their respective corners to wait until you get dinner on the table. Perhaps you're the powerhouse who makes the rules and schedules clear but has no time for somebody breaking the rhythm to have a meltdown. Could be you are the ultimate positive mom who bolsters everybody up but is quick to brush the negative stuff under the rug. At times, you are probably just plain angry, tired, guilty, and resentful—and you make no bones about the fact that it's everybody else's fault. Chances are, you have been and will continue to be all of the above at one time or another. So—get over thinking you have to be the flawless parent. This path is about process, not perfection. Neither you nor your daughter is going to move forward without making a myriad of mistakes from which you'll both learn. That is actually where the good stuff happens.

I believe you are first and foremost your daughter's mother. Not her buddy. Not her BFF. You're her maternal ally as she learns to strike out on her own. You're the one who sets boundaries and warns of consequences and, as Carol Burnett once said, loves her enough to let her hate you sometimes. That doesn't mean you can't be close, share girly times, and treasure each other in a relationship like no other. It does mean frequently making decisions for her that she isn't ready to make yet, decisions that evoke "You don't understand!" when in fact you understand all too well.

I think parenting a tween requires as much change in us as in our daughters. Let's face it—some of what qualifies as good parenting of this age group just doesn't come naturally. Cuddling, rocking, feeding, and diaper changing, though exhausting, may have been almost

Out of the Mouths of

Mini-Women

How Am I Supposed to Honor My Parents When . . .

They make a mistake with me, and even though they admit it, they don't apologize.
They yell at me in front of my friends.
They tell stories about me that they know are embarrassing in front of people who are important to me.
They talk about me like I'm not even in the room.
They read my private journal.
They believe a lie my brother or sister told about me.
They punish me for something I didn't do.
They have fights that really upset me.
I hardly ever see them.
They're abusive.

Responses from tween girls in a Blurry Rules Workshop

instinctive. Early discipline was pretty cut and dried. Here's what "no" means and here's what happens when you say it. But backing off to let your tween daughter make a choice you know isn't going to end well, or watching other kids tease her because she isn't their clone — those things aren't necessarily in your makeup.

Not only that, but at this point your daughter knows which of your buttons to push because by now they are all clearly marked for her. Add to that the fact that she no longer misses a trick in your behavior. Even if you're just an average gossiper, tell a few white lies, and have the occasional maternal meltdown, you're acting in ways that, by zero tolerance standards, wouldn't be allowed in her school. Again, you can't be perfect, but if you want to be good, some alterations in your default reactions may be required.

You may have to change your image of what a "talk" is too. Yeah, I hate it, but 90 percent of "Because I'm the parent and I said so" is going to have to go if you want decent communication with your tween daughter. The 10 percent is reserved for situations where there's no time for an explanation — she has to get out of the way of the oncoming train, for instance. The rest of the time you're looking at dialogue, not just you holding forth and her listening and obeying. First-time obedience is the goal, but it's going to be more likely if she understands the reasoning behind what you want her to do. That wasn't appropriate when she was a toddler or preschooler. Now that she's developing higher levels of thinking, "Just do it" only works for Nike.

Here's the way I look at it: If you both don't come out of a discussion seeing something in a new way, however small, it wasn't a real conversation. That could mean she sees that you aren't the pushover she assumed you were, and you see that she is a lot savvier than you thought she was. Good things to know for future dialogues. It does not mean you have to repeat the conversation every time that topic comes up. It's perfectly okay for you to say, "I refer you to our agreement on October 5," and expect her to get on with it. You'll save yourself a lot of nagging, lecturing, repeating, and yelling, none of which works any better than "Because I'm the mother." Don't think you have time for dialoguing? What about all those aforementioned hours in the car going to and from everywhere?

Mini-Women

"Your daughter will most likely pretend she doesn't want to talk with you by evading your questions. But keep on talking to her, and she'll eventually open up. But if she really DOESN'T want to talk, leave her alone for a while, or you'll damage the relationship."

age 13

As you work and play and talk with your daughter, she can help teach you how she needs to be parented in this new phase of her life. I can offer you tools and suggestions, but those things can only be used in light of what you know about her and what you allow her to show you about who she really is. Everything you read here should go through your personal filter. I respect that with every word I write, and I'll remind you of it ad nauseam.

If you're not enjoying being her mom at least some of the time, that really bears looking at. It's all right to admit that parenting isn't always a blast. Nobody's crazy about getting reluctant students off to school or reining in the first fits of boy craziness. But we can get so caught up in the frenetic, day-to-day job of, as one tween girl with ten siblings put it in an email to me, "making sure we all survive the day," we can forget to laugh at our daughters' jokes (tween girls think they are hilarious) and revel in their discoveries and delight in their growth. We miss out on just about everything that's worthwhile about being parents if we let that slip away unnoticed.

For all of this you are definitely going to need God. You know the verse where Jesus says it's easier for a camel to pass through the eye of a needle than for a rich man to enter the kingdom of God? That no one has a chance of doing it alone but every chance if he sticks with him? Then surely, it's easier for that same camel to pass through the eye of that identical needle than for the parent of a tween girl to guide her into a healthy, well-adjusted, God-loving adolescence without God right smack in the middle of it. Help for doing that is an inherent part of this book.

At the same time, it's wishful thinking to say that a good home life with all the right influences, even being brought up in the church with Jesus all around, guarantees that she will turn out to be a deeply spiritual, highly productive adult. God doesn't promise that. At all. Trust me — I've looked. Even Proverbs 22:6 — "Train a child in the way he should go, and when he is old he will not turn from it (NIV)" — isn't the never-fail promise it appears to be at first glance. If you don't train them up in the way they should go, you definitely won't see good results. But we've all known kids whose parents seemed to epitomize this proverb and who still had messy adolescences and messier twenties. And yet … at some point they eventually realized they needed to make better choices, and had the foundation on which to build a good life. There is no guarantee, not in this very-changed world. But there is giving them the best chance and praying them through.

A word about Dad before we continue. Parenting is such a team effort, as any mother or father trying to raise a child alone will tell you. That becomes more apparent than ever in your daughter's tween years when she encounters Dad's advice about boys (or his refusal to acknowledge them!) and his unspoken effect on her beauty and self-image. His influence is so important, in fact, that I've devoted an entirely separate book — written with my husband — for the dads of tween girls. You can look for *What Happened to My Little Girl?* in the spring of 2011. So while I will refer to Dad from time to time, our focus here is on your special role in your daughter's life. Anything here that rings true for you, by all means share it with him. A united effort is always a stronger one.

Out of the Mouths of

Mini-Women

"I would really enjoy it if my mom would do more things with me … sort of like having a special day for just the two of us. I think that would maybe even strengthen our relationship more, because we'd have a whole girl day to talk about ANYTHING!"

age 11

"I wish the same thing. Except even if I did get a day like that with my mom, I don't know what we would talk about. She's never really invited me to talk or tell her anything or tell her my problems. It's great that some girls are getting closer to their moms now. I wish it was the same for me."

age 12

What We'll Talk About

My work with tween girls has convinced me beyond a doubt that there are four areas of ultimate concern to them, and we ignore those at our peril and theirs. Having provided a book on each of these for the mini-women themselves, I'm offering you a mom's-eye view on these four ultimate issues: (1) Who am I? (2) Am I pretty enough? (3) What's happening to my body? and (4) Do they like me?

Section One: I Tell Her to Be Herself, But She Doesn't Know Who She Is (Identity)

In this part of the book, there's help for imprinting the concept of authenticity before adolescence comes in and tries to wreak havoc on it. You'll find advice here for helping daughters find and be comfortable with their true selves, including encouragement for letting them make mistakes along the way. As a result of this section you'll be able to let your mini-woman discover herself within the Christian parameters of a kind, loving individual, rather than tell her who she is or who she should be. That reinforces what your tween girl can learn in *Everybody Tells Me to Be Myself, But I Don't Know Who I Am.*

Section Two: Well, *I* Think You're Beautiful (Beauty)

It's my intent in this section to give you some help in encouraging soul-image (as opposed to self-image) and inner beauty in your daughter. Yes, you'll find tips for grooming and fashion that are age-appropriate for mini-women. The emphasis, though, is on guiding her toward a healthy attitude about beauty in a decidedly unhealthy beauty culture. What you do as a result of reading this section will reinforce what she can read in *The Skin You're In.*

Section Three: Who Are You, and What Have You Done with My Little Girl? (Puberty)

Here you'll find a mini-handbook for supporting your tween daughter through one of the most challenging periods of her life: puberty and its baffling physical and emotional changes. My purpose is to help you allow that mini-woman of yours to grow into full womanhood naturally and at her own pace, rather than nudging her, if not downright pushing her, into adolescence before she's ready to go there. We'll be all about ten *not* being the new fifteen, something your daughter can embrace in *Body Talk.*

Section Four: Why Can't They Just Get Along? (Friendships)

In this final section, I feel a deep obligation (and an equally deep humility) to offer help for guiding your daughter toward the healthy girl friendships that will shape her future relationships. I hope the suggestions you'll find here will enable you to enjoy your tween girl's totally girlfriend years before boys come in and tangle things up. That includes your looking at yourself and determining honestly how you want to participate in that. Whether you are the mom whose house all the girls flock to or the one-friend-here-at-a-time mama, you'll have a chance to set boundaries that will serve your daughter—and you—well. And speaking of friendship, I hope you'll find through this section ways to nurture a relationship with your daughter that will survive and even flourish in the teen years. What you glean here is reflected in your daughter's book *Girl Politics: Friends, Cliques, and Really Mean Chicks.*

How We'll Talk about It

Each of the sections is divided into chapters that focus on the real and the practical, with their basis in the spiritual and the mysterious, because our tween girls are all four of those things. There's a lot of stuff in there, to be digested while you continue to pack lunches, drive carpools, get yourself to work, and grab a minute or two daily for prayer that isn't interrupted by somebody's cry for clean socks, lost homework, or sibling refereeing. So you can expect features in each chapter that will act as a GPS system for you, whether you go through the book in one journey or take frequent side trips.

What It Looks Like: A real-life scenario used in the introduction to each of the four sections to show you that you are not alone—and that your daughter is deliciously normal.

Getting Clear: A full exploration of the topic, with statistics as well as psychological and developmental background and anecdotes—information you need but don't have time to google. Most of us will do better when we know better—even when we're already doing a pretty good best.

From the Ultimate Parent: The scriptural basis for the importance of the chapter topic. Each of these features includes suggestions for encouraging your daughter in her own faith journey and for helping you deepen your own even when quiet time with God looks like a luxury enjoyed only by those with nannies.

Test Your Own Waters: A self-assessment of how this topic impacts you personally. In a nonjudgmental way this can help you see what you may be unconsciously modeling for your daughter—positively or mistakenly. The kind of information you *couldn't* google even if you had the time.

Going for It: Ways to approach and deal with the chapter topic. This will include general guidelines and hands-on suggestions for applying them in a way that's unique to you and your tween daughter.

Bridging the Gap: Help in praying specifically the most important prayer a mom can lift up: "God, please bridge the gap between what my daughter needs and what I have to give."

Out of the Mouths of Mini-Women: Quotes from tween girls about what they wish their moms would (and wouldn't!) do, what they appreciate about their mothers, and what they wish they knew—everything they don't think they can tell you themselves (but, man, would they like to!).

Out of the Mouths of

Mini-Women

I Want to Be …

I want to be a math book
So I'll get all the questions right.

I want to be a referee
So I'll know what to do in a fight.

I want to be a pencil
So I can be used to create.

I want to be some figure skates
So I can feel a figure 8.

I want to be a flashlight
So I can show people the way.

I want to be a rug
So I can just lie around all day.

I want to be an eraser
So I can help people forget their mistakes.

I want to be a critic
So I can always say what I think.

I want to be a parent
So I can teach my brothers not to whine.

Or even better, I could be me —
And I could do all nine!

Regan Hendricks
age 11

That's it. That's our map. If you're ready—or if you have ten minutes when you aren't immersed in some girl drama—let's set out together. It is my honor to be your companion on a road I myself have traveled. A road I wouldn't have missed for the world.

PART 1

I Tell Her to Be Herself, But She Doesn't Know Who She Is

What It Looks Like

She's been talking about going to summer camp since before there was a sleeping bag small enough to fit her, and she all but pitched a legendary fit every time one of her siblings climbed on the bus and she was left behind to suffer without campfire smoke and lumpy crafts and shaving cream up her nose while she was sleeping.

Finally—and thank heaven for everyone concerned—the summer has come when it's *her* turn to go. For weeks you've been shopping for the perfect swimsuit ("Mo-om, everybody *else* is gonna have a bikini!") and stocking up on a myriad of small bottles of stuff she won't use but has to have (what nine-year-old "needs" facial toner?) and listening to the countdown ("Only eleven more days if you don't count today"—even if it is only six o'clock in the morning). It's all you've heard about in the minivan, all she talks about on the phone to her friends, all she can contribute to dinner table conversation, until her siblings are ready to break out the duct tape. You've started to count the days yourself, because she's driving you nuts.

And then the afternoon before she's to leave, when you're helping her tuck the last new pair of shorts into her suitcase, she turns to you, white-faced and trembling, and says, "I don't think I want to go to camp, Mom."

Although your head threatens to explode, you manage to ask her what on *earth* she's talking about. It all comes out in a torrent of what-ifs—

"What if everybody thinks I'm a loser? What if I don't make any friends? What if I get left out of everything because they all hate me?"

What can you possibly say to that except the obvious? "Honey, don't be silly. Just be yourself and you'll be fine."

She stares at you as if you're in need of serious medication. Because whether she can put it into words for you or not, what is obvious to her is: *How can I be myself when I don't even know who I am?*

———————

A situation like that—or "crisis," depending on which side of the generational fence you're on—brings into clear focus *the* biggest issue a tween faces. She may never voice it. In fact, she might not even be able to identify to herself that funkiness she feels when she approaches a place where nobody knows her name. But unless she is the only perfectly adjusted girl-child who has ever lived, it's going to be there at some point.

For some, it fades the moment she walks in the unfamiliar door and instantly becomes the life of the party (the class, the team, the waiting room). For others it takes some time to find the niche, the voice, the kindred spirits. For still others that sense of not feeling quite real becomes a way of being. Even if you're certain she never feels unsure of her identity (and is never shy about telling you exactly what that is), I hope you'll read on. After all, have *you* never wondered which "self" you're supposed to be in a brand new arena? How about the day you brought that baby girl home from the hospital?

Here's the deal. The question *Who am I?* is a perfectly natural one for a girl between the ages of eight and twelve. She's become gradually aware that she has emerged into a world where, unlike at home, people don't have to love her. She's realizing that how she behaves affects whether people like her, which begs the *next* question: *What if I'm being me and nobody likes that?* What she hasn't figured out is that every other girl in her age bracket is trying to answer those questions too, so they aren't totally reliable mirrors for seeing the real her. All of that natural figuring can take these kinds of shapes:

- Giggling like a nervous hyena. We used to call that "an attack of the sillies" when my daughter was a tween. It's akin to an adult's irresistible urge to laugh during a funeral.
- Crying for no apparent reason. Some of that is hormonal (more on that in a later chapter), but I-don't-know-how-I'm-supposed-to-act-right-now is a common trigger for tears. Think of yourself the first day of a new job. Escape to the nearest restroom, anyone?
- Bringing out the negativity with both barrels. That was my daughter's M.O. I could always tell when she felt unsure of herself because suddenly everybody else was a moron. Seriously —aren't we all crankier with our kids when we're not certain what to do with them?
- Having an abrupt personality transplant. Normally sunny, witty, and roll-with-the-punches, she morphs into the Tasmanian Devil right before your eyes. Always the outgoing, in-your-face type, she flips into terminal shyness and retreats to her bedroom. PMS-style mood swings aren't always responsible for a shift in character. Even kittens hiss and spit when their identity is threatened. I imagine we've all been known to hiss and spit now and then.

So if it's normal, even for us, shouldn't we just let them wrestle with it until they come out real? That would definitely be the easiest route to take, but as we've already pointed out, parenting is anything but simple. If we leave it to our young daughters to figure out who they are and move on, the rare few will do just that without our help. Those would be the ones who are sealed off from the rest of the world. Completely. And even if that were possible (we're talking a cabin up in the Himalayas), the moment she stepped into the real world, she would face an identity crisis that would require years of therapy.

Our job in these tween years is to imprint the concept of authenticity and help our daughters become as comfortable with who they are as possible, before adolescence really puts it to the test. How tough it is to resist negative peer pressure is almost always dependent on how strong and positive the individual's self-concept is. It has almost nothing to do with the set of rules she's been presented with. The time to get to know her true self and to find a place for that self in her world is right now—while the consequences for not doing it don't have the potential to deeply harm her. As a tween, if she wears an outfit because everybody else has one and realizes she looks like Olive Oil in the thing, she'll recover. As a teen, if she tries a hit of ecstasy because everybody else is doing it, she might not.

So, step one on our journey: help her find out who she is. And you'll no doubt discover some things about yourself along the way.

1

Will My Real Daughter Please Step Forward?

Whoever did want him, who believed he was who he claimed and would do what he said, He made to be their true selves, their child-of-God selves.

John 1:11–12

I feel like I'm living a life that is not mine, like I'm in a movie with someone else writing the script telling me what to do.

age 12

Not to put you into a cubbyhole—especially since this section is all about being uniquely oneself—but as a parent, it really is helpful to look at the generation you're part of, because, ten to one, you do embody at least a few of its characteristics, and that does have an effect on the way you understand your daughter's generation.

If you were born between 1974 and 1981, you're part of the much-talked-about Generation X. And can I just say that if I were a Gen X-er instead of a Baby Boomer, I would take serious exception to being called "X"? You have been much maligned for being angsty and materialistic, and for playing the victim, because, after all, you were the latchkey kids. As tweens and teens you definitely had an edge to you, and I admit that when I was teaching high school in the 1990s, you nearly drove *me* to the edge.

But you had every reason to be resentful and push the envelope and express all that was heinous in the world. When we were raising you, many of us Baby Boomer parents were pretty busy "finding ourselves" in the wake of that whole hippie thing—and a lot of us mothers were buying into the superwoman myth that served no one but the creators of antidepressants.

That's putting a pretty dark face on it, but the point is, as a young girl coming of age in your generation, peer pressure was about breaking rules. Anger was cool, and hope was absurd. Seeing how far they could go in blasting through old taboos was the mark of Generation X in their growing-up years. As a teacher, my heart ached, because in my view, it was all done in hopes that somebody would notice and say, "Okay, stop. Just stop. Let's figure out what's really going on here."

Somebody finally did say, "Stop." It was you.

As a generation of young parents, you aren't doing things the way we did. Your children are your treasures, and most of you are bending over backwards cherishing them. They want for nothing. You will sacrifice anything as long as it means they go to the best schools, have their place on the right teams, get the lessons with the top professionals, and possess every electronic device that will enable them to keep up with all of the above. The fact that you care so deeply and are so committed to your kids is the very reason you're reading this book. Your children are blessed to have you raising them.

However (and didn't you know there would be a *however*?), the X-ness is still out there in the world. Take the media, for example.

Even though you may be protective about what your child is exposed to, the world of music, movies, television, and Internet offerings still thinks that this new generation will want to continue to push the limits of acceptability in entertainment the way Boomers and X-ers did. I love what Neil Howe and William Strauss say in their eye-opening book *Millennials Rising*:

> Imagine growing up, as a kid, in a world in which older people provide a trashy lineup for you, tailor it to your vernacular, market it in your media, and then condemn you for participating in it.... That's what it's like to be a teenager today.[1]

Your tween daughter, born after 1982, is a Millennial. She's growing up far differently than you did, but the people making decisions about what media is available to her are still caught up in let's-see-how-far-we-can-take-this. It's not an eight-year-old who is writing the offensive lyrics to the music being sold to her—it's a thirty-something. Ten-year-olds don't make movies full of sex and obscenity—the forty- and fifty-year-olds are responsible for that. She's not seeing a reflection of what *she* thinks and feels and wants in this new world she lives in. She's "being pulled by the license of the adult culture far more than [she] is in any sense pushing it."[2]

So—if your innocent daughter is going to maintain that innocence and be allowed to be a kid, either you're going to have to raise her like an orchid in a hothouse, or you're going to need to help her find out who she is and what she wants, and show her how to maintain that in the face of what *our* generations are throwing at her.

The sad-and-sorry state of media is only one of the reasons that authenticity is as essential to our tween girls as good nutrition and the right ballet teacher. Let's explore five more.

Getting Clear: Why She Has to Be Real

Peer pressure has changed.

Peer pressure basically means: "Friends—who know everything—have way more influence than our parents, who essentially know nothing." Dealing with peer pressure always has been an important part of growing up. Learning who to listen to and trust is vital to well-being—and there has never been a generation of parents who has been successful at pulling off the listen-only-to-what-I-say-and-obey-only-me approach to raising kids. It's not even healthy to go at it that way, since the minute your child goes off to preschool you are no longer the sole influence in her life. She has to learn to sort through all that she's hearing in order to get the good stuff from it, and there is good, valuable stuff to be learned from her relationships with her peers.

The "pressure" part of it starts bearing down when what "everybody is doing" (supposedly—have you ever taken an actual poll of "everybody"?) goes against what she knows is right. At least, that was the way it was for us. "Peer pressure" in both yours and my day came in the form of alcohol, drugs, sex, and, if you really want to go back, protests against the "establishment." In essence, we were pressured to break the rules.

Hard as that was, it was somewhat easier on our parents. The decisions were pretty clear. Do this and this will happen. There you go.

For the Millennials, though, three things have happened. First, they had to have slept through elementary school not to have heard about the evils of drugs, underage drinking, and unprotected sex. They knew "Just say no" before they had the Pledge of Allegiance committed to memory. There's still pressure to participate, but they're much more savvy and not so easily persuaded. That's good news.

But, two, the pressure now is not to break the rules, but to "fit in." And that is a more complicated and much muddier thing to accomplish. You have to own the right stuff, talk the right way, wear the right clothes, and have the right coolness factor, which can change at any moment depending on the whims of the Ruling Class that makes those kinds of determinations, i.e., the Popular Kids. The pressure to figure that all out is much more complex than deciding whether or not to have a beer at a party. The consequences of succumbing to that pressure are not life threatening, but they can be soul threatening.

Third, that kind of pressure starts long before the teen years. Your daughters feel it as early as second or third grade, and it hits its stride in grades four and five, so that by the time they reach middle school, they're being bombarded with it hourly, often in cruel ways.

What that means for parents is that just equipping girls with the rules, a set of rights and wrongs, is, though important, not enough. If a tween girl isn't developing a strong sense of who she really is, her true self can be swept away in the rush to belong in a community that doesn't even know what *it* is from one minute to the next. The eight- to twelve-year-olds I talk to on a daily basis know not to drink, smoke, do drugs, or get physically involved with boys. Y'know, like, du-uh. But they are already sick of trying to be cool and popular and part of the clique. They are crying out to be real. You can help them.

School is becoming more standardized.

No Child Left Behind (or as my educator friends call it, No Teacher Left Standing) has shed the spotlight on the shortcomings of our public education system and made schools more accountable, at least for standardized test scores. Their response has been to return to a more structured curriculum, more order in the classroom (in the form of zero tolerance), and more emphasis on the basics. Have you noticed that your daughter has more homework and more demanding teachers than you did? Is she more excited about math and science than you were, as opposed to the previously more "girly" subjects like humanities and history and the arts? Does she perhaps balk at the assignments that don't call for black-and-white answers? Does she stress about getting it "right"?

The result of "teaching to standards," which educators are now called upon to do, has its upside as test scores improve nationwide. Yet there is a downside, which is that we cannot expect school to be a place where our daughters can express themselves in authentic ways. The trend toward cutting arts programs in these tough economic times speaks to that. In Nashville, where I live, there is one music teacher for every seven hundred students in the school district. Drama and band programs are seen as "nonessentials"—in other words, there's no standardized test for those, and we have to be getting them ready to score well in math and language arts, so let's not waste time and money on frills. Self-expression, however, is not a frill. It's a very real part of helping kids discover who they are, which is just as vital to their education as their basic academic skills.

So the job of allowing your daughter to express herself into a true sense of who she is falls to you. Her generation is becoming left-brained.[3] But her soul doesn't reside there.

Technology can eat away at individuality.

Before you write me off as a technology-resistant fifty-something who just doesn't *get* how important technology is to daily life in the new world—seriously, I do. I sit now before a computer with two screens. My email signals me every time I have a new message. My laptop waits in its bag for my next trip to a coffee shop that has free wireless. I own an iPhone that practically reminds me to pee, and if I don't blog and Facebook (which, I understand, is now a verb) daily, I hear about it. Especially from your daughters.

I wouldn't be able to do what I do without technology, and chances are you wouldn't either. The kinds of schedules you keep up with for your kids boggle my mind, and I know you can't pull it off without at least a BlackBerry. Again, I really do get it.

I also get that your daughters are what Dr. Mary Manz Simon, the guru of trend-savvy parenting, calls "digital natives."[4] Even if you didn't have a Blue Tooth device in your ear during labor, your child has no doubt always been very aware that electronics define much of her world. Computers are as natural to her as VCRs were to you. She's not afraid of technology. In fact, it gives her a certain air of superiority to know that she can operate devices with far more ease than her elders. My sister's eleven-year-old granddaughter recently taught her how to text. Tween girls who post on my blog are not shy about telling me if I would do this, this, and this, my pictures would load more easily or I could change fonts, you know, so it wouldn't be boring. No offense.

I don't begrudge them the labor-saving devices they get to use in their education. Who wouldn't rather look up facts on the Internet than plow through the Encyclopedia Britannica? Even as I'm writing this book, I'm remembering the agony of typing footnotes on an electric typewriter on erasable bond paper. Only on my crankiest days do I resent the fact that our tween girls will never have to endure that.

But I still have concerns. Will our mini-women depend so much on technology they'll become isolated from the very people they're constantly connecting with? I have a blog for young teens on which posters are constantly saying, "I wish I could be as real with my face-to-face friends as I can with all of you." I am so saddened by that.

I also worry that they are limited in expressing their uniqueness. There is a certain sameness in texting and Facebooking that, no matter how much they customize and personalize, seems to compromise their individuality. I see them in danger of being cookie-cuttered, only allowed to be creative within the limits of a MySpace page or a cell phone screen.

Another problem is that constant emailing and texting and Twittering and cell phoning could make them so dependent on peer support, they don't even know if they're okay unless they have their BFF within an instant's reach. It used to be bad enough to eat alone in the cafeteria. Now if no one's emailed them in the last five minutes, they wonder if there's something wrong with them. It's far easier to be in the loop than it is to be real.

Scheduling is now the biggest part of parenting.

Moms these days don't mean for it to be, but so often it's the truth. By the time you get them to school, participate in the book fairs and field trips—whether by physical presence or yet another check made out to the school because you yourself have a job to pay for all of the following—make sure they get to the after-school activities, make some kind of meal happen, supervise (or referee) homework, and get everybody ready to do the whole thing again tomorrow—is there actually time for all the things you thought parenting was about? You know, like teaching life lessons, sharing everybody's day at the dinner table, lingering over the tucking-in to say prayers and tell stories. You dreamed of that, didn't you?

And then the world took over. Sure, you could take your daughter out of everything and try to recreate a nostalgic fifties' cookies-and-milk-after-school atmosphere in your home, but a nagging anxiety would creep in that you were cheating her of all that's out there for her, all the things her friends are taking part in. You'd sense that she was perhaps falling behind and would soon become a gymnastics-less, soccer-challenged, piano-deprived misfit. You're a good mom. You can't do that to her. It's the way things are and you're coping with it, and probably pretty well.

I really do believe that, so please know that this is not at all a criticism. It's merely an observation that you might want to look at. Yes, I'm seeing tween girls who are gaining great confidence and team spirit from participating in sports, who are exhibiting tremendous poise and grace from performing in dance, gymnastics, and musical endeavors, who have a deep spiritual awareness because of their involvement in church life. At the same time, when I suggest to them that they take some time to dream or journal or talk to God, I often get very adult-sounding responses:

- "My schedule's pretty tight. I don't know if I have time."
- "My plate's already full."
- "If I add another thing to my day, my head's going to explode!"

These are nine-, ten-, eleven-, and twelve-year-olds. Most of them love what they're doing, or they at least know the importance of it, and no doubt they're learning things about themselves in the process. But when do they sort that through? When do they process it? What chance do they have to express it or experiment with it or even have a good cry over it?

I have a very real fear that they will become capable, efficient, accomplished young women who have no clue what lies under all their achievements. The more they add to their résumés—and at twelve many of them are already thinking about what their college applications need to look like—the more what they do defines who they are. That's certainly a part of the big picture, but it isn't all of it. The discovery of self that used to naturally occur when kids took off on their bikes after school and weren't seen again until Dad stood out in the front yard and gave the family whistle doesn't happen now unless the parents are intentional in finding other ways for their daughters to simply *be*.

Failure isn't an option.

It used to be, as recently as the early nineties, that grades didn't really "count" until high school. A student could barely scrape through middle school, suddenly decide to make the honor roll, and emerge as valedictorian. It *didn't* usually happen that way, but kids were told it *could*, and some actually did gear up for freshman year, knowing that now it "mattered."

These days, it starts "mattering" in kindergarten, sometimes even before, as moms shop for preschools the moment that little blue line comes up on the pregnancy test. Success in kindergarten means reading on a second-grade level. Virtually babies still, first and second graders have hours of homework. Fourth and fifth graders carry

Mini-Women

"I'd like for my mom to know that sometimes we have to face stuff on our own, and sometimes we need to be alone to figure it out."

age 11

backpacks that not only make them look like Quasimodo, but are sentencing them to years of chiropractic treatment. My own observations indicate that tweens are either stressing to compete for the top grades, or they've already defined themselves as "losers" and have basically given up.

And it's not just in the classroom where the pressure's on to excel. Girls are competing in sports earlier than ever, and even the least likely to ever kick a ball professionally are being assured that if they work hard enough, they can get an athletic scholarship. Not that college is on their minds at ten, but hey, we have to prepare for the future, right? Could some promise shown in gymnastics or skating mean the Olympics are a possibility? If she plays the piano or the violin this well now, should we be thinking about Julliard? Carnegie Hall?

I am *not* saying that we shouldn't dream big for our daughters, or even that we should refrain from encouraging them to dream for themselves. What little girl who has ever put on a pair of ballet slippers and a tutu hasn't dreamed of debuting as Clara in *The Nutcracker*? The issue we can run into in today's culture is the seriousness behind it all. These are uncertain financial times; where is the money for college going to come from? The number of college applicants is increasing, but the number of colleges isn't. Nineteen thousand high school seniors applied to Vanderbilt University last year. Sixteen hundred were accepted. If our daughters are going to be able to compete in that arena, don't we have to start preparing them now?

And what about failure in life choices? Having sex still carries with it the danger of pregnancy or STDs—but now we've added HPV, which is linked to cervical cancer. If we don't make *sure* she remains a virgin, couldn't she actually die? Twelve- to seventeen-year-olds made up 8 percent of substance abuse treatment admission in 2006, and made up nearly half of all admissions who say they used inhalants, which can cause severe damage, even death.[5] One bad decision and might we not lose her forever?

And what about her soul? There are so many religious options ... don't we have to guarantee that she won't stray from the Christian faith, even for a moment? Don't we have to shelter them so there's no chance that they'll turn out to be shoplifters or exotic dancers?

Talk about the pressure your daughter is under—*you* are dealing with 10,000 PSI on her behalf. There's no margin for error. She has to get it right, and you're responsible for that.

Or at least that's the way it seems. After a certain point, I tend to disagree. Your daughter is eight, nine, ten, eleven, or twelve years old. There is no way she is not going to come up short on something. And why not? So much of her education about herself and how she fits into the world comes from the mistakes she makes, the bad choices she opts for, the immature decisions that happen on the spur of the moment. If she isn't allowed to make some personal choices now and suffer consequences that are not life-threatening, she is only going to know how to be "good," maybe a "high achiever," perhaps a "success" in some field. But she's not going to know what makes her who she is as an individual. If you never allow her to "fail," she most assuredly will.

It may be harder than it has ever been for a tween girl to discover who she is. But who she is, is in there. She can either become an unconscious, twisted version of it, or she can be the deliberately true version. With society being what it is, you are her best chance of discovering and living into the latter. Even with all the other voices calling to her, yours is still the one she hears most clearly.

It won't be that way forever. You will still have influence on her when she becomes a teenager, but exerting it then can be far more of a battle than it is when she's a tween. Why not connect with her now, when it can be delightful for both of you—before you hear yourself saying what the mother of a young teenager said to me just this morning: "I have never been as annoying to another human being as I am to my thirteen-year-old daughter." As I recall, just last year she was telling me what a great relationship they had.

Yeah. Do it now.

From the Ultimate Parent

I'm convinced, especially after writing the features for the *FaithGirlz Bible*, that the whole gospel is about authenticity. Seriously. Jesus talks about real faith—the true worshipers worshiping in spirit and in truth. He gets into the faces of the Pharisees for being hypocrites, and holds up children, the most transparent of beings, as examples for us all. He's constantly telling us to get real, because we can't be truly saved any other way. I quote again the passage you found at the beginning of this chapter: "Whoever did want him, who believed he was who he claimed and would do what he said, he made to be their true selves, their child-of-God selves" (John 1:11–12).

You don't have to take my word for it that authenticity is essential to your tween daughter. Jesus beat me to it a long time ago. "It's who you are, not what you say and do, that counts," he says in Luke 6:45. "Your true being brims over into true words and deeds."

In John 3:6, he tells us, "When you look at a baby, it's just that: a body you can look at and touch. But the person who takes shape within is formed by something you can't see and touch—the Spirit—and becomes a living Spirit."

That concept was familiar to his listeners. "He has shaped each person in turn," a psalmist had written centuries before. "Now he watches everything we do" (Psalm 33:15).

I don't think we can deny that God put a "self" in that baby girl long before you knew her, so it pretty much follows that you as her mom have a responsibility to help her coax it out and embrace it. Isaiah, bless his outspoken, prophetic heart, puts it in even stronger terms: "You have no right to argue with your Creator. You are merely a clay pot shaped by a potter. The clay doesn't ask, 'Why did you make me this way?'" (Isaiah 45:9). I have to admit I prefer the way one of my favorite Christian nonfiction authors, Dan Allender, expresses it: "We read our children as God wrote them."[6]

There it is. God says it. But as always there's the question—"Okay, but what does that *look* like?" You're convinced she needs to be herself, but how does God mean for you to help her do that? We're going to talk about a number of things you can look at and try. The following are the ones I see as arising directly from the Spirit.

Be content with who she truly is.

If she isn't a math whiz, so be it. Okay, so yeah, the best jobs of the future may require a solid arithmetic skill set, but if that isn't

"I told her she needed to be herself, that God had made her exactly the way he wants her to be for the things that he has planned for her. What she said next was heartbreaking. She said, 'I don't even know who I am.'
Mother of a
12-year-old

her, it isn't her. God's got something else planned. She's not as out-going as you think she needs to be in order to survive the looming giant, middle school? You're not going to turn her into an extrovert, so don't try. You can mold a basic sense of caring and consideration (because children are born totally self-centered, after all!), but you can't "make" her into anything she isn't. She's destined by God to take a certain shape. Don't re-form it. Just love it. Only things that go against what you know of God are not "her." "You're blessed when you're content with just who you are—no more, no less," Jesus says in his marvelous recounting of the Beatitudes. "That's the moment you find yourselves proud owners of everything that can't be bought" (Matthew 5:5).

Give her opportunities to serve, rather than constantly being served.

She's privately chauffeured, provided with every chance to experience whatever she wants to, and sheltered like a crown princess. That speaks well of you as a parent. It also explains why this era of child-raising is already known as the Age of Entitlement.[7] You can be an even better parent if you require consistent help around the house, a commitment to treating members of the family with respect, and encouragement to do things for other people when she really doesn't "have to"—as in, there's nothing in it for her. And yet there is.

"Do you want to stand out?" Jesus says. "Then step down. Be a servant. If you puff yourself up, you'll get the wind knocked out of you. But if you're content to simply be yourself, your life will count for plenty" (Matthew 23:12). It's almost impossible to be anything other than genuine when you're absorbed in meeting someone else's needs. Your daughter isn't too young to experience that.

Teach her to let Jesus lead.

All of us Christians say it: "Jesus Christ is master of my life." And then most of us go ahead and do what we want or what the world expects or what's going to get us through the next half hour without smacking somebody. The reason for that, of course, is that our lives are so full and complicated and downright frenetic. But despite their crowded schedules, tween girls aren't faced with the same degree of complexity that we are. It's so much simpler for them to take each issue they face to the Lord and then clearly see how it's resolved. I love this passage:

> *Then Jesus went to work on his disciples. "Anyone who intends to come with me has to let me lead. You're not in the driver's seat; I am. Don't run from suffering; embrace it. Follow me and I'll show you how. Self-help is no help at all. Self-sacrifice is the way, my way, to finding yourself, your true self. What kind of deal is it to get everything you want but lose yourself? What could you ever trade your soul for?"*

> *Matthew 16:24–26*

Model authentic worship.

When Jesus was coaxing the genuine article out of the woman at the well, he said to her: "It's who you are and the way you live that count before God. Your worship must engage your spirit in the pursuit of truth. That's the kind of people the Father is out looking for: those who are simply and honestly themselves before him in their worship." And just in case she didn't get it (most of us don't the first time through), he added: "God is sheer being itself—Spirit. Those who worship him must do it out of their very being, their spirits, their true selves, in adoration."

When I read that, I don't get an image of a chaotic Sunday morning getting everybody dressed, fed, and out of the house—fighting en route about who didn't brush their teeth and who doesn't want to go to Sunday school—delivering everyone to their respective classrooms—catching about half of what goes on in your own class because you're still reliving the fight in the car—regrouping all of them for the worship service and going through the motions while you try to keep your brood from scribbling on the back of the pew, texting during the sermon, and dozing off while the anthem is being sung. And that's just your husband.

Okay, so I'm exaggerating, but I've never known a churchgoing mother yet who didn't own up to the fact that her "true worship" was compromised by squirming, whispering, yawning children. Some of that's unavoidable. Kids aren't programmed to sit still, and let's face it, most sermons aren't written with them in mind. But some of it comes from focusing on whether your offspring are bothering any-body. Tween girls are seldom the culprits. Can the younger ones hang out in the nursery (or be administered a dose of Dramamine—JK!) so you and your daughter can share a worship experience?

Can you bring *your* true self to the occasion? Are you naturally inclined to sing your heart out? Raise your hands in the air? Respond verbally to the sermon? (Hopefully not with, "You lie, brother!") Or is it more you to become quiet and reverent, hands folded, lips whis-pering? Whatever is natural when you go into the house of the Lord, that's what your daughter needs to see—not to copy it, but to know that it is a good and joyful thing to get real when you worship.

Again, if authentic worship means waiting until younger children can do the same before dragging them into the sanctuary, their spiri-tual formation won't be stunted. If it takes shedding some of your church commitments so you can concentrate on praising and pray-ing and filling your well, the place isn't going to fall down around you. Seriously, if your young daughter can't be herself before God, how can we expect her to be so in front of people who don't love her unconditionally the way he does? Sounds like a priority to me.

Honor her doubts and questions.

I know it seems like if we could just indoctrinate them in the faith now, give them a solid, certain foundation, they'll never waver. To some moms that translates as never exposing them to any other religion, making sure they have only Christian friends, only going to church-sponsored social events, sacrificing so they can go to a Christian school, or making the *supreme* sacrifice and homeschool-ing them. None of those things are harmful in and of themselves. Certainly we want our girls to know as much about Jesus Christ as they possibly can and to love him and serve him and follow him.

Where I cringe is when I hear girls say: "Is it okay that sometimes I wonder if God's really there? I'm asking you because I'm afraid to ask my mom." Is there any one of us who can honestly say she hasn't agonized over a failed relationship or mourned the untimely loss of

Out of the Mouths of
Mini-Women

"The most important thing my mom taught me is to love God and have a relationship with him. They've always encouraged me in this area, which I know I do take for granted — not everyone's parents are Christians, which can make life kind of harder."

age 12

a loved one or rocked a screaming baby and thought, "Where *are* you, God? What—did you lose my address?" When God answers in some concrete way or in his still, small voice, "I'm here. What do you need?" our faith is strengthened beyond the mere recitation of the creed. Doubting and questioning are an integral part of the growth of our faith—and it's no different for our daughters.

I look at it this way:

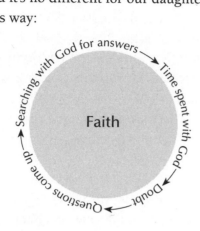

You have faith, so you spend time with God. While you're hanging out—praying, reading the Bible, meditating on your experiences and how they're lining up, or not lining up, with what you think you know of God, questions come up. Why do bad things happen when I'm being so faithful? Why are some people literally getting away with murder? Why is he saying one minute that I'm mere dust in the wind, and the next he's saying I own the universe? Those questions naturally create doubt. You want those doubts resolved, so you hang out more with God, searching together for the answers. When you find them, you have even more faith, which means more time spent with God, which leads to even deeper questions, more troubling doubts, more stunning answers, and a faith that grows more solid with every new question.

I can almost hear you protesting: *I can do that. I'm an adult.* But who's to say my daughter won't be led off on some tangent while she's doing all this questioning?

First of all, nobody said she'd be doing this by herself. You'll be the one teaching her about the things that will hold her up in the process. Conversations with God in prayer. Learning to read the Bible. Authentic worship. And mentors—like you. If you allow it, you are the one she will come to with her questions and her doubts; you'll be the one who assures her that doubt is not the opposite of faith, but an important part of it. You'll be the one who refuses to judge her or pitch a hissy fit if she says, "Did Jesus really come back from the grave? I mean, seriously?" You are the one who will say, without horror, "He really did—but why do you ask?"

Undergirding all of that, of course, is God himself. Remember the parent who came to Jesus asking him to heal his child who had suffered from seizures all his young life? He himself was stricken with a certain amount of doubt. "If you can do anything," he said, "do it. Have a heart and help us!" (Mark 9:22).

"If?" Jesus says. "There are no 'ifs' among believers. Anything can happen" (v. 23). To which the father responds, "Then I believe. Help me with my doubts!" (v. 24).

You can show your daughter that God understands the questions and the doubts and will help her through them. If you don't, if you're shocked by anything but an at-all-times-unshakable faith, one of two things is likely to happen:

1. She's going to interpret that to mean that having doubts makes her a bad person, so she might as well give up on Christianity—and she will as soon as she's out of the house.
2. She'll shove her doubts and questions under the rug and know only a rigid version of "faith" that keeps God and joy at a distance.

Is it necessary to say that both you and God want something more for your precious angel-child?

Test Your Own Waters

Before we move on to forming a plan for putting that into action, let's take a few minutes to look at you and where *you* are in being your true self. This is not a matter of determining that you're a fraudulent mess so how can you possibly teach your daughter the first thing about being real. I actually think it's more about discovering how genuine you really are, and how much you have to offer your resident

Out of the Mouths of Mini-Women

"My mom has taught me all about God and his Word. Even things she doesn't say I have learned from her. Like listening to God."

age 10

mini-woman. I know that I am constantly surprised at how "myself" I've become when I wasn't looking, and I suspect you'll find out much the same thing. This is affirmation, ladies, not condemnation. (Not with me having this rather large beam in my eye ...)

I know you probably don't have time to write out answers to essay questions. But at the same time, I don't want to give you one of those magazine-style quizzes where you pick *a*, *b*, or *c* and read a paragraph that tells you what kind of friend, mother, cook, or Christian you are. This is about *not* putting yourself into some artificial slot, right? So— I've simply provided you with some things to think about. They can become part of your quiet time with God (you have managed to carve some into your day, yes?). If you're a journaler, these might be topics. Or you could simply ponder them while you're waiting for your daughter to get out of soccer practice, piano lessons, play rehearsal—you know, instead of catching up on your phone calls. If you're the quintessential extrovert who doesn't know exactly what she thinks until it comes out of her mouth (I often fall into that category myself), you could use these as discussion starters with other moms you trust. However you approach them, I hope they'll lead you to a clear awareness of the part your trueness plays in the raising of your tween daughter.

- Do you believe that women have a special wisdom when it comes to their children? That they instinctively know who their daughters are—even if that's not who they want them to be? Do you know that wisdom is inside you, providing the strength and power you need to raise your daughter authentically? No matter what anybody else is telling you, do you know that?

- Are you using that wisdom with your daughter? Are you accepting who she is—or are you trying to shape her into who you think she needs to be in order to do well in this world? Do you know her natural personality is going to make it hard for her to fit in, and so you're trying to change her to make her life easier? Or are you looking for ways to help her be who she is and still find a sense of belonging?

- Do you take time to cultivate your own interests? Do you make space in your schedule so you can have quiet moments with

God? Do you insist on respect for who you are? Or are you always, always available to fill every request? Do you put one more activity for your daughter ahead of that Bible study you think you'd really benefit from? Do you find yourself wishing you could go to the bathroom without somebody pounding on the door wanting to know when you're going to take her to her BFF's house? Do you find yourself wishing you could buy a one-way ticket to the Cayman Islands, just so you could think your own thoughts?

- Do you work very hard at trying to be a perfect parent? Does that leave you feeling not perfect, never good enough? Do you ever resent your daughter for not allowing you to be the perfect parent? Or do you learn from your shortfalls? Let yourself be human? Refuse to let your kids criticize you for not being infinitely patient, kind, and understanding, when it's they who are driving you up the wall?

- If someone asked you (like I'm doing now) to tell a story from your daughter's recent history that would sum up who she is, what would it be? Would it be delightful to spin out that tale? Would it bring tears to your eyes? Would it break your heart? Would it make you want to go hug her?

- If you asked her to tell a story from her recent history of you that would sum up who you are, do you think she could do it? Does she know you well enough? What tale do you think she'd tell? I dare you to give it a go.

Are you getting a sense of what an incredible mother you are and can be just by being your authentic self? Your journey is a model for her. Continually discovering yourself and being that to the best of your human ability will go farther than anything else in insuring that your daughter will do the same.

Going for It

I will probably say this no less than fifty times in this book: I can't tell you how to be the best parent to your tween daughter. I can only offer some concrete ways to get to what's going to work best for both of you.

Using all of the above, here's what I've come up with for guiding your mini-woman toward her true self.

Give her space and time to wonder and experiment and try out who she is.

You can feel like you need computer software to figure out how much after-school activity is too much—and which activities are helping her discover who she is and which are stressing her out—and which are helping her socially and which fall into the category of "everybody's doing it." Not only that, but there really are so many great opportunities for kids now—everything from classes in composing your own songs to travelling soccer teams. What if you're responsible for her missing out on something amazing?

Actually, the only "program" you need is your understanding of your own daughter. Some thrive on a busy schedule—although I still advise leaving at least two afternoons a week open. Some determine early on that they want to focus on one activity and knock everybody's socks off with it. Others just simply need a lot of down time. Go with what you know. Try not to let what's being done by all the other moms determine how you and your daughter structure her out-of-school time. (*You* don't have to do what everybody else is doing anymore!)

When your daughter does have some time to wonder, be her ally (or her security guard if you have to be) in insuring her some privacy. Seriously, wouldn't *you* enjoy an hour to sort through what the day has brought, without somebody yelling, "Hurry up! It's time to go!"

Don't label her.

We Christians are so guilty of that with the personality tests we take in church groups. "Oh, she's a sanguine. She just doesn't get worked up about things." "Not mine. She's such a melancholic. Cries over everything." Myers-Briggs, the Enneagram, spiritual giftings, that thing where you're a golden retriever or a weasel or whatever—all of those are helpful in working with and getting along with adults, and even in teaching your kids if you homeschool them or help them with homework. But an eight- to twelve-year-old girl, though she has a specific nature, hasn't grown into it yet. She may have been a high-spirited handful right from the delivery room, but to tell her, "You're a choleric, which means (what *does* it mean—I've never been able to keep those straight) …" is to make it far less likely that she's going to explore *all* that she is. Personality "types" are useful tools. They aren't labels that tell us what's in our souls. We humans are far too rich and complex to be defined by one word.

Help her say what she means.

She might not always know, but that provides you with an opportunity to help her find out and put it into words that heal rather than hurt, that open people up rather than shut them down, that resolve issues rather than turn them into international incidents. It's about helping her to find her voice. If she's prone to screaming like the proverbial banshee when she's crossed, you can help her find a way to state her case without alienating everyone within a hundred yards. If she tends to go off and pout, you can draw her out and make it safe for her to say what she's feeling. Again, she might not know exactly what that is, much less how to express it effectively, but that's where you come in.

One of the things I did do "right" as the mother of a tween daughter was to approach Marijean's tirades with, "Okay, let's find out what's really going on here." I believed that "going off" isn't really who anybody "is," and if I could teach her to get in touch with what she was feeling and talk about *that*, instead of lashing out at whoever was within tongue's reach, I would be helping her find out who she *actually* was. It seems to have worked. It went something like:

"Okay, so Mrs. Luzzie is stupid, everybody in your class is stupid, *I'm* apparently stupid for making you go to school. Since none of that is probably true"—pause for her to eventually and perhaps reluctantly nod—"did something happen today that made *you* feel stupid?" That usually resulted in an immediate torrent of tears, much preferable to the previous near-apoplexy, and a joint effort in determining how she could deal with her imaginary stupidness and move on.

Granted, Marijean was an only child. But at the same time, I was working as a teacher, running a children's theatre, and trying to get my writing career off the ground. Going through that with her took time it wouldn't appear that I had. I made time. What I didn't make time for was keeping up with the laundry, putting fabulous meals on the table, or getting those papers graded within a week of the assignment. There are only so many hours in the day. Using some of them to help your daughter find her voice sounds like a good use of time to me.

When she speaks in her own voice, listen to her.

That sounds pretty simple. If she's like many tween girls (my own included), she never *stops* talking. How can you help but listen, right? Actually, I think most of us moms do a pretty good job of *not* tuning in. Even today, there are times when my grown daughter calls me while I'm working and I find myself going, "Uh-huh. Really. Wow." In response to what, I have no idea. We often have to go on autopilot just to maintain our sanity.

And yet. Isn't there a maternal antenna that goes up when your daughter takes that tone that says, "I'm in trouble here"? Doesn't everything in you say you need to stop what you're doing and find out what this is about? Those are the times when she's going to tell you who she is—in the way she handles stress, in the way she responds to hurt, in the way she approaches problems. This is where you discover that raising her isn't all about making rules and applying them—though that has to happen too. It's about reading who she is and parenting her accordingly. She's giving you a glimpse. Don't miss it.

Let her make mistakes.

I know this is where I might lose you, but I'm taking the chance that you'll hear me out. We've already talked about the fallacy in *Failure isn't an option*. You can put that into practice in ways that aren't going to throw your daughter into harm's way, and may keep her out of it in the future.

First let's talk about the difference between "protecting" and "sheltering."

Protecting means providing a safe place to live. Making sure she eats right and dresses appropriately for the weather so she has a better chance of avoiding illness. Not letting her wander off alone in stores. Keeping a close watch on her Internet access. Preventing her brothers from leaving bruises on her. Protection is a response to your deep love for her and your desire for her to grow up strong and healthy and whole.

Sheltering is something else entirely. It's preventing her from ever coming into contact with something that might potentially give her a peek at a path that differs from the one you are determined she's going to follow no matter what. It's reading every book she wants to read before you let her open the cover. Not allowing her to watch a movie, listen to a song, or view a TV show that doesn't have overtly Christian content. (*Are* there any TV shows with Christian content?) Requiring her to keep her bedroom door open at all times. Telling her she shouldn't even be thinking about boys until she's eighteen.

Moms who shelter in these ways love their children fiercely. We should all have had mothers who cared that impeccably about us. But the sheltering decisions they make aren't based on love. They're based on fear. And while parenting is surely a terrifying task, it should never be directed by the fear that one misstep is going to ruin the child for life—perhaps even for eternity.

If you are a shelterer, then yes, what I'm about to advise may seem horrifying to you, but I'm begging you to at least pray about it as a possibility. Here it is. When your daughter was learning to walk, you weren't constantly picking her up every time she came down on her diaper-padded little fanny. You didn't say, "Don't let go of that table or you'll fall." She had to experiment, she had to try and fall down and get back up and try again in order to eventually move forward.

She still does.

That doesn't mean throwing up your hands and saying, "Do what you want to do, but don't come crying to me if it doesn't work out." It does mean that in the case of something where the consequences of a bad choice will not be dire, but rather provide the teachable moment, you can wisely say: "Okay, if you treat your friend this way today, she probably isn't going to be your friend tomorrow," and let her go. There may be tears, but who ever grew up without shedding a few?

"I am not going to stand over you again tonight until you get your worksheet done. You decide whether you're going to do it or not, but if you don't, the sleepover tomorrow night is out." Then stick by it. When she hears Monday morning about what a blast the slumber party was, doing that worksheet is going to seem like a small price to pay to get back into the loop.

You will obviously decide which decisions can safely be left up to her and which ones are totally in your court. When my daughter was only two and I was struggling with the constant arguments (she was never one to throw a tantrum—she just wanted to debate everything), a counselor friend showed me a technique we used with her until she graduated from high school.

My husband Jim and I drew a box on a piece of paper. Inside the box, we wrote down all the things that she might as well not argue about because that was the way they were going to be. Since she wasn't even reading yet, we drew a picture beside each one. The box contained things like "Go to bed at 7:30," "Sit at the table while you eat. If you get down you're done. Period." "Say please and thank you." "Ask 'Why?' instead of saying 'No' when we tell you to do something." It was a pretty big box. But there was still a little room on the piece of paper outside its lines. There she could put the things that were her decision. Which toy to play with. Which outfit to wear of the three Mom puts on your bed. Which book to have read to you before bed.

It worked like a charm most of the time. All we had to do was say, "Uh, I believe that's in the box," and the whining eventually faded. She felt pretty good about her sweet self getting to make some choices, and the "Wait, this one, not that one—no I wanted THAT one!" was eliminated. "You picked it, darlin', so here we go."

As Marijean got older, the box got gradually smaller. We redid it every so often as it seemed appropriate, until she didn't need the visual drawing anymore, just the sense that some things were still in our hands and some were up to her—with the full knowledge that there are always consequences for the decisions you make and you can't blame anybody else for them.

Through the years, Marijean and I have discussed the fact that some girls didn't seem to have a box. That they rode roughshod over their parents and ended up a danger to themselves and others. Their potential for a free and happy life was down to nil. On the other hand, some girls operated with a box that filled up the whole page, no matter how old they were. Interesting how they too ended up a danger to themselves and others, without the possibility of an authentic journey. I try not to be smug—but again, I swear by this.

You still have the brakes. You can still intervene if a decision she's about to make suddenly threatens to get ugly. You're like the driver's ed teacher who gives the young driver the wheel, lets her stall out, and watches her knock over a few pylons before she gets the hang of parallel parking. But he doesn't take her out on the interstate until she's ready—and he's always prepared to grab the wheel or come down on that brake he has on his side of the car. Eventually he'll let her take off on her own—way on down the road from now—but that won't happen if they never leave the parking lot now.

Realize that the things that drive you crazy about her now may become the best things about her in the future.

Does she argue about absolutely everything? You can put limits on that (see the box technique above), but try not to stifle it completely. She could be headed toward becoming a great debater, perhaps an attorney (so she can support you in your old age). Does she have an opinion about absolutely everything? You can teach her to express those in appropriate ways, but I wouldn't try to stop her from having them. Who's to say she isn't destined to be a social critic? Does she spend long hours daydreaming when she's supposed to be setting the table? Definitely train her to take care of her responsibilities, but make sure she has plenty of "legal" dreaming time. Great feats always begin with great visions.

Above all, enjoy her.

The best way to instill a love for who she truly is—is simply to show her that she is truly adored. That you treasure her precious self. That you are delighted with who she is, no matter who she is. No, you aren't going to giggle with glee when she's slamming her bedroom door because you've told her she can't have an iPhone. But there are plenty of moments when she isn't practicing to be the Wicked Witch of the West—in fact, that's probably most of the time. That's when you can show her that she is the joy of your world, not because of anything she does to "earn" that, but simply because she's your daughter.

As a tween she's experiencing a certain confidence, perhaps a sense of adventure that's typical of her age. Revel in that. Have fun getting to know her. Watch, listen, study, figure out—who did God make her to be? And love doing it. Purely and simply, love it.

For example, some of the discussions you'll have with your girl as she grows up are going to be on the heavy side, but the question "Who are you?" can be one of the lighter ones to entertain.

What if on one of those afternoons spent in the car dropping kids off and picking them up, you and your mini-woman ask each other:

- If you were a dog, which breed do you think you'd be? (Not which one you want to be, but which one fits your personality.)
- If Dad were a chef back in the kitchen of a restaurant, what would you order that would let him know you were there in the dining room?
- What color says it all about you?
- If you could ask God one specific question and have him answer in an audible voice, what would it be?

The only rule in this game is that you don't get to say, "No, I don't think you're an Irish setter—you're more like a Chihuahua." The point is to find out what she knows about herself. The fun comes in the surprises.

Enjoy. Yes, enjoy.

Bridging the Gap

Lord God, thank you for making _____ everything you want her to be. Please help me to see what that is. Please guide me in guiding her to embrace her me-ness. I know I can't do it for her, so please, please, bridge the gap between what she needs in order to be truly authentic, and what help I have to give.

Thanks be to you, God. Thanks be to you. Amen.

2

Is She Herself, or Is She You?

[Jesus] said, "Why were you looking for me? Didn't you know that I had to be here, dealing with the things of my Father?" But they had no idea what he was talking about.

Luke 2:49–50

Near your birthday, the mom and the daughter should have a mommy/daughter day. Moms should do that often to get to know their child.

age 10

When Marijean was eight years old, she and I visited a friend of mine we hadn't seen since Mj was a toddler. My friend and I watched Mj interact with her kids, and after only about an hour, my friend turned to me and said something that rocked my maternal world.

"The learned behaviors are definitely you," she said, "but the raw material? Totally Jim."

There it was. I'd molded and shaped, chiseled and refined—and my child was still turning out to be just like her father.

Not that being like Jim Rue is a bad thing, mind you. Both he and Marijean are passionate, opinionated, generous, energetic people who never leave you in doubt as to where you stand with them. No pair of people could be more loyal, more fascinatingly verbal, more full of the love of life. Between the two of them, I'm kept in joyful hysterics hourly, and when a crisis occurs, there is no one else I want there, because they will have the situation under control before the paramedics arrive.

Still, the years have proven that Marijean is neither completely "her father's daughter," nor is she a dead ringer for me. She is her own person, in many ways a combination of her parents, and in many more ways a unique, one-of-a-kind individual. Neither Jim nor I possess her instinct for healing. Her stand-up-comic sense of humor is unmatched by either of us. And where on *earth* did she get her financial sense? She is not a photocopy of her parents.

No daughter is.

Yet so often we try to raise them as little Us-es. You want to go in with me and take a look at what that's about?

Getting Clear: She's Not You

It's evident early on.

You've known who your daughter was from the first weeks of her life. She demonstrated right out of the womb whether she was a cuddler or a straight-armer. It took only a few days to determine whether she was going to be sensitive to loud noises or snooze her way through the Fourth of July fireworks. By the time she was a month old you were saying things like "She has a temper" or "She's a laid-back baby." Although your mother may have claimed that as an infant you were just like your newborn, she wasn't to be believed. If you've had more than one child, you know every baby is different.

That means not only different from every other baby, but from every adult. Including you.

I recall sitting next to Jim with two-day-old Marijean positioned on Jim's propped-up legs and watching her glare — I'm serious, *glare* — at us, the skin between her little eyebrows pinched, eyes suspicious, as if to say, "Things better improve a whole lot around here, or I'm going back where I came from. And don't think I won't."

We recognized her intensity then, and it's been present ever since as a force to be reckoned with. The basic personality is there, pre-birth, in every baby, and it has nothing to do — yet — with anything you've done or haven't done. Doesn't matter whether you listened to Mozart or Alan Jackson or Celtic Woman during your pregnancy. That kid is who she is. And she's not you.

Mom's own personality, however, is her natural, first-instinct approach to parenting.

As a child I was a pleaser, a personality trait I still struggle with at times. Praise, approval, and the threat of shame "worked" in raising me. At least, that approach kept me on the straight and narrow, kept me from giving my mother an instant of trouble during my tween years. Thinking back, I must have been an incredibly easy child to have brought up. I let my mother off way too easy.

It was natural, then, for me to expect that the same style would work with my daughter. Uh-huh. When she was two, I was already asking: Why aren't praise and approval motivation for her? Why does she have to have the last word (yes, at two) when she knows that's going to make me want to flush her down the toilet? Why isn't she a pleaser? I hated that in myself, but it would have been so much *easier* if the very thought of making me frown was enough to pull her away from that wall with that crayon.

By the time she was eight, I had more questions: Why doesn't she seem to care what her classmates think of her? Why doesn't it bother her to get an "unsatisfactory" on an assignment? Why will she endure an endless lecture from me and *still* say, "Okay, but that doesn't mean I think you're right, Mom."

I knew that what worked for me wasn't tailor-made for her, and yet, what else did I know? I didn't *get* somebody who wasn't motivated by the promise of approval and the threat of shame.

You may have a daughter who would do cartwheels (perhaps literally) for a compliment, and yet you aren't one to dole out the praise because you yourself don't need much of it. Yours might do best when she has clear-cut rules, presented in triplicate, while you are more one to wing it. That doesn't mean you have to become like her in order to parent her effectively. I think you just have to know what does work for her, and somehow pull that off using your particular set of traits. Not to panic—I'll give suggestions shortly. For now, just know that she's going to respond best to mothering that takes her individuality into account.

Even if she is a lot like you, she's not an extension of you.

You know that book-turned-film *Sisterhood of the Traveling Pants*? The premise is that one of a close-knit group of teenage girls buys a pair of jeans that look sensational on each of them, even though they all have completely different body types. (This is obviously fiction …) That's the way I view the daughter who seems to be so much like her mother. She may share some of your characteristics—your total generosity, your witty sarcasm, your love of all things girly-girl, your no-nonsense approach to just about everything. But even those traits are going to look different on her than they do on you. Just as fabulous, but different.

For instance, both Marijean and I love children and they, for some reason, seem to like us too. However, when I see a baby, I go ga-ga over the poor child. I am reduced to complete idiocy as I gurgle and squeal and use baby talk that no self-respecting infant should respond to—and yet they do, with gurgling and squealing and jabbering of their own. Marijean, on the other hand, never changes her tone or her facial expression from the way she presents herself to adults. "Hi, buddy," she says to a boy-child as if they went to graduate school together, and the baby breaks into a slobbering grin from one earlobe to the other. Go figure.

You may share a deep spirituality with your daughter, and yet while she expresses that by doing all the motions to "Father Abraham," you meditate whenever you find a spare moment. You may be the clichéd two-peas-in-a-pod when it comes to being intelligent, but she's a math whiz, where you can spout history facts more accurately than a Williamsburg tour guide.

Many of those differences-in-the-sameness are due to age, of course. Your daughter may actually become an attorney or a social activist or a minister just like you because of the traits you have in common, but obviously she's not going to display those traits that way as a ten-year-old. Other variations on a theme arise from the differences in generations. For example, where your generation was often more into individual achievement, theirs tends to go for team-work, group efforts, community building.

Whatever the reason, any personal characteristic she has that reminds you vaguely of yourself is clearly going to have her unique mark on it. Just as when she gets older and starts borrowing your clothes, you will find yourself wondering if they look that way on you. (Just a heads-up for the future: they don't. You might want to steer her away from your closet.)

Nowhere do the differences between mom and daughter become more apparent than when they're shopping for clothes.

Yeah, well, duh.

You may be blessed with a daughter who loves everything you pick out, or agrees to whatever you like because she wants to make you happy. That is a gift from God and you should cherish it as you do life itself.

For the rest of us, a shopping excursion can run the gamut from careful negotiation to all-out war.

That's because the clothes she wears are an expression of who she is, and she chooses her apparel accordingly even before she's aware that she's doing it. In that respect, why would she be any different from you? How many times have you yourself been shopping with a friend who pulled out a garment and said, "What about this?" and you've said, "That just isn't me."

Yes, naturally you're going to gravitate toward clothes for your daughter that *you* like. But you can't count on her liking them as well, especially if her personality is far different from yours. It's easy to be hurt when she turns her nose up at that adorable sweater set you've just presented to her, but I think it's wrong to assume she's just doing that to be contrary. Most tweens aren't there. They really do just want to dress in a way that makes them feel comfortable and cute and a part of the group. We'll talk more later about why they often want to dress like every other girl their age (see pages 91–92). For now it's enough to know that even that is part of who they are. The sense of belonging is vital, so much so that she'll wear purple Crocs because her BFFs all have them, even though she secretly thinks they border on hideous.

Out of the Mouths of

Mini-Women

"I wish my mom would understand who I am and what I wear and do — stuff like that."

age 10

Instead of becoming a battleground, the girls' clothing department can be a great place for you to discover some things about your daughter you hadn't picked up on before. It was hard for me to bypass the cute little pleated skirts and cardigan sweaters when Marijean was nine and wanted to wear nothing but leggings and enormous sweatshirts. (It was the eighties, after all.) I look at old pictures now and think how darling she looked—big teeth, high-top tennies and all. At the time, it taught me that she was far less concerned about appearance than I was, and that her passions and pleasures required lots of free movement. I came to love that about her, and perhaps even envy it a little.

A mom's dreams for her daughter can't be whatever she hasn't fulfilled for herself.

We all want far better for our kids than we ourselves had. But trust me, you're providing that. In spades. I so admire your generation for the sacrifices of time and money and self that you're making for your daughters. It's inspiring, really.

I'd just be careful that "better" doesn't mean "what I wanted."

An extreme example is that horrific reality show in which mothers of girls even younger than their tween years are carting them all over the country in a quest for beauty queen titles. "She loves it," they say to the camera—while their girl-children are screaming because they hate the curling iron and the false eyelashes and—come to think of it—them. Almost every one of those mothers has a wistfully beautiful face and a body she has long ago abandoned as she focuses on her young daughter's "perfection." I always want the interviewer to ask, "How many times did you not make the cut in your day?"

Most of us don't go that far as moms of tween daughters, but many move unconsciously in that general direction. "My mom makes me take piano lessons because she never got to," tweens tell me repeatedly. "I kind of don't like it." I've met miniature cheerleaders reliving their mothers' glory days, when it's so obvious they would rather be out there playing football with the boys and young soccer players who barely finish the season before they're on the court playing basketball, with an eye toward those softball sign-ups—all because their moms were pre-Title IX and didn't have those opportunities.

I am *not* saying that your daughter shouldn't be given the chance to excel at something you had high hopes in for yourself. I always wanted to act—something I didn't do until I was in my thirties. Once I received a second bachelor's degree in theater, founded a children's theater with my husband, and began teaching high school drama, Marijean was hooked too. In high school she excelled as an actress and did community theater when there wasn't something going on at her drama department. I've long since left the stage behind, and so has she, but we still share a love for live theater. I like knowing I instilled that in her. However, if she hadn't shown an interest, I would have been just as pleased with her playing volleyball or taking up pottery. What I loved was that she was a kid. I never saw any of it as a dream for the future—mine or hers.

What I *am* saying is that the real dreams come from God—his mouth to their souls. Our job is to provide the opportunities for them to pursue those dreams and to keep them from going off some tween deep end in the process. It's a whole lot more fun to watch that unfold naturally, and to recapture our own dreams for our own lives.

It helps to know how her learning style differs from yours.

You are a lot of things to your daughter—nurse, confidant, play-mate, parole officer—but most of all you're her teacher. When are you not teaching her something, whether it's how to actually get the dirty clothes into the hamper or how to work through a rift with her BFF? You're teaching her even when you don't think she's aware you exist. Trust me, she's watching you.

So since you are her most influential instructor in the things of life for these few years, doesn't it make sense to understand how she learns, and how that jives—or doesn't—with how you teach? I know, I know, I've said I wasn't wild about pigeonholing people into personality types. But what I'm about to offer you is a really simple way to get a general idea of your daughter's learning style and your teaching approach. It's not hard and fast. Most of us are in fact a combination of styles. But to have a basic picture can be helpful in eliminating a lot of unnecessary battles. We're all about that, yes?

For the sake of simplicity, a group of professors at Brigham Young University assigned a color to each combination of the middle two letters of the Myers-Briggs designations.[1] If your eyes are already glazing over, take heart. That's the last of the technical jargon. This is my interpretation, which I use to help homeschooling parents and which I've adapted for you.

Tween Girls' Learning Styles

BLUE

- Takes in information through emotions and instincts. (She just gets a feeling about something.)
- Hates to hurt other people's feelings or have hers hurt. (She may spend a lot of time crying during her tween years.)
- Prefers to talk about feelings and relationships and the effects of events on individuals. (In other words, she often tells you more than you really want to know about who said what to whom and why.)
- Has trouble with criticism. (Even if you give fifteen positive comments and one negative, she'll dwell on the negative. And probably cry.)

GOLD

- Takes in information in a very organized way. (She seldom forgets what you've told her, even when you wish she would.)
- Likes to know what the rules are, what the structure is. (As long as she knows what's expected of her, she'll usually do it, perhaps more efficiently than you would.)
- Has trouble just letting go and thinking outside the box. (One of the few times *she* cries is when she has to do a creative assignment.)
- Usually does things right the first time. (Often doesn't understand why everybody else doesn't too, which makes her anathema to the brothers she is constantly correcting and tattling on.)

GREEN

- Takes in information very logically. (Her favorite question is still "Why?")
- Likes facts, likes to know how stuff works, and likes to invent things. (Don't be surprised if she takes the toaster apart; that activity is not confined to males.)
- Will do just about anything you ask as long as there's a reason. ("Because I said so" is an invitation to an argument, which she will enjoy and may win.)
- Can take criticism straight out as long as it's not abusive and, again, there's a reason for it. (She does very *little* crying in her tween years.)

ORANGE

- Takes in information by getting it on her. (You can tell her it's hot until you're blue in the face, and she will still have to put her finger through that candle flame just one time.)
- Likes to take risks before she asks questions. (She's all about experiencing it now and worrying later about whether that was a good idea.)
- Likes to do creative things in which she can look at the world sideways. (If she is required to do something boring, she either won't do it, or she'll get somebody else to do it for her, which she's so good at, Tom Sawyer could take lessons from her.)
- Shrugs off criticism or ignores it unless someone (you) gets right in her face. (She does *no* crying in her tween years. Door slamming, yes, but no crying.)

Moms' Teaching Styles
BLUE

- Creates structure that feels right (which means there always is one, it just changes from time to time).
- Tailors the routine to her kids (and tends to sacrifice her own rhythm in the process).
- Makes everything personal (which is great in relationships, overkill in folding laundry).

Out of the Mouths of

Mini-Women

"I wish my mom understood my personality better, the way I do things, and not get mad at me if I don't do it her way. That would save us a lot of fights."

age 10

- Great at teaching relationship skills and personal development (but feels bad if she can't also help with math homework).

GOLD

- Very structured in all endeavors (i.e. the kids' schedules are on the frig, color coded, and the backpacks are loaded and by the door before she goes to bed).
- Loves routine, especially one she creates (everybody has a bedtime, a scheduled after-school activity, a day to sit in the front seat).
- Is excellent at spelling out the rules in a clear, concise way (if any daughter in her house is in doubt, she need only refer to the list on the refrigerator, next to the schedule).
- Is great at teaching the black-and-white things every girl needs to know (her daughters can load a dishwasher, program numbers into a cell phone, and say no to gossip).

GREEN

- Creates structure that is functional and flexible. (It's never a crisis when somebody misses the bus or forgets a lunch. There is always a Plan B in place).
- Fits her routine to the task at hand. (No time to cook because her daughter waited until today to announce she has a science project due tomorrow? No problem. There's a pizza in the freezer—and what's more fun than a science project?)
- Likes to let her daughter figure things out on her own. (You'll hear a lot of "What do *you* think you should do in this situation?" at her house.)
- Is truly the best when it comes to teaching how to find things out. (Her daughters know how to locate any piece of information online.)

ORANGE

- Structure? What is that? (Her daughter is taking her academic career in her hands if she gives this mom papers that have to be signed and returned to school.)

- Resists routine and really has to work to create it when it's necessary. (Her daughters learn to expect the unexpected.)
- Likes to create "guidelines" (do we have to call them "rules"?) when a situation arises. (Her consequences for inappropriate behavior are creative works in themselves.)
- Shines when it comes to allowing her daughters to be truly themselves. (Which means she—and her kids—are often seen by other mothers as being "a little out there.")

It isn't hard to see how the combination of your teaching style and your daughter's approach to learning can either allow you two to work like a well-oiled machine, or start a bonfire every time you speak.

Mini-Women

"She acts like she can read my mind and say I'm doing something because of this when that isn't it AT ALL. That's what frustrates me the most."

age 11

- ORANGE moms can push their GOLD and GREEN daughters over the edge with their ever-changing routines—or complete lack of them.
- GOLD moms don't get why their ORANGE girl-children can't just follow the rules and make everybody's life easier, including their own.
- GREEN moms may constantly hurt their already sensitive BLUE daughters' feelings with rational explanations for things that clearly defy reason (like BFFs and boys and mood swings).
- BLUE moms can embarrass the socks off of their GOLD girls with effusive shows of praise and affection in front of their friends.

But—

- Get an ORANGE mom and a GREEN daughter together and there will be both fun and function.
- Pair up the BLUE mom with the ORANGE daughter and they will make each other laugh and feel good about their respective selves.
- Let a GREEN mom and a GOLD daughter go and there will be peace in the valley.
- Put a GOLD mom with her BLUE daughter and they can practically create a ministry in the living room.

What happens when identical colors cohabitate?

- BLUE/BLUE can either be a hothouse of female emotion or a place where understanding abounds.
- GREEN/GREEN has the potential to become a clinical lab (think Spock as the mother of a mini-me) or a forum for the satisfying exchange of ideas.
- GOLD/GOLD can go either way: a stress-laced drive to get it all right, or a smooth-running lifestyle that leaves room for growing and talking and trying things out (within those Gold limits, of course).
- ORANGE/ORANGE—uh, do I need to point out the possibilities in *that* arrangement? We're talking about sheer chaos, or an atmosphere of delicious fulfillment of potential.

Most daughters—and moms, for that matter—are a combination of colors that make them the rich, enchanting individuals they are. Even so, finding out which stripes or polka dots kick in when can go a long way toward understanding your mini-woman and discovering that, once again, she is so *not* you.

From the Ultimate Parent

Years (and *years!*) ago I wrote my first book, with a coauthor, entitled *Home: Love It and Leave It.* (I think approximately sixty copies were purchased, thirty of those by my mother.) It was a nonfiction book for teenagers in which marriage and family counselor David Wayne and I put forth the truth that it isn't up to parents to launch their children from the nest when it's time for them to strike out on their own; it's the responsibility of the young adult to spread those wings and fly. Our premise was based on Genesis 2:24: "Therefore a man *leaves* his father and mother and embraces his wife." The Scripture doesn't say, "The father and mother will push the man out and he will find a wife to pick up where they left off." (Although some men seem to think it reads that way.) It's the son—or daughter—who has to do the leaving.

So even biblically, the act of parenting is one long process of letting go. It's a *slow* process, and its steps have to be appropriate for

Out of the Mouths of

Mini-Women

"My mom taught me that it is okay to have to get away. She's a mom to eight of us, and life gets pretty crazy sometimes (okay, a lot of the time). But she has shown me that when that happens, it is better to take five minutes, leave the mess, and pray. Clear your thoughts by talking to God and being reminded that he doesn't care about the toy mess or the messy bathroom — all he wants is my heart and attention."

—age 12

where Daughter currently is on her path, but the end goal is for her to feel confident enough someday to make her own life. Your time for helping her to shape it is relatively short, and the tween years are the *prime* time. You won't be pushing her out. Her impulse to leave will later be strong in her and she'll go. The question is, will she be authentic enough to do more than just hold her own out there? That's your job, and it needs to be under way *today*.

That would be daunting, if not for the fact that who she truly, genuinely, authentically is has already been decided. Her soul, the very realness of her, is, according to Scripture, preordained. The psalmist David says it so beautifully:

> *Oh yes, you shaped me first inside, then out;*
> > *you formed me in my mother's womb....*
> *You know me inside and out,*
> > *you know every bone in my body;*
> *You know exactly how I was made, bit by bit,*
> > *how I was sculpted from nothing into something.*
> *Like an open book, you watched me grow from conception*
> > > *to birth;*
> > *all the stages of my life were spread out before you,*
> *The days of my life all prepared*
> > *before I'd even lived one day.*
>
> > > > > *Psalm 139:13, 15–16*

That pretty much leaves no doubt that your daughter's identity is (a) already a done deal and (b) unique to her and no one else, including you. That is not to say that you throw in the towel and proclaim, "I don't understand her at all, but she is who she is so what can I do?" There are certain things that *everybody* needs to adhere to in order to be a loving, giving, thriving part of God's world. The rest of the Bible is all about that, right? What it does mean is that *how* you "help this child to grow into the full stature of Christ" is unique to *your* "prayers and witness,"[2] and what that eventually looks like in your daughter is unique to *her*.

Once I realized that, I found it incredibly freeing, for both my daughter and me. I didn't have to decide who she was supposed to be. I didn't have to shape her into me. And thank heaven God was going to play a far bigger role in helping her find herself than I was.

Thank heaven.

Test Your Own Waters

It's really no wonder some of us automatically think our daughters are going to respond the same way we do. More than a few of our own mothers assumed the same thing about us. I don't know about you, but the mother tape recordings that play in my head were never louder than when I was navigating the tween years with my daughter.

"You be nice, Nancy," it said. "People won't like you if you're not nice."

"Don't you be a show-off, now." And in the next breath, "I'm going to ask you to play your piano for the Johnsons when they come over, and I don't want any argument."

"Tears again?" was its finale. "You're such a crybaby."

My mother herself—bless her heart—was polite, modest, and emotionally controlled. Not bad things to be, except that trying to be all of that myself pretty much stifled me for a long time. I tried to be nice to absolutely everybody, which often required a degree of falseness and not a few outright lies. I had a natural tendency to perform, but that was coupled with the learned habit of beating myself up after I kicked into theatrical mode. As for those tears—somewhere in there, I forgot how to cry.

When I became a mother myself, I was immediately a basket case. I didn't want Marijean to "act ugly," as we always said at our house. But at the same time I didn't want her to be everybody's doormat. Was that okay? Or did it mean I was setting her up to be a real shrew? Would people like her?

It became apparent to me that as much as I told myself I was my own person now, my mother's voice was screaming in my head. I had to put her on mute, or Marijean, who was most assuredly not a pleaser, was going to stage a grand mutiny that might go on until her twenty-first birthday.

Don't get me wrong. I also had valuable, positive tapes in my head, compliments of my mom.

- "You need to stay in touch with … (basically everyone related to you)."
- "Have you written a thank-you note for that?"
- "Set a nice table every time you sit down to eat." (Placemats required.)
- "Make your home as nice as you can for your family."
- "Make friends wherever you are."
- "The church is the center of your life."

None of those things went against who I was, or, for that matter, who anybody is. I then shared with Marijean those mother-things that had brought me personal joy and successful relationships and closeness to God. In the process I learned two things I want to pass on to you.

First, those positive lessons have a fresh new look in a new generation. My mother brought out the pink tablecloth and Desert Rose Franciscan china. I'm all about white ironstone and bright yellow placemats. At Mj's table we sit down to bamboo and hand-glazed pottery. My mother would be pleased. Puzzled, perhaps, but pleased.

Second, the my-mother-did-it-this-way lessons that go against a daughter's natural grain will haunt her. Just like they haunt you. Neither my daughter nor I can put a pretty face on an ugly situation. I tried and ended up in therapy. Marijean has escaped that.

So why not try putting the unwanted legacy to its final rest? Just recognizing your mother tape recordings and turning down the volume (if not erasing them completely — good luck with that) will help more than you can imagine. Here are some questions to ponder in your own personal way:

- In what situations do you "hear" your mother's voice in your head? (Using your full name, of course!)
- Do you have a knee-jerk reaction to that tape? Does the hair on the back of your neck bristle, or do you feel guilty enough

to follow her instructions? (Just to get her off your mental back.)

- Now that you think of it, are you unwittingly playing that tape for your daughter?
- Do you hear yourself repeating things your mother said to you growing up that you swore you were never going to say to your kids? (Starting with "Because I said so.")
- On the brighter side, are there things your mom taught you that you haven't thanked her for yet? (Since by now she doubtless knows all the things you didn't appreciate.)

You can look at it this way. Nobody uses cassette tapes anymore because there's nothing to play them on. You can refuse to allow your parenting mind to be a dinosaur Walkman—and customize your parenting playlist. Okay, cheesy, but you get the idea.

Going for It

Now that we've slogged through all of that, it's time for the fun part. These are suggestions for exploring both how different you are and what you have in common. They are to be—you guessed it—chosen and personalized for you and your mini-woman.

Make a list of fun activities.

Grab a sheet of paper, divide it down the middle vertically, and write "ALIKE" at the top of one column and "DIFFERENT" at the top of the other. With your daughter, think of the supposed-to-be-fun kind of activities that each of you enjoys. (Most tweens won't think this is lame!) As you discuss the possibilities, put them in the appropriate column. Just avoid making statements along the way like "I know you like to bake cookies, but I would rather be shot than go into that kitchen when I don't have to." Just put cookie baking in the DIFFERENT column and move on. Expect the same respect from your daughter. Once you've written down all you can think of, choose one activity from the ALIKE column and do it together. Both like to eat ice cream? Take an hour and slip away to Ben & Jerry's. Share a love

Out of the Mouths of

Mini-Women

"I deal with things a lot different than my sisters. I think moms need to get to know each child and know the difference. My sister and my mom are totally alike, and I'm the complete opposite of them. It's a problem."

age 10

for music? Pick a fave song each and listen over lemonade. Discovered she'd like to learn to plant flowers like you do? Shove aside your fear that she's going to kill the petunias and show her how it's done.

Do something your daughter enjoys.

At some point, pick one of the activities in the DIFFERENCES column, one she enjoys and you, well, don't. Give it a try with her. You might be surprised that you actually like playing DDR or heading a soccer ball or painting your toenails purple. Participating in something she loves, even if it's out of your comfort zone, will help you appreciate the traits she doesn't share with you.

Do something you enjoy.

Try the reverse—do something *you* enjoy—without the expectation that she's going to fall in love with quilting, tennis, or haiku. If she does, great. The point of the thing is for her to respect your individuality, just as you've shown that you honor hers. (You might want to lay some ground rules for this: no eye rolling, dramatic yawning, or use of the L word—*lame*—from either of you.)

Make a collage together.

Pull together a stack of magazines, two pairs of scissors, two glue sources, and two large pieces of paper or poster board. Set a timer for ten minutes. In that ten minutes, each of you will pull out pix from the magazines that appeal to you. Don't stop to analyze why; if it catches your eye, cut it out. When the timer dings, each of you will make a collage using the images you've gathered. Place your finished pieces side by side. One glance is going to show how marvelously unique you both are. You'll never again think of her as a carbon copy.

Make a list of expectations.

Make a list of the expectations you have for your daughter, both now and for the future. Honestly examine them to see if any of them conflict with what you know about who she is. You may find yourself crossing out *Keep her room neat* for your on-the-go tomboy, or

Participate in sports for your Anne of Green Gables dreamer. You'll find yourself letting both of you off a hook neither of you needs to be on.

Name what needs to be changed.

As you're enjoying all this, you may also come up against some obstacles, some things about your daughter that, despite your best efforts, you just can't wrap your mind around. You know in your heart that the way you do it really would be better for her. We can call those kinds of things "The Way NOBODY Just 'Is.'" Things like:

- Going off to pout every time she's crossed.
- Using shyness as a reason to be rude.
- Pitching a royal fit.
- Doing whatever it takes to get her way.
- Lying.
- Treating you like her personal assistant.

It doesn't matter what personality color she is. It makes no difference whether she's an introvert or an extrovert, a gifted athlete or a musical prodigy, the middle child, only child, or genius child.

Out of the Mouths of

Mini-Women

"There are some movies and books and clothes that I enjoy that Mom just hates. I feel like I have to appreciate what she does and dislike what she dislikes. Sometimes I just don't feel the mutual understanding that Mom and I don't have to love the same things. We are different people. This has nothing to do with morals or values, just tastes. I love my mom and just don't want to risk hurting her feelings or anything if I acted like I hated the kind of music she likes, or act like I feel bad if she puts down my taste."

age 12

None of the above is part of anybody's natural personality, physical makeup, or personal destiny. They just plain aren't okay. You can use her learning style to decide how to nip those behaviors in the tween bud—but please, please do it.

Yeah, there might be a reason why your hitherto honest daughter starts telling whoppers. Go ahead and find out what that is. But it would be wise not to use it as an excuse to let her get away with it. There are acceptable ways to express those funky emotions, and I think it's one of your most important jobs to lead her to those. "That's just the way she is" doesn't apply when she's staging a coup on your household.

Play "what if."

The tweens I've worked with love to play "what if." You probably did too, although you might be a little rusty. I know your daughter will be glad to help you.

These "what ifs" may help you be more comfortable with the "her" that isn't "you":

- What if—we each got a thousand dollars to do whatever we wanted with?
- What if—we were going on a week's vacation, just us two? Where could we agree to go? What could we do together?
- What if—we could each help one person? Who would it be and what would we do?
- What if—we could each ask the other that one question we've always been afraid to put out there?

Bridging the Gap

Merciful God,

I confess that I've sometimes read _____ wrong because I was seeing myself instead of her as you made her. Please be my guide in discovering her uniqueness and in helping her grow from there. I'm going to fall short in that at times, I know. Please bridge the gap between my ability to see her and how completely she needs to be seen. Through Christ our Lord. Amen.

3

Why Can't She Just Be Herself?

"There's trouble ahead when you live only for the approval of others, saying what flatters them, doing what indulges them. Popularity contests are not truth contests.... Your task is to be true, not popular."

Luke 6:26

"I wish my mom understood more about how hard fitting in is. Even though people keep telling you it will be all right, it's normal to be really scared."

age 11

We've established that being one-of-a-kind, genuinely real is hugely important for a tween girl. Now all you have to do is let her have at it. Right?

Oh, that it were that simple. For any of us, actually, but particularly for her. Just when she's realizing that she has a self of her own and comes to like the idea that her tastes and interests and idiosyncrasies are unique to her alone, the world around her clears its throat and says, in tween vernacular, "Okay, you're just *weird.*"

You might expect that for a girl who, shall we say, marches to the beat of a decidedly different drummer (and we'll deal with that specifically). But does an "average" girl—whatever that is—come up against it too?

She does. A tweenie doesn't have to be a championship chess player to be considered "different." Any aberration from the norm is held suspect in the tween world. Even the girl who seems to *set* the standards for what's in and what's out has to work pretty hard to maintain her position as coolness monitor.

It isn't only her peers who make it hard for her to "just be herself." Factors from the way her school is run to the way the gospel is preached can call her view of who she is into question before she really has a chance to bring it into focus.

One of those factors may unknowingly be you.

At the same time, you are the person most likely to notice if she isn't being true to herself. You of all people can tell the difference between Daughter Feeling Comfortable and Daughter Floundering. Have you ever watched her at a party where she doesn't know many of the kids? Is she a mere shadow of her former self as she cases the situation and decides whether to join in or run for the restroom? Does she hold her usually warm-fuzzy self aloof until she's sure it's safe to venture in? It's the rare eight- to twelve-year-old girl who propels herself into the middle of this unknown and says, "I'm here—let the games begin!" And if she does, she's going to immediately be pinned as "weird," and we're back where we started.

What's that all about?

Getting Clear: What Gets in Her Way?

There are numerous obstacles that block your daughter from truly living into the self she's just starting to find. Some of those barriers are "out there" in her world, things you may not even be aware of because now she's spending more awake time away from you than with you. Even if she's homeschooled, the outside stuff finds its way to her and makes it a challenge for her to behave authentically.

The other is comprised of roadblocks that can exist at home— again things you may not know about because they're often silent. Before we move on, please remember that none of this is meant to make you look in the mirror and cry, "I'm the worst mother ever! She's going to be in therapy for the rest of her life!" This is just information that may or may not apply to your daughter and you, so under no circumstances should you beat yourself up. Please just take what fits and use it to become an even better parent than you already are—and allow yourself a little pat on the back for the things you've managed to avoid.

Before we go on, be aware that different girls hit this wall at different times, and the rare few not at all. Your daughter may breeze through her tweens so self-assured you're convinced she's a social prodigy, and suddenly freeze when she's thirteen. Others seem to struggle from the fourth grade on. Even the girl who truly doesn't care what other people think is aware that others just don't get that and find her strange.

Roadblock #1: She gets labeled.

Some of you will rush to say that you protect your tween daughter from as much secularity as possible so that she isn't exposed to the current culture. But really, every girl has a culture, a small society that she's growing up in. Your daughter's may largely be a Christian school and the church community. Or her private school and the local youth athletics program. Or public school and her gymnastics/dance/cheerleading world. Or the homeschool co-op and her large extended family. Her surroundings and the people she spends the most time with constitute a culture for her, and what that culture expects is on a continuum between allowing her to flourish as an individual and demanding that she conform in every detail.

Within that small world, she has probably already earned a label for herself, whether she wants it or not. If you listen to her conversations with friends, you may hear things like, "She's that girl who always tells on everybody to Mrs. So-and-So." That "girl" has been labeled "The Ratter Outer"—don't anybody trust her. The poor kid may just have a strong sense of responsibility. Your daughter may have that as well, but to keep from also being dubbed as a dreaded "Ratter Outer," she's going to hide that important part of herself.

The same is true for "The one who dresses up all the time" ("Miss Priss") and "That one girl that raises her hand, like, every five minutes" ("Teacher's Pet"). Sure, the labels can be flattering: "That girl that dances so good" ("The Ballerina"), "You know, the girl with the really pretty hair" ("Girly Girl"), or "She's the one everybody copies" ("The Popular Girl"). Tweens can actually be quite complimentary and even idealize each other, but a girl who's up on the dance pedestal may feel like she can't sign up for soccer, and the little scholar who makes a B- will make a beeline for the girls' restroom to cry.

Roadblock #2: She knows what a girl is "supposed" to be.

In addition, somehow, no matter how sheltered they are, tweens pick up on what a "girl" is "supposed" to be. Her BFFs may accept her without question, but she would have to be in total isolation from the world not to get wind of the larger culture's expectations for a female. We'll talk more about the beauty culture in a later chapter, but there's more to it than what she's expected to look like. Her generation of girls gets the message that they have to be the best at everything they do, should be liked by all, and must wear, do, say, and own all that is currently considered cool — whatever that is at the moment.

If that sounds a lot like the teenage world, it is — and there's your trouble. A tween girl has barely gotten a whiff of what psychologist Emily Hancock calls her "root identity,"[1] and she's already in a position of having to defend it or compromise it — because of course nobody's root identity is to excel at everything she tries, maintain constant popularity, and be at the top of the trends at all times. That doesn't even describe a real person! A teen girl has known herself longer and has a somewhat better chance of holding onto her root identity if she has actually found it. The naturally carefree, basically confident eight-year-old is far more at risk for losing that identity because she's so easily influenced, so much more trusting, so readily bruised. Without encouragement and validation, that carefree confidence can be gone before she's ten.

Roadblock #3: Other people call the shots.

When I do authenticity workshops with tween girls, I always ask them why it's so hard to just be them. The hands go up, because they know the roadblocks.

A tween girl knows what's generally accepted as cool and what isn't. She can go ahead and get a perm even though nobody else has one, but she better be prepared to be called everything from "Annie" to "Labradoodle." She collects stamps? I doubt she's going to admit that to the girls with iPods in their backpacks.

What the popular kids might think, even if they're not her friends, matters a lot to tweens. This is wrapped up in what's cool and what isn't, only on a more personal level. This isn't just the general coolness factor; this is about acceptability to the people who can control just how miserable her life will be. Teenage girls can be masters at this, handing down judgments in subtle ways. Tweens don't have that kind of finesse yet, so the decisions about who has fallen from grace are often expressed rather brutally. "You're not eating at this table. You smell." "Go away, Brainiac." "I don't know why I don't like you. I just don't." Anyone who says she would rather have someone tell her straight out how she feels rather than couch it in subtleties never went to elementary school.

A tween girl learns quickly to cover up anything that's going to make her the object of a Popular Crowd attack. This is not to say that if your daughter is a leader and has a lot of friends she's automatically cruel. Such a position merely offers up that temptation, which, again, we'll talk about in a later section. Just know that raw judgment runs rampant in the tween world and has a tremendous impact on authenticity.

Even if they don't worry about their peers in general, they often care what their friends might think. A BFF is a most sacred thing. So much of a tween girl's identity is wrapped up in that special mirror of a person. She knows who she is partly because of what's reflected back to her by this friend she can't live without. She doesn't consciously see it that way, of course. For her it's this—lose the BFF, and who will she sit with at lunch or giggle with in the restroom or call to find out what they're wearing today? She has a good chance of being left to go it alone, because BFF often takes the rest of the friends with her when she inexplicably goes. More on that in section four, where we cover girl politics. For now, just know that many tweens will hide parts of themselves rather than risk losing best friend status.

Roadblock #4: She has to hide certain things.

Every tween has things she thinks she has to hide. This applies to things she herself thinks of as "bad." It isn't just a matter of being laughed at or excluded. It's about "everybody" knowing what a horrible little person she is, in her estimation. She still sucks her thumb in private. She wets the bed. She has a learning disability. Her parents fight all the time, which she believes is somehow her fault. She has been sexually abused and she hasn't told anyone. She just somehow knows she isn't as good as other people and she would die before she would let anybody know it.

Many, many times, especially on the younger end of her tween years, a girl doesn't realize how much of herself she's burying just so no one will find out the "truth" about her. As a result of going underground, she is likely to act in ways that are in themselves "weird" to the rest of the kids, so that she's pushed even farther from acceptance and can't figure out why. Their saying she "is just annoying" tells her nothing about what she's doing to make her the class misfit.

Roadblock #5: She thinks she has to be perfect.

Not all tween girls are perfectionists. I'm sure there are some mothers who wish their daughters were, just for a day or two! It does look like that almost-perfect girl-child would be a dream to raise, but any mom of a junior perfectionist knows her daughter is in constant turmoil. "What if I spill something on my outfit? What if I don't make an A on the test? What if I make some weird noise when I'm laughing? What if I ask too many questions? What if I don't ask enough? What if I ask the wrong ones?" In that quest to reach an unobtainable goal, there's very little room for discovering what's real about her.

Roadblock #6: She's undeniably unique.

On the other end of the spectrum from the perfectionist is the tween girl who is so—um—untypical that even you, her mother, wonder how she's ever going to fit in. She's obsessed with fantasy or history and tends to live in a world of her own. She's incredibly bright and isn't afraid to tell everybody else how much they don't know.

She's a little mystic or a mini-prophet and alienates people with her pronouncements about their doom. You love her, you even get where she's coming from, and you're sure her eccentricities are going to be of great service to the world someday. But right now you fear for her, and rightfully so. Though it would seem that the child who doesn't seem to care what anybody thinks is most herself, deep down she does care about acceptance, and that sense of belonging is going to elude her without balance in her life. She is the tween most likely to get in her own way.

Roadblock #7: She has a physical, mental, or emotional challenge.

It's a jungle out there for tweens with physical disabilities, difficulties with learning, and behavioral conditions such as ADHD. Being true to self is harder for no one. No one. They live in a world that is still uneducated in how to accept them as the "regular people" they are. They have special needs, are in special education and special programs, but their peers don't treat them as special. They treat them as anomalies. It's the rare person of any age who can get past that to a real identity.

Roadblock #8: She's overprotected.

With the next few roadblocks I know I'm treading into delicate territory, because you're very likely to think I'm telling you what you're doing "wrong" in your own house. Truly, I'm not. I am only offering up what I've learned and what people far wiser than I have determined, just so you can examine what you're doing and see if it might need to be tweaked. I'm operating under the assumption that you wouldn't be reading this book at all if you weren't looking for ideas and support—and this is meant to be both.

So here goes—there are things that frequently happen at home which can be barriers to a daughter feeling confident to be who she is. I'll start with the danger of overprotection.

I'm not talking about refusing to let your daughter watch R-rated movies or walk to her friend's house a half mile away or wait for you outside the dance studio alone in the dark. That sounds like responsible parenting to me. So does monitoring her Internet usage and checking out the parents when she's invited to spend the night at a new friend's house. I especially love it when moms allow their daughters to be little girls for as long as they want to — playing with dolls, playing dress-up, pretending to be Superwoman, sleeping with her soccer ball. To me, that's the kind of protection a girl needs from her mom.

The kind I'm referring to is "protection" from making choices. We've touched on this before, but I want to make it plain. We know we have had to struggle and fail and even suffer at least a little in order to grow into our truly mature selves. (If you're like me, you're still doing it.) But it's easy for us to forget that our kids have to do the same thing. We cannot do it for them, any more than we can continue to brush their teeth for them. What we can do is teach them how to make decisions. We do them a disservice if we make every single choice on their behalf.

That has a huge impact on their perception of themselves. A tween girl who is constantly told what to wear, what to read, what activities to participate in, which girls to be friends with, and how to spend every minute of her time — all things she could appropriately have some say in without the results being catastrophic — will be insecure about her own preferences and tastes and ideas. She will constantly look to you to make sure what she thinks is "okay" — and her peers will have a great deal more influence on her than you want them to, trust me.

Roadblock #9: She lives in a rule-heavy home.

No one is more aware than I am that you have to have rules at your house or chaos will reign and tweens already feeling entitled will try to take over the whole operation, and sometimes succeed. I've seen it happen, and it isn't pretty. I'm also a big proponent of setting limits early on. Parents who don't do that until their daughters are teenagers and are suddenly facing potentially dangerous choices will themselves face rebellion from kids who understandably say, "Where is THIS coming from?" So, yes, rules now. Definitely.

However, in many Christian homes I've observed, a well-intentioned attempt to raise godly children has stricter standards than a monastery. I can't say it better than Dan Allender, author of *How Children Raise Parents*:

> A conservative home characterized by stringent rules, clear consequences, and high demands on the children ... often lacks warmth, humility, laughter, and tears. The children perform well, obey the rules, and succeed through hard work and perseverance. What they lack is passion, whimsy, playfulness, and vision.[2]

What they lack is the freedom to explore what makes them all they can be. The moms and dads are using the Bible like an instruction manual, their faith like a curriculum. It's all about the rules they think Jesus handed down (I have yet to find them in the gospel), rather than about relationship with God (which I *have* found there). I refer back to the Box example in chapter 1 (page 53). Some things need to be covered by hard-and-fast rules. Other things can be open for respectful discussion. Otherwise you run the risk of raising "generic" kids. No parent really wants that. Overprotection just erupts from the kind of fear we all feel when faced with raising a daughter in this day and age.

Roadblock #10: She is overscheduled.

We've been here before, so I won't beat a dead dog. Just know that in terms of blocks to authenticity, this looms tall. While we're wearing ourselves and our kids out giving them opportunities and providing them with a leg up, as it were, we're not giving them much time to process what they're experiencing and to figure out if it really reflects who they are. Once they're committed to soccer, piano lessons, tennis lessons, junior cheerleading, youth choir, and Wednesday night church programs, they often feel stuck with all of the above and deny any inner whispers of, "I'm sick of soccer," "I would rather read than take piano," "I think cheerleading is sort of lame." They won't let themselves be "quitters," "slackers," or "couch potatoes" — but by staying silent they become inauthentic and miserable and learn to do things that are supposed to be fun and aren't. Nobody shines under those circumstances.

Roadblock #11: Her parents expect too much of her.

It is true that kids, especially tween girls, will rise to the occasion, so to speak. When we raise the bar, they step up and show us all. To a point. Your daughter is already living in a time when *average* is a bad word. Competition for college acceptance, and even more so for scholarships, has become fierce, and parents are paddling like mad to get their kids up to the front, ahead of everybody else. The demands on the kids can easily become too much, and they lose themselves in grades, trophies, certificates, ribbons, honors, and awards. Everything they are is displayed on a shelf or the refrigerator door. No parent means for it to happen. We all know there's more to them than that. But do they?

Roadblock #12: You are too concerned that she isn't fitting in.

This can get confusing. Above I said that when a tween girl is truly—what did I call it?—"untypical"—that can stand in the way of her finding out about all that she is, and it can separate her from her peers, which deep down makes her unhappy.

Now am I saying that your worry about her being separated from her peers can also keep her from being all that she is?

Yes, but I'm talking about worry that creates a barrier of its own. I learned about this when I researched ADHD in girls for a teen novel I wrote. Experts say that too often when mothers see their daughters aren't fitting in, due to their being "different," they panic and "unwittingly send their girls the message that their differences are a weakness and a cause for shame."[3] Rather than helping them to achieve balance while seeing themselves as "gifted non-conformists,"[4] anxious moms may try to erase that ultra-individuality altogether. They can't pull it off, but the trying can do some damage.

Roadblock #13: Her brothers and sisters get in the way.

While sibling rivalry is as inevitable as a dog fight when you have only one bone, it can be tough on the development of individuality if brothers and sisters are allowed to put each other down however they want to. It's one thing to fight over whose turn it is to unload the dishwasher, and another to say, "You're still playing with dolls? What a baby." Or "Mom, don't let her wear that—I don't want my friends seeing me with her in that outfit. They'll think I'm a geek too." Thousands of reinforcements of "You're weird" can occur in a home where a girl is growing up and trying to be who she is.

From the Ultimate Parent

God pays no attention to what others say (or what you think) about you. He makes up his own mind.

Romans 2:11

I said earlier that the Bible isn't an instruction manual, and the Christian faith isn't a curriculum. There were times when I was raising my daughter that I wished that *were* the case, but I'm glad now that it isn't. How much more satisfying and meaningful—and at times memorable!—is it to come to understand the concepts found in the Word of the Lord and apply them to that unique little creature known as your girl-child? Somehow it makes the Bible even more miraculous when we realize that what it teaches works in every single unique individual's life, without forcing all of those lives to look alike.

There are several passages of Scripture that speak to the issue of overcoming the blocks to authenticity.

The first is the one we opened this chapter with:

"There's trouble ahead when you live only for the approval of others, saying what flatters them, doing what indulges them. Popularity contests are not truth contests.... Your task is to be true, not popular."

Luke 6:26

Jesus understands what tweens are up against. He also points out to us as parents that we constantly struggle with the same thing. Which to me means that we need to offer our girls compassion when they start "living for the approval of others." As women, we are the best equipped to "get" that being true and being popular aren't likely to exist together, and we are the best equipped to help our daughters figure out which is most important. Just knowing that *of course* it's more godly to be honest than well-liked doesn't automatically make it easy to live that way. But Jesus says here that it's possible. We can show them how.

If we actually *know* how. Jesus doesn't fail us there either. He spells it out clearly in Matthew 5:14–16.

> *"You're here to be light, bringing out the God-colors in the world. God is not a secret to be kept. We're going public with this, as public as a city on a hill. If I make you light-bearers, you don't think I'm going to hide you under a bucket, do you? I'm putting you on a light stand. Now that I've put you there ... shine!*
>
> *Keep open house; be generous with your lives."*

The light he's talking about is *reflected* light from what he's given us—not what we try to be to stand out. I see in this passage three things you can instill in your daughter.

Never hide who you are.

Never hide who you are—not by refusing to raise your hand in class so people won't think you're a brainiac, not by holding back in choir so people won't call you a show-off, not by crumpling up your drawings because somebody might say they're stupid. As a mom, your encouragement (not your pushing), your honest praise, your help when someone does call her a name, will make it safe for her to come out from under that bucket. The happy by-product: this will make her more likely to share her faith effectively, something she won't be able to do if she's ashamed of who she is.

Shine as brightly as you can.

That doesn't equate to "Be the best at everything you do." It simply means, "Be the most authentic light you can be in your daily round." Rather than just give her the opportunity to be the MVP of her soccer team or get to Level 3 in dance, you also need to teach her to smile a real smile—give genuine hugs—say sincere, encouraging words—take an interest in other people—find joy in the little stuff. She will radiate in her own way the light God is shining on her as a person, not just as a student, an athlete, a performer, or an obedient offspring. Your appreciation for who she is will bring that glow to her face and into her actions.

Be generous with yourself.

Let me clarify that for those of you who are so generous with yourselves you don't know how to say no and are so overcommitted you're living on Starbucks and adrenalin. This isn't about time. It's about being present. A mentoree of mine said to me the other day, "What I love about you is that when I'm with you, you make me feel like I'm the only one you have to think about, even though I know you have about a thousand other things you should be doing." I think she caught me on a good day, but I basked in that compliment because that *is* how I want the young women I work with to feel. And that's how our daughters want to feel. And that's how God wants them to be for their friends, their tasks, and their time with him. You do have other things to do besides listen to the latest tween girl drama in her life. But if you can give her five minutes of undivided attention, she will learn to be that kind of person as well.

The blocks to her authenticity will still be there even if you do all those things. Society will still try to tell her who to be. So will her friends, the popular kids, her fellow siblings, and sometimes even you (subliminally). But she will be so much better equipped to knock them down, get around them, or ignore them if she's consciously reflecting the love of the Lord. Help her do that now, when this will sound exciting and fun and special to her. As a tween she is at the perfect place developmentally to embrace the concept that God loves her and wants her to sparkle for him. Do it — and bring on the sunglasses.

Test Your Own Waters

There are several things I'd love for you to think about as you strive to be your daughter's ally in her journey to become herself. As always, handle them in a way that works for — of course — the authentic you.

Remember a time when ...

In order to get your empathetic juices flowing, get in touch with your sense of humor and think of a time when you:

- told a lie so you'd fit in or wouldn't feel like a weirdo.
- wore an outfit like everybody else had and felt totally self-conscious the entire time.
- were at a party where you felt like an alien.
- couldn't think of a thing to say when somebody you really wanted to be friends with started to talk to you.
- snubbed somebody you liked because you were with people who probably wouldn't accept that person.
- pretended to be fine when you weren't so nobody would know what you were really feeling.
- not said what you knew because people might think you were a know-it-all.

If you can both laugh at yourself now but remember the pain then, you can be compassionate with your daughter and even share those experiences with her. Female misery truly does love company.

This is a little darker, but if you're willing to look at it, I think it may prove helpful. Did you ever deny your authenticity and find yourself:

- putting on a persona that *so* wasn't you?
- becoming resentful and blaming other people for stifling you?
- never feeling quite at ease?
- losing your connection with God?
- not being able to discover your purpose?
- just doing what other people expected you to do?
- rebelling against other people's expectations but not knowing what your own were?
- suffering from anorexia, bulimia, depression, constant anger, or frenetic busyness?

Can you buck popular opinion?

If you have ever said or been tempted to say to your daughter, "Don't worry about what other people think," ask yourself if you honestly pull that off yourself all the time. See if you can remember the last time you kicked yourself for not saying what needed to be said or doing what should have been done because you were scared off by opinions. We're not talking *mea culpa* here. This is just another way to understand what your daughter is going through.

For a little practice in being yourself, try this:

- Make a list of five things (maybe even ten) that you would do if nobody would think you were strange for doing it. Take pictures of insects? Try skateboarding? Dust off the old cassette player and listen to eighties' music wearing leg warmers? Let your kids cook dinner under your supervision? Choose one and just do it. Enjoy it to the hilt.
- Dream of how it would be if you parented like nobody was watching.

Going for It

I'm sure that just from reading about the obstacles, you've already come up with ideas for how to help your daughter get past them to her true self. Just in case you're still baffled, I'm putting some suggestions out there for you to ponder and perhaps choose from. They're organized by the specific barriers your tween may face so you can pay particular attention to the ones that apply to her.

She insists on being the clone of the girls in her world.

If you can barely tell which one she is when they all get off the bus, your daughter falls into this category, and actually, that isn't all bad. First of all, to a certain degree, wanting what "everybody else" has makes sense in this stage of her development. She wants the same Crocs, headband, and hoodie the entire tween girl population owns because a sense of belonging is hugely important to her. As I've said before, this is her first foray out into the world where people don't have to love her. She's quite rightly trying to find a safe place in it, and her first step is to look like she belongs. We might actually be doing the same thing ourselves when we give that jacket with the shoulder pads to the Goodwill and shop for one of those cute cropped blazers "they" are all wearing.

Secondly, when she gets to school or church and her outer trappings are just like the other girls', she avoids being visually set apart, which actually gives her a better chance of being able to express other parts of herself authentically. If she isn't considered "weird" in the way she dresses, her friends probably aren't going to think she's "weird" when she says she'd rather paint this afternoon than practice cheers in the backyard again.

The trouble comes in when she thinks she has to have the latest trend for people to like her. You can help her change that particular conviction — the one that sounds like "Mo-om, they won't hang out with me if I wear tha-at!" But you won't do it by forcing her to wear "embarrassing" clothes that make her look like a misfit right out of the chute. Nobody's her best self when people are pointing and laughing in that way only tween girls can. You won't be teaching her how to be a strong individual. You'll be teaching her what it feels like to be mortified. The object is to let her look like she belongs to the pack but still encourage her to be an individual within that group. You can do it by:

- putting a reasonable limit on spending for the next big thing, as well as on the number of shopping trips that will be made.
- making it a fun thing to discover her own style (more on that in the next few chapters).
- coaching her privately when you see her talking, laughing, scowling, and hair-tossing *exactly* like her friends when you know her actions don't ring true.

Some of the "cloning" also has to do with tween role models. The clothes they "all" want are often patterned after teen idols. Wanting an outfit like Hannah Montana doesn't mean your daughter's trying to be somebody she's not. I would, however, monitor the celebrities she adores. So far Taylor Swift and Miley Cyrus haven't fallen into the Lindsey Lohan/Britney Spears trap, so there's not a lot of harm in your daughter wanting to somehow capture their look. Just make sure you're there if her faves start shaving their heads and getting arrested for DUI.

Since she's already primed to look up to people, this is a great time to encourage your daughter to look at even better role models. A lot of tween girls devour biographies, so some doses of Clara Barton, Florence Nightingale, Corrie ten Boom, Maya Angelou, and Eleanor Roosevelt would go down really easily and give them amazing footsteps to follow in.

Another step is to get your daughter involved in something bigger than herself and her material wants and her obsession with fitting in. Volunteer work as a family, sponsorship of a Compassion child, a way for her to serve at church — activities like this not only get her mind off of doing-saying-wearing the right things; they bring out marvelous qualities she didn't know she had.

The cloning thing usually passes, but when it's here it provides some great teachable moments.

She seems dependent on the approval of her friends, especially her BFF.

Some questions you need to ask yourself include:

- Are there other things she'd like to do but won't because her BFF doesn't do them?
- Does she always give in to her friend's choices about what to do with their leisure time together?
- Has she abandoned former relationships or pastimes to spend more time with her BFF? Does she seem content with that — or is she whining, arguing, and talking back more than usual?

If the answers concern you, tell her what you're observing and ask her if she sees it too. Tween girls usually have an uncanny way of stepping outside themselves and looking at themselves objectively — far better than their teenage sisters. She's discovering "self-reflection" for the first time in these years[5] and she loves doing it with some guidance. The girls on my tween blog are all over it when I ask them to comment on what color says it all about them, or how they react when somebody hurts their feelings. Their insights into themselves put some adults I know to shame. So this is a perfect time to process together how much of what they're doing is

BFF dependence and how much is a new part of themselves they're discovering.

She shows evidence of self-hatred.

When Marijean was in her tween years, she exhibited some mild-to-moderately disturbing behaviors that didn't fit with the way we were raising her: outbursts of anger if someone told her she was pretty, uncharacteristic resistance to dressing up (except in costumes), and outright refusal to improve anything about her appearance because people might look at her and make a big deal out of it. Given her self-confidence and zest for life in other areas, that made no sense to us. Then when she was twenty-one her girl cousins, ages twelve and fifteen, revealed that their father had sexually molested the two of them all their lives. In his belongings, pornographic pictures of our daughter at age three were found.

She has no recollection of the situation, but hindsight explains her tweenage aversion to attention paid to her body, as well as other things that went down during her teen years. Jim and I like to think that the things we did right by her as she grew up kept the effects of that traumatic experience from being worse than they were. But if we'd known, we could have gotten her the help she needed. We would have handled some things differently. She might not have had to struggle with hating her own body.

I'm not suggesting that if your daughter is angry or self-sabotaging that means she's been sexually abused. But it does mean something is going on, and even if it doesn't seem monumental to you, if it manifests itself in any of these ways, it's something that can cause her to turn on herself:

- unexplained anger
- sleep disturbances
- physical complaints not accounted for medically
- circles under her eyes
- general lethargy
- unfounded fears
- regression into old behaviors

It isn't a normal part of being a tween to dislike herself. If it's evident that she does, talk to her gently about what might be bothering her. If her relationships, schoolwork, and general well-being are being adversely affected, don't hesitate to get professional help. Self-hatred in the sunniest years is such a loss.

She's a perfectionist.

In spite of her straight A's and her flawless appearance and her spectacular-for-a-tween accomplishments, she is never quite satisfied, and she can wring everybody around her out with her anxiety over what she isn't getting right—things nobody else can even see. What to do? You can't really say, "I only want you to get B's from now on," or "For the rest of the season, you need to give only 75 percent on the soccer field." Her desire for excellence is part of who she is. It just isn't *all* that she is—so I suggest providing opportunities for her to do things that (a) she can have fun doing but doesn't have to be good at (games that totally rely on chance or non-competitive activities like tubing and jumping rope and climbing trees) and (b) that *nobody* has to be good at to enjoy (journaling, watching movies, reading, playing with hairstyles, throwing snowballs). She needs plenty of activities with no evaluation involved. Anything she can do for the pure joy of it will help her ease off on what she demands of herself.

You can expect meltdowns from a perfectionist, but don't let her wallow in her perceived failures. What went wrong? Can you fix it? Okay, let's move on. Help her honor her own mistakes. In the meantime, check yourself to make sure you aren't either modeling perfectionism or registering shock when she doesn't excel.

She has special needs.

Challenges your daughter took in stride up until second grade may now make her feel like a freak of nature, most of which is due to the reactions of other kids who haven't been taught that people with handicaps actually have feelings. While you can and should be her advocate in making sure her educational needs are met, you can't control the reactions of her peers, even when they stand in the way of her feeling at ease enough to be herself. But you can help her take charge of her own actions by:

- Not making everything about her a part of her limp or her lisp or her dyslexia. Those things impact her life, but by keeping them in perspective, you can help her see herself as somebody other than "That girl who talks (walks, breathes) funny."
- Not making a huge production out of your advocacy. If you have to complain to the principal about the lack of wheelchair ramps or closed captioning on the audio visuals, keep that out of earshot of her classmates. She wants them to see her as normal. In so many ways she is, so give her that chance, rather than always calling the not-normal-for-everybody-else things to everyone's attention.
- Realizing it's ultra-important for her to be like the other girls in whatever ways she can—her clothes, her "stuff," her language, her music. She already knows what makes her different. In order to feel comfortable enough to be an individual, she has to also know how she's the same.

She is, shall we say, eccentric.

You would think the way-far-out-there girl is the one being most herself, and that is sometimes true. The job of the mom is to make sure she isn't using her I'm-not-like-anybody-else status as a shield against hurt feelings. A nine-year-old friend of mine told me she wanted to be weird. When I asked her how she thought she was weird, she said she didn't know, she just wanted to be. A little more probing revealed that she wasn't where the other girls in her fourth grade class were in terms of clothes, boys (*boys*?), and "stuff" (iPods, Webkinz collections, etc.). Since keeping up was the only way to be accepted, and she had no hope of doing that, or actually any desire, she'd decided to just "be weird" and act as if she wouldn't be a part of the non-weird crowd if they begged her to. If you're sure your daughter is only pretending to be a "freak show," you can help her find and get comfortable with her normal.

First get her to spend time doing things the rest of the family does, as well as her own "thing." Raking leaves, topping pizzas, playing board games, helping with the grocery shopping, cheering for a basket-ball team—those kinds of communal activities at home can give her the sense of belonging there that she can take into her world. The idea that "I'm good enough to belong in this group" will get her a long way.

Talk to her about what it takes to be a part of things in her world. Then address whether she really wants to fulfill those expectations. Ask her if she's going so far in the other direction so she won't have to risk trying and failing. Could she gather other girls around her who don't want to be tween clones either and enjoy them?

Don't tell her she's right and "they" are wrong. But don't try to convince her she needs to either conform or hush up about it because that's the way the world is, either. The truth is somewhere between those two extremes: conforming enough to get along, yet still main-taining her unique identity.

There is a very good chance that your daughter really is a breed apart. How cool is that, really? My daughter was—still is!—one of those, and although it was hard for her at times, the struggle to maintain her individuality without becoming a social leper made her both a unique and a compassionate young woman. I would suggest:

- talking about why people don't get her and practicing with her ways she could respond that would not only make her less of a "weirdo" in other people's eyes but would allow her to share her gifts and talents.
- teaching her to respect other people's right to be "normal"; just because the other girls aren't artists, computer geeks, or experts on life during the Civil War doesn't mean they're shallow.
- helping her find other girls she has things in common with.
- letting her know it's okay to be like everybody else in some ways.
- helping her see that in the future, it will be more and more okay to be "different," but be aware that middle school is the most painful place to live outside the box.
- pointing out that in the future, as her social circle expands, she is also more likely to find other people who share her

personality or interests and who themselves were probably labeled "different" too.

You know you're more than moderately protective.

If your heretofore non-whiner is complaining that all the other moms are letting their daughters post on an age-appropriate blog, stay home for ten minutes by themselves, or go to a sleepover without an affidavit on the parents of every girl who's going to be there, that could be a sign that it's time to look at your protectiveness quotient. The amount of overseeing you need to do does change over time, but the entrance to the tween years happens without a lot of fanfare, so you may not have noticed that your daughter can handle a little more freedom and trust than when she was six or seven. The key, I think, is to ask yourself: Have I made this rule for me, or for her?

For example:

- Not letting her surf the Net at will is totally for her safety; not letting her get on the Internet at all saves you the trouble of setting parental controls and monitoring the sites she visits.
- Making sure you know the parents of the girls she's spending the night with may eliminate issues she's not ready to deal with; making a rule against all sleepovers saves you the time and maybe the awkwardness of talking to people you don't know.
- Only letting her spend time with boys in groups allows her to learn to be friends with the opposite sex without undue drama; prohibiting her from even thinking about boys (like you can really enforce that . . .) lets you think your little girl isn't growing up.

If you can loosen the reins here and there, self-confidence and realness will blossom in your daughter. You are, after all, trusting her in areas where she's shown a desire to *be* trusted. Tell her she's earned that from you, and she probably won't abuse it. If she does, the consequences are built in: she loses the privilege. And meanwhile, you don't have to micromanage.

You're afraid not to have a rule for everything.

And she is pushing the envelope on every one of them! Rules are meant to let kids know their limits, which in turn makes them feel secure. When a tween girl makes noises about how "un-FAIR-er" a rule is, she no longer feels secure—she feels like she's in lockdown. Then it's time to take a look at whether she really still needs to follow that rule.

Try making a list of all the rules you have for her. All of them.

Decide which ones are no longer necessary by using *this* rule of thumb: *What would the consequences be if I let her decide that for herself?*

Let's say the rule is: *Bedtime is 8:30.* If you let her determine what time she turns out the light, mornings are going to turn into Dante's Third Circle, she'll be falling asleep at her desk, and she'll get every illness that comes around. That rule is a keeper. But depending on her personality, you might let her stay up late a few times just to show her how non-functional she is without the proper rest. Doing so shows her that your rules have good reason behind them—and clues her in on the self-care she's going to take on someday anyway (more on that in chapter 8, "The Care and Feeding of a Tween").

How about: *Bedroom doors must be left open.* If you let her determine when she wants her door open and when she needs privacy just to think and dream and be, she'll experience healthy freedom and be less cranky and, actually, less secretive. A compromise might be: *Bedroom doors must be left unlocked but everyone will knock before entering*, and explain that that's for safety reasons. The same rule will, of course, apply to *your* door.

You might want to announce the elimination of rules one at a time so you'll have a chance to see how decision-making is working. Praise for good handling of choices is always an excellent idea. Letting her learn from not-so-wise choices is an even better one. After all, you already know the consequences aren't dire.

One more thing: Too-stringent rules set us up for failure, as Paul points out in Romans 8. In chapter 7 he talks about the conundrum of not doing this right thing over here that he really wants to, but doing this wrong thing over here that he really doesn't want to. In chapter 8, he offers a solution: focus on God, rather than on following rules. The law code, he says in verse 3, could never set the "disordered mess of struggling humanity ... right once and for all." Through Christ, God did that by showing us how to "embrace what the Spirit is doing in us" (verse 4) and in *that* way overcome the control of sin.

So—in addition to the necessary regulations for running a household—thou shalt put a new roll on if thou usest the last of the toilet paper—there can be discussion of what Jesus would do in a situation—or how God's people in the Bible approached tough problems—or how God's love makes you want to behave. Your daughter will be able to say not just "I follow the rules," but "I know how to do what's right."

She has an abundance of scheduled after-school activities.

Some girls may thrive on that, so how do you know if she's doing too much? These are common signs that it's time to re-examine her schedule:

- She acts tired long before bedtime on a regular basis. Tween girls usually have to be marshaled into bed unless they've had a big soccer game or dance recital or day at Disney World. Ongoing fatigue isn't normal.
- She's cranky more often than not. Cranky is for tired toddlers and angsty teenagers. The tween years are naturally upbeat ones, unless there's something going on.
- She comes up with excuses not to participate in activities, even ones she picked out. Their boundless energy usually makes tweens up for anything, but even the most wound-up have their limits.
- She complains of physical ailments that magically disappear when she has some free time. She may not be "faking it"—her body is probably rebelling against overuse.

The problem is that the thought of not doing the things her friends are all involved in may be monstrous in her mind. You are the perfect one to help her get that in perspective. I suggest having her look at her list of commitments and talk about which ones she actually enjoys. If there are any that aren't personally fun for her, but her BFFs are all there, count up with her the number of hours she still has with her besties even without tap dancing class or the guitar lessons they take together. Tell her you'll help arrange some fun gigs with her buds—because she'll have more time for just hanging out together.

While we're on the subject of extracurricular activities, don't be concerned if she changes her mind a lot about what she wants to do. One of my nieces requires her daughter to choose one activity per semester to do after school. It is never the same from one season to the next. Now eleven, she's played T-ball and soccer. She's won medals in swimming and has currently moved on to basketball. After experiencing the dance world, she chose to take part in a sewing course. My niece is not concerned that her daughter will never be able to stick to anything. Uh, she's eleven years old. And she loves church, her friends, and playing with her baby brother, none of which she shows any signs of wanting to give up. She's one of the most well-rounded, best-adjusted tween girls I know (even taking into account the familial bias!). My niece's advice: Don't buy equipment; just rent it.

It's natural and healthy for your daughter to want to "try on" versions of herself, even in her unscheduled time. One day she's climbing trees, the next she wants to wear pearls to school. She doesn't have as many opportunities to do that if she's always doing some kind of structured activity that limits exploration. I'm certainly not saying dump everything, because things like sports instill so many valuable qualities. But so does learning what to do with unstructured time.

You might think she'll be bored, and at first she may claim to be. That's the time to suggest ways for her to explore the options. Do you have a dress-up box she and her friends can go nuts with? Assign them to come up with three totally different looks and model them for you. Got a mishmash of art supplies? Bring them all out and challenge her (and her BFFs) to draw or paint three different "Future Lives" each. Want to get her off the couch? Turn off the TV, present her with a stack of magazines, and have her make a collage of anything active that appeals to her. Encourage the kind of "pretending"

Mini-Women

"Me and my friends like to do this thing when we have sleepovers where we totally change who we are just to see how it feels. Like, my one friend, she's not girly at all, but she let us put makeup on her and curl her hair and teach her a cheer. She's still a tomboy but sometimes she wears a bracelet now or something like that and nobody says, 'That's not you. You play soccer.' I love that we did that."

age 11

she did as a little girl, updated for tweendom, and see how that plays out in her freedom to experiment with who she might be.

Above all, try not to let what other people are going to think interfere with allowing your daughter some free time. When another mother says, "Aren't you afraid she'll fall behind?" smile and offer her another piece of chocolate.

If you're still not convinced, look at your own stress level. According to Elium and Elium, authors of *Raising a Daughter*, one of the most common complaints from parents of tween girls is having to be "on the go all the time."[6] Consider all of that stress, along with the million other things you're doing, and then ask yourself, "Would I love to ditch about half that stuff and have a chance to enjoy a cup of coffee someplace other than the car?" You will do a great service not only to yourself but to your daughter if you teach her how to slow down, spend time alone, and pace her activities.[7]

You've realized your expectations might be unrealistic.

How to back off of that? In a different way than you might think:

- Don't compare her to other girls her age—even in your own thoughts. Let her be perfectly good enough for you.
- Don't pigeonhole her. A lot of girls her age are in love with horses, sports, and that one sweatshirt they don't want to take off long enough for you to launder it. Those same girls also come alive when you take them out for tea, let them choose a toenail polish (no matter how hideous you may think Petrified Purple is), teach them how to knit, or give them free rein to set the table. The only thing you can really expect is for a tween girl to be ready to try anything, especially if she hasn't already been told she'll never be girly or she's too much of a klutz to ever enjoy athletics. The jury is still out on who she'll become. Quite frankly, I think the jury is always out. (Just this year, at fifty-seven, I took surfing lessons and learned to water ski, bookworm klutz that I am. Was.)
- Check out what you expect of yourself (i.e., flawless appearance, impeccable housekeeping, conflict-free relationships, sin-free Christian walk, and perfectly behaved children) and

don't project that onto your daughter. Lighten up on yourself some and it'll be more natural to let up on her too.

You're afraid she's not fitting in.

This applies to the mother of the late bloomer, the early blossomer, the super smart, the uncannily gifted, and the simply quirky. The first thing to ask yourself is whether she's the one who's unhappy and not you. Not every girl wants a gang of friends. They don't all covet a place in the spotlight, even if you did. Your daughter may actually be rejecting the shallowness she sees around her, and she could be content with a friend or two that she feels close to. If she truly doesn't seem to be bothered by not belonging to the in crowd, you shouldn't be either!

If she's showing indications of being *completely* friendless and unhappy, if you're seeing her being *totally* left out, that's another matter. If it is the case, be the voice that confirms that who she truly *is* is okay. Then you can help her determine and fix behaviors that put people off (which we'll talk about in a later chapter), but support her essence with your voice and she'll develop a voice of her own.

Whatever you do, don't try to make her like everybody else—let her have her rough edges and her funky quirks and her off-the-wall preferences within the limits of manners, safety, and morals. After all, a vanilla life is not what we want for our daughters. Mint chocolate chip is so much more interesting.

She suffers an undue amount of teasing from her fellow siblings.

Some teasing is normal among brothers and sisters, but don't allow other kids in the family to tease her or criticize her for being who she is or trying to discover who she is. Standing up for her will show her that you're her ally in this. That isn't the same as taking sides. Be clear about rules of respect for everyone, including her, which might include:

- If teasing isn't fun for both the giver and the receiver, knock if off. *Stop* means stop.

- No putting down somebody's idea. You can disagree without disrespecting the person.
- Name-calling is strictly forbidden.
- The following words are taboo when used on each other: *dumb, lame, stupid, loser, gay, weird,* and *retarded.*

I'm not opposed to charging a penalty every time a rule is broken, but genuine apologies and, of course, changed behavior, are the real goal.

———

For any tween daughter, no matter how confident and well-adjusted she may be, the best thing you can do for her as her mom is to be a role model for authenticity. Value your own individuality. Live a life that proclaims "This is me!" even as you practice kindness, consideration, compassion, and an acceptance of other people's uniqueness—especially your daughter's. Don't forget: she's watching.

Bridging the Gap

Most Gracious God, my heart aches over the obstacles that stand in the way of _____ being all you've made her to be every minute of her young life. Please forgive me for any I've created myself, including _____. Most of all, please, bridge the gap between the blocks to herself that she has to knock down and my ability to teach her how. Through Jesus Christ, our Lord. Amen.

PART 2

Well, *I* Think You're Beautiful

What It Looks Like

She has always been, shall we say, "casual" about her appearance. It's been a fight since age two to get her into the bathtub, and hair brushing has only been accomplished under the threat of permanent grounding. Not that she doesn't want to be adorable. She thought she already was, because everybody from her grandmother to the clerk at the supermarket has told her so. She has always been ready to grin for a camera, slip into her swimsuit, and don the ridiculous party hat for anybody's birthday.

And then one day she comes out of the bathroom, tears brimming, and says, "I hate my clothes. My hair is stupid. And I never smell good!"

The tears become out-and-out sobbing, and you are left momentarily speechless. When you finally do think of something to say to comfort her, it's along the lines of, "Honey, it's okay. *I* think you're beautiful."

That's apparently wrong, because she glares up at you, face blotchy, eyes swollen, soul smashed, and says, "You *have* to say that. You're my mother!"

The crying crescendos, a door may slam, and you are left wondering, *What just happened?*

Those were the sounds of a tween daughter discovering that "beauty" is one more thing she has to freak out over.

Your own mini-woman can be anywhere on a continuum of beauty awareness that is considered "normal" for the eight-to-twelve age group:

- Couldn't care less about her appearance yet. She may never be all about her looks, but the realization that they at least matter will kick in sometime.
- Still thinks it's fun to shop for clothes and get dressed up for events, but usually comes home from said occasions looking like she hasn't seen a brush or, for that matter, a mirror all day. (I recall that about myself in fourth grade, when I overheard one of the Pretty Girls remarking, "Nancy Naylor never combs her hair.")
- Shows signs of self-consciousness about her appearance (wants to constantly wear a hat, perhaps) but is just as self-conscious doing anything about it (refuses a new haircut because people might look at her).
- Has become fixated on her appearance and is asking when she can wear makeup and try on a pair of heels.
- Obviously thinks she is the cutest little chicky-woman who has ever lived and has already taken on the role of *femme fatale*.
- Is obsessed with her own ugliness, convinced she is bag-over-the-head hideous.

Wherever your little beauty falls on that gamut of possibilities, certain beauty issues are cropping up in her world. It is normal for her to:

- want to look like her friends (a phenomenon we've already discussed).
- be more critical of her looks than she used to be, from going into cardiac arrest over a microscopic pimple to being vaguely aware that she doesn't look the same in leggings as her skinny best friend.

- admire older girls (though not necessarily you!) and does little things to try to look like them; at age twelve, Marijean suddenly wanted to use the same shampoo as her quite lovely nineteen-year-old cousin.

- begin to compare herself to other girls, especially if they're considered cool.

- have firmer likes and dislikes than she used to; purple is no longer just her fave color—she *has* to wear it.

- be torn between your approval of her appearance and that of her BFFs.

- react with more volatility to sibling teasing about her appearance than she once did.

What is your role in this new act in your daughter's life? It's a leading one. As soon as she shows interest in what she looks like in any of the above ways, she has already started to form an image of herself as a woman. Anything you do or say in relation to her appearance becomes part of that image.

Even though I was a tween fifty years ago, I think my experience still provides a good example. When I look at pictures of myself from age eight to age twelve, I can see that I could have been a cute kid. Big brown eyes. Freckles dancing across my nose. A big ol' smile. What kept that from being entirely so was my hair. Throughout those five years, my tresses were never more than two inches long, and I am not exaggerating. I had neither the head nor the face for the pixie look, yet every four weeks my mother overrode my protests and took me to the local beauty salon where I was sheared to within an inch of my life. I looked like a boy. I felt like a boy. Worst of all, the other kids teased me about looking like a boy.

In sixth grade when the hormones kicked in, my hair became curly, coinciding with a growth spurt that included my nose. Even from the objective viewpoint of an adult, I still look at those late-tween photos and think, *You poor baby. Why did they do that to you?*

I eventually grew into myself and won the battle for somewhat longer hair, although until I was out of high school and away at college, it was always (literally) short of what was currently considered stylish, much less feminine. I was in my thirties before I could think of myself as an attractive woman. I'd never had the pleasure of sitting in front of a mirror brushing my hair, or flipping it over my shoulders in coquettish fashion, or piling it into a curled thingie on top of my head for the prom, and somehow that made a difference.

Bless my mother's heart (as we say here in the South), she had no idea she was allowing me to think of myself as gawky and unfeminine. Here's the deal, though: You won't in the end determine how your daughter looks, but you will play the biggest role in influencing how she feels about it.

And that makes *all* the difference.

4

What Does She See When She Looks in the Mirror?

I praise you because I am fearfully and wonderfully made;
your works are wonderful,
I know that full well.

Psalm 139:14 NIV

"My whole life my mom has brought me up telling me how beautiful I am. I think she really does believe it. That doesn't sound stuck-up or anything, does it?"

age 12

The words Marijean said to me that day when she was eleven years old still bring a pang to my mother-heart when I think of them. They're the very words I used in the scenario in this section's introduction.

"I hate my clothes. My hair is stupid. And I never smell good!"

I responded differently than the sample mom. I was, in fact, ecstatic that my child was taking an interest in looking like she actually *had* a mother, and I whisked her immediately to the mall where we picked out some cute clothes and I let her choose any perfume she wanted. Teen Spirit was, I think, her selection. On the way home we stopped at the drugstore and bought a perm-in-a-box (it was the eighties, remember) and spent the evening doing a makeover. Great fun.

Mini-Women

But if I had it to do over again, I would handle it in another way. Because, at the time, I didn't realize that her outburst wasn't really about a sudden interest in her appearance. It was about believing she was ugly—and smelly—and uncool. Given a second chance, I would go there first.

So let's go there now. Many of you already do, but I hope you'll still find information you can use with your beautiful mini-woman.

Getting Clear: Her Beauty Challenges

As I've said, every tween girl eventually notices that the way she looks matters. It's normal, healthy, and usually delightful. The dream of shopping together, doing hair, and painting toenails is what makes a lot of moms want to have a little girl in the first place.

What keeps it from being "the funnest thing ever," as the mini-women themselves would put it, are actually two things:

1. The current Beauty Culture, and
2. Its implantation of a skewed physical self-image.

Right now, you are the one person in your daughter's life who can get her through her tweenhood with a clear, accurate, lovely concept of herself as a young woman. You still have that kind of influence. It's so strong that you can also unknowingly lead her to one that's distorted, self-critical, and exquisitely painful. Fortunately it isn't overwhelmingly difficult to do the former, as long as you start out understanding these six things.

1. What the beauty culture is

As I've mentioned before, your daughter would have to be growing up in a cave for her not to be aware of what is currently considered beautiful. The standards for beauty change, as we all know from looking at pictures of our grandmothers, mothers, and even ourselves when young and fashion-conscious. In the thirties my mother was all about hats and straight, mid-calf skirts. In the early seventies I wore miniskirts so mini I won't show those pictures to the teen girls I mentor! If you grew up in the eighties you knew that big hair, big shoulder pads, and even bigger earrings made a woman look fabulous. (I kind of wish we'd go back to shoulder pads; they make your waist look smaller ...) If you go even further back to the Raphaelite period, plump, fleshy, voluptuous women were considered the most magnificent. I want to know when we're going to return to *that*.

Unfortunately, today's societal image of "beautiful" is impossible for about 98 percent of women. Flawlessly thin—we're talking maybe 14 percent body fat. C or D-cup breasts—and if you know anyone who naturally has a bosom like that on an otherwise skeletal body, you get out more than I do. Thick, straight, ultra-shiny hair—make it blonde—cascading down the back with nary a hint of a split end. Lips so full they could be used as fold-out couches. Nails that owe their perfection to a weekly manicure. And the ultimate: perfect teeth in a blinding shade of white that does not exist in nature.

Nobody looks like that. Models in magazines who appear to look like that don't look like that. Cindy Crawford is reported to have said, "*I* don't even wake up looking like Cindy Crawford!" Photoshop is a miraculous thing. That photo of me on the back cover? I told the photographer not to touch up anything. Except the teeth. Could he just de-yellow those teeth a little? I drink a lot of tea ...

We all agree that it's ridiculous to expect ourselves to resemble anything close to that standard. But there it is in our faces all the time. Don't think your daughter doesn't notice it too. In the Beauty Workshop that I often do with tweens, I ask them to go through magazines and tear out pictures of what are considered beautiful girls. Together they make a collage—and then they enumerate everything I've outlined above. I ask them, "Do you see anybody in this room who fits the bill?" There is much giggling, because of course most of them are still hipless and have no bra in their near futures. "Does this mean we're not beautiful?" I ask. There is a resounding, "No!"

Ask that of a group of teenage girls and the response will be quite different. Hence the urgency for you to get to your tween daughter before she loses sight of how absurd society's expectations are and actually starts trying to live up to them. Even if she's just in middle school, you may have some catching up to do. Remember what it

Mini-Women

"My mom didn't really teach me about being modest. I just grew up with that. She never wore yuck clothes or anything, so I saw that and compared it to other ladies who did — and was like, 'I don't want to do that.'"

age 12

was like for you in fifth, sixth, and seventh grades when it came to the way you looked. Then multiply that times ten to account for your faded memory and the way times have changed. That will give you some clue to what she's facing.

The good news is that there have been some improvements in the modeling industry, which is the main perpetuator of the impossibly thin beauty image. After three South American models died of anorexia-related health problems in 2006, Spanish and Italian fashion organizations banned models with a body-mass index under 18 (anything under 18.5 is considered unhealthy). Spanish government officials and designers have also agreed not to show clothing under a size 6 in shop windows.[1]

The bad news? The US has a way to go to catch up to that wisdom. While some models themselves are taking on the mission to make American modeling healthier, many agencies continue to demand more gauntness. Says one agency owner, "I'm dying to find kids who are too thin. I've got forty-two models in my agency, and I'm trying to get them to lose weight. In fact, I *wish* they'd come down with some anorexia."[2]

Again, the trickle-down effect reaches our tweens. Studies show that girls as young as five already understand a woman's body is supposed to be perfect. By age nine, they begin to compare their bodies to the standard and see how they measure up. "Indeed," say Elium and Elium, "as many as 80 percent of nine-year-old suburban girls are concerned about dieting and their weight."[3]

"I wish my mom understood what the pressure is today to look like a starving model," one reader wrote to me. She was twelve.

Where are they *getting* this?

That leads us to the second thing you'll want to understand.

2. The influence adults have on the beauty culture

We're shocked when our young daughters think they're fat at age eight, or pick out clothes on the rack most of us moms consider provocative, or "desperately want to wear makeup," as one ten-year-old told me. But as Howe and Strauss put it in their book *Millennials Rising*: "Few adults express any particular shock at the thirty-year-olds who write it, the fifty-year-olds who produce it, or the seventy-year-olds whose portfolios profit by it."[4]

They're speaking, of course, of the film industry, although the same can be said of almost all media. It isn't the kids who are setting themselves up to fail in the looks department. It's the very adults who ought to be protecting them. They are the ones sending the messages that affect girls' self-image and, unfortunately, their self-worth—and those messages are everywhere. Blasting loudly from television commercials supposedly selling soap, cereal, or dog food, for Pete's sake. Plastered on billboards daughters can't miss from the backseat of the car. Kids' programs where the girl characters are already svelte. Magazines that carry more ads for cosmetics and fashion than articles.[4]

Again, try as you might, you're hard-pressed to shield your daughter from every medium that sends the message: "Honey, if you don't look like this, you better either get hot, or give up."

3. The influence of their peers

We've already talked (probably to death!) about the power of "the other kids," and that influence extends into matters of appearance. It's natural for a tween girl to measure herself against her girl peers. We all did it when we were growing up. Linda Porter (I can still see her face) was always the prettiest girl from third grade up, and I always knew I wasn't as adorable as she was (not with *my* hairdo!). But I don't remember a crowd of girls that made the rest of us feel like pond scum. I'm afraid things are different now. We'll discuss girl politics more in section four. For now, just know that these kinds of thoughts are bound to enter your daughter's mind:

- Her hair is way blonder than mine.
- She's got longer eyelashes than I do.
- My clothes aren't as cute as hers.
- She doesn't have to wear stupid glasses like I do.

That's fairly normal. What isn't is the importance the results of those comparisons seems to have these days. Tweens wanting highlights in their hair. Angling for mascara. Begging for contact lenses. The things of which teenagers used to be the sole proprietors have invaded the tween world, where they're far too young to be fixated on what they look like—even though they aren't going to look anything like what they look like now in a year or two.

Boys aren't usually much help here either. Girls this age often tell me they don't care what the boys think, but they can't help hearing them because they're so loud. If you have sons too, you know that as they're going through their *own* prepubescent stuff, a lot of them think they have to be funny all the time—in a way far different than what cracks up a girl and her BFFs. Tween boys think it's hilarious to call a girl Helen Keller when she gets glasses or hold his nose when she stands next to him. Even though any self-respecting tween girl will tell you a boy like that is just an ALC (Absurd Little Creep), she is likely to have her feelings hurt—and her self-image taken down a notch or two.

4. The effect you have on her

The mistake I most regret in raising my daughter is that I modeled a harmful body perception for her. I'm not thrilled about sharing this with you because it describes me at my worst, but I'm doing it because it's so incredibly important that you know the power your example can have.

I was in my thirties when Marijean was a tween of nine and ten. Jim and I were both in school earning theater degrees, which meant involvement in the Nevada Repertory Theater as well as classes and homework. We were both working part-time jobs to support our little family, and we were running a professional nonprofit children's theater. I was also trying to keep my still-budding writing career afloat. I know. Crazy. The stress began to whittle away at my weight, and somehow I got the idea that in the midst of the chaos of my life, this might be one thing I could control.

So I lived on Diet Coke and Slim-Fast during the day, was obsessive about doing a daily one-hour Jane Fonda workout, rode my bike everywhere instead of driving the car, and ate a dinner with my family each evening that was barely more than Gandhi consumed. At my then five-foot-seven frame, I got down to 111 pounds. Pictures of me from that era show me gaunt and drawn. The only things that "stuck out" on my body were my bones.

Mini-Women

"I've never thought about what my mom thinks I look like. She's never told me outright, 'I think you're beautiful.' Since I dance, we talked one day about who had a dancer's body. When I said I didn't, she didn't deny it or try to make me feel better about it. She just kind of ignored the comment."

age 12

I actually thought I was keeping my anorexic habits nicely concealed. Many people complimented me on my slim figure, which made me even more determined to lose another pound or two. No one said, "Are you okay? You look like you were just released from a concentration camp." Jim expressed some concern, but he was as wrapped up in our frenetic life as I was, so he was easily reassured by my insistence that I felt great.

It seems that Marijean was the only one who noticed. I didn't learn until years later that she knew the container I'd pulled the label off of and called "protein powder" was really Slim-Fast. That she was aware of my frowning every time I looked in the mirror. That she heard my muttered comments to myself about "feeling fat." She's told me since then that she would look in her own mirror, at her healthy, robust, ten-year-old's body, and think, *If Mom thinks* she's *fat, she must think I'm Jabba the Hutt.*

In addition to her early molestation, that was another reason for her choice of baggy sweaters and sweatshirts, her agony over putting on a swimsuit, her I-give-up-I'm-a-couch-potato attitude when anyone suggested sports. All that before she was eleven years old.

Although I only remained in full anorexic mode for two years, and didn't do any serious damage to my body except cause the early onset of osteoporosis, I maintained what my gifted therapist Glenda Allen calls "anorexic-style thinking." So did Marijean. When she became a teenager, she got on a roller coaster of weight gain and loss, with a cloud of self-deprecation always over her head, that lasted until she was twenty-five years old. And yet through it all she has been and still is a beautiful young woman with a stunning figure. I take responsibility for the fact that she has seldom been able to enjoy it.

"It's not what you do or even what you say about her that makes the difference," Glenda Allen told me. "It's what you say about yourself."

Enough said.

5. The effect Christianity has on her

I recently spoke at a mother-daughter tea, held at a lovely church where all the moms and tween girls were dressed to the nines and had their hair curled and their nails polished and their purses hung stylishly over their shoulders. I was licking my chops, because the topic they'd asked me to speak on was "Inner Beauty."

"How many of you have ever been told that it doesn't matter what you look like on the outside?" I asked them.

Many hands went up. So far so good.

"How many of you believed it?" I asked next.

Every hand stayed up. In fact, a few additional ones were raised.

Okay. That was not the response I expected.

Thinking the girls were only giving the reaction they thought their moms wanted them to give, I told the mothers to close their eyes, and then I asked the question again. The girls looked like the proverbial deer in the headlights as they glanced nervously at each other and then at their temporarily sightless mothers. About half of them kept their hands up. The other half looked like they were about to cry.

Everything in me wanted to shout, "It's okay to be honest!"

Did they really, truly believe that what you look like on the outside doesn't matter at *all*? Or were they parroting what they'd been taught by these same Christian women who could have gone from the tea to a photo shoot and been paid as models?

That actually shouldn't have been a surprise to me. I've seen it over and over again in workshops, at events, in online discussions. Well-meaning Sunday school teachers and youth pastors and conscientious moms seem to have misinterpreted for tweens the scriptural passages that pertain to outward appearance.

In Matthew 6:25, for instance, Jesus says, "If you decide for God, living a life of God-worship, it follows that you don't fuss about ... whether the clothes in your closet are in fashion. There is far more to your life ... than the clothes you hang on your body." Christian adults tell their wide-eyed listeners, "That means your clothes don't count at all." That's a little confusing when the adults delivering the message are in full fashionable regalia. Besides, it doesn't mean that anyway. Jesus is saying, "Clothes aren't *all* that you are. They're not even the most important thing about you. But they're there to be dealt with, nevertheless." If she doesn't get that, the tween girl emerges from Sunday school feeling like she's a total sinner because she *does* care what she's wearing—or she figures, "Oh well, I guess I'm rotten to the core, so I might as well give up trying to be a good Christian."

The birds of the air and the lilies of the field often lead to similar misinterpretations and confusion (Matthew 6:26–30). Jesus says, "Seek *first* his kingdom and his righteousness" (Matthew 6:33 NIV, emphasis mine). He doesn't say, "And while you're doing it, go ahead and dress like a slob and let your hair turn into a rat's nest." In 1 Peter 3:3–4, we're told that our "beauty should not come from outward adornment. . . . Instead, it should be that of your inner self" (NIV). He's telling us that God is more interested in how we live than in how we dress. That doesn't translate into what some girls are hearing from their teachers: that it's wrong to even think about "outward adornment." At all. That they're vain to give it a thought. I don't see that in there. I hear the passage saying that beauty does matter a great deal—that we are to have the "unfading beauty of a gentle and quiet spirit, which is of great worth in God's sight." Beauty doesn't come from a trendy haircut and some lip gloss, but beauty needs to be there nevertheless.

And then there's the other extreme that I've experienced in churches, where a woman's appearance is seen as a direct and singular reflection of her devotion to God. It's the interpretation of Proverbs 31 that reflects its true meaning about as accurately as a funhouse mirror. The model wife described there is certainly something for a woman to aspire to spiritually. A *literal* exegesis leads us to believe we've got to make ourselves a wardrobe of fabulous clothes and wear them while we're preparing breakfast, selling fields, mending the winter coats, and keeping everybody in the household busy and productive. I suspect a number of the Christian weight-loss programs that imply we are not living up to God's expectations if we're packing a few extra pounds are a direct result of that kind of scriptural distortion.

Yeah, the very faith that is supposed to make the path clear for our daughters can definitely throw some booby traps in their way.

With all of that going on in her world, no tween girl would have a chance of entering her adolescence with a decent image of her own beauty if she didn't have a mentor to help her sort it through and throw out what's damaging and cruel and just plain false. You are that mentor. Let's build the foundation for your approach with, of course, our God.

From the Ultimate Parent

I'm offering this to you the same way I present it to the mini-women who read *Beauty Lab*. Same Scripture, same explanation, same everything. It still applies to you, even though you are now a taller tween.

You believe in God, right? You believe God's in charge because God's perfect, yes? So you agree with all the things David says about God in Psalm 139:

- God knows everything about you (vv. 1–4).
- God is everywhere (vv. 5–12).
- God created your "inmost being" (v. 13 NIV).

And if you believe that, then you can say this right along with David:

> *I praise you because I am fearfully and wonderfully made;*
>   *your works are wonderful,*
>   *I know that full well.*
>
> v. 14 NIV

"Fearfully" doesn't mean like Dr. Frankenstein's monster (although even he turned out to have a soft spot). It means "awesomely." You were made to be awesome and wonderful. There it is, right in the Bible. God knit you together with love in every stitch. He thought of you, and you *became*.

You are the result of God's precious thought. You're not some modeling agency's thought (though there's nothing wrong in theory with being a model). Not a Cool Girl's thought (although a lot of Cool Girls are really nice). Or that Boy's thought (which he doesn't even understand himself!). None of those. Just God's thought.

You are a beautiful person. Believe it.

And — God doesn't just want you to *know* you're beautiful. God wants you to show it — not by plastering on makeup or spending a bajillion dollars on clothes, but by shining from the inside. Jesus talked about that in his teaching.

You can—and should—let God's "precious thought" out where it can shine like a light. Be every bit the beauty God created you to be, so other people will see Christ in you and be drawn to you. Then you can love them and show them more about God's works. No one can do that when she's hiding her beautiful self.

Okay … go ahead and ask it. You know you want to: "But aren't some girls more 'precious' than others? Don't some just naturally 'shine' brighter?"

All right, picture God creating a new baby girl. Imagine the God whose works are wonderful saying, "Oops, I didn't make little Megan as precious as baby Brittany. I hate it when that happens."

Uh, no. Every tiny being God creates has the divine fingerprints on her. She's shaped with love and "breathed through" with her own gifts and special brightness. Each child is an original. Each one is God's art. Each is priceless.

And that includes you, Precious Thought. You are fearfully and wonderfully made. Your part is to uncover the beauty—inside and out. It's a journey. Are you ready to begin?[5]

That's what I tell them. I hope you'll take it to heart yourself.

Test Your Own Waters

Whether your daughter ever admits it or not, she learns how to be beautiful—or not—from you. So your next step is to get centered with your view of both your daughter and yourself. Will you try to do these two things? (As always, in the way that comes naturally to you—whether that be journal, mural, or a rousing dialogue with a friend over mochas—with whipped cream.)

- First, describe your daughter to yourself. What does she look like to you? What, if anything, about her could be called un-lovely? Where does her beauty lie?
- Now describe yourself to yourself. How do you name your beauty? What about your appearance do you (fiercely) wish were different, if anything? How does your beauty manifest itself?

If you resist doing this exercise, try your best to do it anyway. None of the following will make sense if you don't have a context within which to work. If you think it's narcissistic, you might want to go back and read #5!

Going for It

Everything I'm about to suggest here takes time and attention, the same kind you devoted to your daughter when she was a baby and needed to be fed, changed, and cooed at. I'm sure you never said, "I do *not* have time for this child right now!" Why say it at this point in her life either? She needs you.

Listen.

Really listen. Most of us aren't as good at it as we think we are. I would probably want to curl up in the fetal position if I had a tape recording of some of my past conversations with my daughter. But with some awareness we can all get better at it.

Provide at least a little time on a regular basis to talk to your daughter by herself. "It's really hard for me to get alone time with my mom," one tween confided to me, "'cause I've got too many sisters. If we go somewhere, so does another sibling." It can be tough to carve out chunks of time for just the two of you, but there are things she probably won't talk about if there's an audience. While sometimes it's less awkward to chat while you're both engaged in something else at the same time, like riding in the car or doing the dishes or folding laundry, it's better not to try to squeeze in a mother-daughter conversation while checking your email, texting your husband, or filling out your tax return. Think about the last time you tried to communicate with your spouse while he was watching a football game and you'll get the idea.

Be prepared for her to act like she doesn't know exactly what to say. The older she gets, the more common it is for her to give you, "I don't know," or "What do *you* think?" That's just a signal that she needs a boost to her confidence. If you assure her that nothing she says is going to be deemed "silly" or "wrong," that you're not going

Mini-Women

"I'm afraid. When I ask something like if I can wear makeup, what will she say? That's because she's never invited me to tell her things or ask questions about anything."

age 12

to come back with "Are you serious? Where did you ever get an idea like that?" she's more likely to ask those questions that are burning in her mind, and less likely to doubt herself.

Don't be quick to judge. If she's asking a question about what you think of makeup or skinny jeans or tattoos, that doesn't mean she's thinking of putting on any of the above. She's just asking for your opinion. Hearing her out doesn't mean you agree or condone. You're just honoring her right to an opinion, a desire, a bit of curiosity. She will, in turn, honor yours — eventually. (You might train her to warn you when she's about to bring up something with potential shock value by saying, "Okay, so Mom, promise you won't freak out.")

Hang in there, even if she starts into territory you weren't expecting to be dragged into just yet. In fact, how much your daughter will open up to you will depend on how much you're willing to hear!

Have an intentional conversation about what's beautiful and feminine.

This can be one of the best discussions you ever have with your tween *if* you allow it to be a two-sided dialogue. This isn't about you sitting her down and giving her your rendition, resulting in yet another set of rules for her to add to the list. It's about coming up with "what beautiful is" together. How on earth do you do that? I have three suggestions.

First, you can both bemoan the fact that to hear people talk, you'd think the only girls who could be considered beautiful are pencil skinny with flawless complexions and dress only in the trends that just started this morning. You can be in agreement on that, for sure. Then together you can think about all the girls and women you know that you consider beautiful. Do they all look like the above? No, you'll decide. You'll discover that the people you've named are all people you love. They're beautiful because you love them. Your definition of feminine beauty can start from there.

Second, do the collage activity described on page 73. You might follow that with a collage of all the people you listed in the above exercise. Comparing the two will say it all.

And finally, you might want to read either *The Skin You're In* or *The Beauty Book* with her. They're both books you "do" rather than just read, and are broken down to fit into those snippets of time you make for your daughter. Enjoy!

Establish parameters.

Now that you've both agreed on what really makes a girl or woman beautiful, you can set some parameters on what's okay and what isn't that will not only save you much wailing and gnashing of teeth (from both you *and* your daughter), but allow your daughter to be more at ease talking to you.

If you've already agreed that a woman is most beautiful when she's as natural as possible, you can simply point that out if your mini-woman decides eyeliner at age nine might be a nice touch. If you two have established before you hit the mall that two inches above the knee is short enough, you can remind her of that if she whips a micro-miniskirt off the rack. If you've come to a compromise that she can have only one trendy item (i.e., it will go out of style before she outgrows it), you'll find her making her choices oh-so-carefully. Setting up parameters is a great way to help you choose your battles. Is it really such a big deal if she wants everything pink? Why tell her you think she looks like a walking bottle of Pepto-Bismol and bring out the unbeautiful in yourself?

Allow some experimentation within those parameters.

She's going to want to know what this idea of "beautiful" looks like on her. We'll talk later about letting her play with makeup and funky do's at home. Right now I'm referring more to giving her chances to practice feeling beautiful in her unique way. That could mean announcing that we're all dressing for dinner tonight and bringing out the candles and china. Or having high tea, complete with hats and gloves for the two of you. Or taking a walk together at dawn and letting the breeze and the light kiss your faces. She won't know what it means to be a truly beautiful her unless she feels it. When she does, she's more likely to replicate it, over and over, and abandon the things that don't work for her.

Mini-Women

"If I try to talk to my mom about, you know, 'stuff,' she puts me down for just asking about makeup and stylish clothes, so I don't even like to talk to her."

age 11

Take as many opportunities as you can to reinforce her confidence in her own special brand of good looks.

That doesn't mean a constant verbal stream of compliments. That'll grow thin, and you'll be rewarded with an eye roll. What about an approving look when she heads out for school looking put together? How about the occasional surprise when she gets into the car: "I hardly recognized you coming out the door! You've grown up overnight." Can you take pictures of her kicking a soccer ball, casting a fishing line, stepping back to view her latest artwork? Anyone doing something they love to do is beautiful. You won't even have to tell her that. She'll know.

Avoid empty praise.

Don't give empty praise or comments like the one that opened this section ("Well, *I* think you're beautiful"), especially when someone has just put her down or she's feeling ugly for no reason at all. Better to help her figure out why she's upset and come up with a plan, or simply break out the popcorn and turn on a feel-good movie. To say, "I don't know what you're going to do when you really have problems" is, of course, not even an option.

Most important of all, be careful what you say about yourself.

We can't instill a positive, healthy, realistic beauty image in our daughters if we don't demonstrate one ourselves. You can tell her all day long that she's beautiful just the way she is, but the minute you stand in front of that mirror and say, "I am disgusting. I have *got* to lose at least twenty pounds"—you might as well have saved yourself a day's worth of words, because everything you said about her has just gone out with the garbage. Try not to do any of these things, not just in front of your daughter, but ever, for your benefit and hers:

- Complain about how fat you are.
- Have a tizzy if someone comes by unexpectedly when you don't have your "face" on.
- Make a big deal out of having to wear something "last year" because you don't have the money for new wardrobe pieces.

- Insist that you and she have to be coiffed and polished when you walk out the door, but let your son go out looking like a homeless person.
- Pick yourself apart: your brows are too thick, your lips are too thin, your hips are too wide, your shoulders are too narrow. While you're picking yourself clean, she's picking up ammunition to use on her own self-image.
- Act like being beautiful is a battle against nature. If you treat self-care as a chore, you take away one of the joys of being a woman—from both of you.

If that seems like the most challenging thing I've asked you to do yet, take a little time to do something that makes *you* feel beautiful. Do it now. In fact, pretty mama, do it often.

Bridging the Gap

Holy Father, Great Creator,

Thank you for making _____ the beautiful child she is. Forgive me if I've bruised her image of herself in any way. And please, please bridge the gap between what she needs to see when she looks in the mirror, and what I can do to help her love it. In Christ's name, amen.

5

Passing the Beauty Care Baton

Didn't you realize that your body is a sacred place, the place of the Holy Spirit? ... The physical part of you is not some piece of property belonging to the spiritual part of you. God owns the whole works. So let people see God in and through your body.

1 Corinthians 6:19–20

"My mom always says when I have an issue, I should come to her and tell her. But I kinda wish she would just say, 'Hey, do you want to try a different haircut or go shopping for some new clothes?' It can get really uncomfortable always having to ask. I want her to be interested in all of me."

age 12

Whether she's a complete non-groomer or she's mirror-obsessed or she's the little beauty who pushes every limit, sooner or later the care and keeping of your daughter's physical appearance is going to lie entirely in *her* hands. Which means that in her tween years, she's standing somewhere on the bridge between you tying her shoes and her buying her own. And you're the one who will walk her across the expanse.

Hopefully you're clear at this point on *why* her relationship with her own appearance has to be healthy, strong, positive, and God-centered. Now let's look at *what* you can do, physically, to help her across that bridge—without hurling one or both of you over the side.

In fact, if you aren't actually grinning (giggling, maybe?) by the end of this chapter, I haven't accomplished what I want to, which is to help you make the trip across the bridge belly-laugh-'til-you-can't-breathe fun. For your daughter *and* you.

Getting Clear: Tween Beauty Isn't an Oxymoron

Dealing with appearance *won't* be fun—not even close—unless you know what to expect in tweenhood. Some of the stuff your daughter might toss out onto the family table could throw you off balance—as in "You want to *what?*"—if you aren't prepared. These are the issues that commonly come up during the eight-to-twelve years. Keep in mind, as always, that these are the "usual" traits. Your daughter may not exhibit any of them yet, and in rare cases never will. But to be forewarned is to be forearmed!

Self-criticism

Most little girls think they're precious—because they are. They *still* are when they turn eight, but somewhere in the tween years they start chipping away at that. Their naturally developing ability to scrutinize and analyze isn't limited to science projects and what's-wrong-with-boys. Sooner or later, most of them turn it on themselves. You may hear:

- I'm fat.
- My lips are huge.
- My hair is gross.
- I hate my freckles (my ears, my nostrils).
- Why did I have to get Dad's nose?
- I wish I looked like Miley Cyrus.
- I'll never look like Miley Cyrus.
- I think I hate Miley Cyrus.
- I think I hate me.

Mind you, in the next breath she may inform you that she's glad she's blonde (or red-headed or curly-haired), or just happily skip out the door to whack a soccer ball around the backyard. But *intermit-*

tent critical assessment of herself in the bathroom mirror (while her brothers bang on the door) is to be expected.

An in-between body

It used to be so simple. When she was a baby, the clothes were marked *3 months, 6 months, 12 months.* As the mom of a toddler you could count on 2T, 3T, 4T. As a preschooler she graduated to the "big girl" sizes in rapid succession, the only hiccup perhaps being an X behind the number. And then it started to get complicated. 6X is big enough around but way too short. Size 8 is slim enough but those legs seem to be coming right out of her neck. Her body is ready for junior sizes, but the style is much too sophisticated for a ten-year-old.

It's absolutely normal for the hormonal craziness she's experiencing to put her little body through several interesting permutations that refuse to fit into off-the-rack sizes. But trying on clothes can become a dismal affair in which that cute new style that "everybody" is wearing just won't hang right from her chubby center or her newfound hips. Tears in the fitting room are not uncommon. But then neither is complete blindness to the fact that this is not her best look. You never can tell. (From one shopping trip to the next.)

If your daughter's body really strays from the "norm"—she's taller than everyone in her grade, she's the class shrimp, she's the first one to be visited by the breast fairy—she may get hung up on that from time to time, unwilling to believe she isn't doomed to weirdness for the rest of her life.

A sudden, unexplained desire to look like a teenager

We've talked about how the marketing world is pushing for age ten to be the new fifteen. Eighty percent of mothers in one study said the fashions they're finding in the girls' department are too provocative.[1] That's a function of our times. However, there is also a *natural* wistfulness in a tween girl to be "grown up," which can show itself in a crush on one of the Jonas Brothers, the doubling of her use of the word "whatever!"—and the belief that makeup is the key to the meaning of life.

Mini-Women

"My mom hasn't given me much advice on beauty. Mostly she says wear clothes that actually fit you, but not so tight they emphasize all your bits of fat."

age 10

In another recent study, 35 to 54 percent of tween girls said they're not too young to wear lipstick, mascara, and eye shadow.[2] Even if your daughter would rather have her face painted at a carnival than wear lip gloss "for real," she will at some point think about what it's like to dress, flirt, style her hair, and apply eyeliner like a sixteen-year-old. Wanting to experiment with a blush brush now is perfectly normal.

Confusion about modesty

While *you* are already concerned about her showing too much cleavage—whenever she gets some—your tween daughter doesn't yet think of herself as a sexual being. She may appear to be boy crazy, mimic the bumping-and-grinding of the high school cheerleader next door, and beg for the skinny jeans that reveal her brand of underwear, but she isn't doing any of that because she wants to be "sexy." No matter how precocious her body is, she doesn't know anything about being seductive. Most of that is the imitation of all things teenage we talked about above. If she stares at you like you've grown a second head when you refuse to buy that pair of microshorts, she's not headed toward becoming an exotic dancer. She really doesn't get it yet.

Very real angst over "beauty bummers"

Your daughter may have had that mole on her cheek since birth or worn glasses from the time she was four without complaint, but it's not uncommon in the tween years for that to abruptly become an obsession. Nobody in the family has teased her about her lazy eye, but she suddenly wants to all but pluck it out. Please can she have that microscopic wart on her finger removed? Her "Dumbo" ears fixed?

Even the changes *all* the girls are going through can loom like King Kong. It has always seemed a cruel twist of fate to me that just when a girl is starting to care about her looks, puberty kicks in and brings with it a whole raft of beauty challenges: pimples, greasy hair, weight gain, and hairy legs. We suffer a lot of the same things in middle age, come to think of it, but by then we hopefully have the wisdom and experience to cope with it. Who faces it with aplomb at age ten, eleven, or twelve?

Mini-Women

"I don't feel ugly anymore when I have new clothes — I feel pretty. I know I shouldn't feel that way, but I do. I wish my mom understood that clothes aren't the only thing that's important to me — but that they matter."

age 11

Some interest in basic beauty care

Those hours of watching you apply toner to your face and do your nails when she was a sweet little baby girlfriend, were a warm-up for the time when she'll want to do those things to herself. But not necessarily on a regular basis in the tween years. Life's too full of other important things like sleepovers, BFFs, and maneuvering her way out of her turn to do the dishes. But you may find her lingering over cosmetics ads in magazines or smelling your night cream. Tomboys might squirm at the introduction of conditioner to the hair-washing routine, but don't kid yourself. They secretly like those soft, shiny results.

Questions about taboos

You may be taken aback—if not horrified—by questions like, "What's wrong with piercing your belly button anyway?" "What would you do if I ever got a tattoo?" "Why do grown-ups hate it when kids dye their hair green?" But there's really no need to consider an exorcism—or launch into a lecture. It's just a question about something she hasn't quite figured out, and you are still the resident expert on all things. So—she sees the college student with the multiringed nose when she accompanies you to Starbucks. The high school kid who bags your groceries has enough ink on his arms to pen the Declaration of Independence. These people smile at her and chat with you, so she knows they aren't serial killers. Yet she also knows you don't approve of face piercing and body art. Naturally she's going to want to know what that's about. Her asking doesn't mean she's considering slipping out to the nearest tattoo parlor.

That may all be "normal," you say—but it's also a little bit scary for you. What if she comes out of this phase wanting to dress like a hoochie mama or . . . ?

Okay—so think of it this way. When your daughter passed her second birthday, she blurted out the occasional "No!" at the very least, and you didn't assume she had oppositional defiant disorder. If she mastered the classic temper tantrum, you didn't rush her off to the child psychologist. You just knew the terrible twos had invaded your home. The same can be safely assumed if she exhibits the above signs now. She isn't vain, shallow, or bound to turn her skin into a mural. She's only being a tween girl. And just as you taught her the inappropriateness of pitching a fit when she was a preschooler (how many times did you lock yourself in the bathroom during *that* process?), you can help her work through the stuff of tweenhood too. A look at some divine guidance to start.

From the Ultimate Parent

The "body as a temple" passage from 1 Corinthians, quoted at the beginning of the chapter, is usually used in reference to not trashing it with promiscuity. That makes sense in the context, since Paul is railing on the believers in Corinth for wasting themselves in loose living.

But I think it's a mistake to stop with the "Don't indulge in illicit sex" interpretation, saving this deep piece of Scripture for after you've had "the talk" (or planning to use it *instead* of the talk!). That "sacred place" (v. 19) Paul refers to isn't just your daughter's genitalia. It's also that crop of blonde curls. Those chocolate-brown eyes. Her soon-to-be-graceful hands. The cute space between her front teeth that causes her no end of prepubescent grief. Why not impart to her now that she can honor God by honoring her face and her grace and the way she's put together, which are just as important a part of her body as her sexuality? If she emerges into full womanhood knowing that when she shines light on the unique beauty God has given her, she shines light on him, that belief will provide a foundation for her entire physical life.

"The physical part of you is not some piece of property belonging to the spiritual part of you," Paul writes to the errant Corinthians. "God owns the whole works. So let people see God in and through your body" (v. 20).

Do I hear an amen to that?

Test Your Own Waters

This is the self-check I offer tweens in the book *The Skin You're In.* We call it "That Is SO Me." It might be revealing for you to take the quiz, just to give yourself more information as you and your young beauty make your way across the bridge.

Here's what I tell the girls:

Be really honest with yourself as you read these possible thoughts. Put a star (*) next to each one you've ever had for more than, like, two seconds. Even if you don't *believe* the thought, but it nags at you sometimes, give it a star. There's no right or wrong. No good or bad. There's just you.

(Moms: These have been tweaked for your benefit, but the meaning is the same.)

That Is SO Me Quiz

____ I'm fat.

____ I'm unattractive.

____ I don't look that bad except for my _____.

____ I'm too tall (or short) to be considered beautiful.

____ I have my mother/father/Aunt Mildred's _____, which is not good.

____ I hate having to wear _____ (glasses, a padded bra, that frumpy uniform for work).

____ I'd secretly love to look good enough for the cover of *Vogue* (*Redbook, Today's Christian Woman*).

____ There is *no way* I'd ever look good enough for a magazine cover (no matter how extreme the makeover).

____ People who tell me I'm attractive are just trying to make me feel good.

____ When someone implies that I'm not attractive, I'm right on the same page with them.

____ I don't do much to improve my looks because I know it wouldn't make much difference.

____ If I were better looking, I'd probably have more friends.

____ I really don't care that much about how I look. I'm just not the girly type.

If you have between 11 and 13 stars, you seem to be having a tough time seeing your own beauty.

If you have between 4 and 10 stars, you're like most girls your age who go back and forth between thinking they're not so bad and deciding they're total freaks.

If you have between 0 and 3 stars, a lot of the time you're seeing the beautiful person you were made to be.[3]

Just something to think about, Mom. (True confession: I scored a 2 today. Ask me again tomorrow . . .)

Going for It

Now for the fun part!

I mean it. Helping your daughter refine her natural beauty doesn't require—nor should it include—anything resembling hard work. That's why each of the suggestions I'm offering here includes a celebration, a party, or a goofy way to play yourselves into discovery. In my delightful dealings with tween girls at events and workshops, I've found that they will get on board with just about anything as long as it has the potential for fun. Most of the time, their moms are right in there with them. I get the giggles myself just watching them clap and dance and dive for flying inflatable frogs (you had to be there)—together. So many mothers have emailed me saying what great conversations they had with their daughters on the way home in the car.

I just smile.

There is no reason why the discovery of blossoming beauty has to be such a serious business. Blow-drying your hair and finding something to wear may have become a chore to you, but (a) it's still something of an adventure to the daughter who has only recently given up playing in the sandbox, and (b) wouldn't you like to put a little charm back into your own life too?

So c'mon. Leave the lectures and the worrying and the nagging for other things and dance with your daughter across that bridge. Some suggestions:

Dealing with self-criticism

If your daughter has made a science out of detecting flaws not visible to anybody else's naked eye, or has become fixated on some physical funkiness, it's time for you to do a little detective work of your own. Until you can name what's really causing her to flip out—outside or inwardly—she'll continue to beat herself up—or you. It's highly unlikely that she's going to come to you and say, "I cry at the dinner table every night because the other girls tease me about being fat so I'm trying not to eat—but I'm hungry!" She's more likely to burst into tears when you serve the spaghetti and leave you to figure out what just went down.

Your first step is to get her acting out into perspective. Neither of these is true:

- She's overreacting.
- There's something psychologically or emotionally wrong with her.

This is just the teachable moment—so give her a quiz. It might be something like this:

Okay, Emily (Hannah, Madison, Katie . . .)—pick a letter:

(a) Some RMG (Really Mean Girl) or ALC (Absurd Little Creep, not excluding brothers) made fun of you today.
(b) I said something that made you feel Bag-Over-the-Head Hideous even though I didn't mean to, but sometimes it happens because my kids have stolen my brain cells.
(c) You have an oral report coming up and you're nervous about standing up in front of everybody.
(d) _____ (insert BFF's name) is getting all this attention from boys (or the Cool Girls, or the New Pretty Girl) and you aren't.
(e) all of the above
(f) none of the above

If she chooses *f*, she'll probably blurt out her "reason," if she hasn't done it already. Obviously I'm not suggesting that you commit this exact "quiz" to memory—although if you feel so inclined, by all means knock yourself out! What I'm offering is simply the multiple choice idea, fashioned to your personality and your daughter's. It isn't a matter of being glib. It's about using a non-threatening, mood-lightening way to give her possible causes for her sudden self-hatred so that (a) she can see that the negative thoughts she's having about herself aren't accurate—they're just reactions, and (b) she can learn to figure out what's going on with herself without you telling her (because chances are she isn't going to believe you anyway; after all, Mom, "you just don't under*stand!*")

Even simply, "Are the RMGs at it again, or is there some other reason you have your hood over your face?" will get her thinking beyond, "My zits look like leprosy!" It's all about an understanding tone and as much humor as you can introduce without you yourself belittling her temporary pain. In a less angst-ridden moment you can even bring her in on the creation of the quiz. Mini-women I know have come up with some succinct choices—*RMG Attack, ALC Alert, OSA* (Older Sister Again), *BFF Issues,* to mention a few.

Once you two name it, the nit-picking at herself will probably subside as together you explore the real issue. It may turn out that she's just ready to look better and wants some help with her hair, but was afraid to put that into words. Great. That's the simplest—and most fun—fix of all.

Your next move is to get her focused on the positive, rather than the things she's convinced are ruining her life. You can't do it by pointing out her pretty features yourself. That's sure to elicit—"You *have* to say that stuff because you're my mom!" Nor will you get the desired result by making it sound like a consolation prize—"Okay, so you have a beak like a fledgling eagle, but look at your nice smile" (or, worse, how good you are at piano). The best approach is to get her to appreciate her finer qualities on her own. This is a fun thing we do in the Beauty Workshop. It's called "So You Think You Aren't Beautiful? Think Again!"

1. Go to your respective mirrors with paper and pen (colored gel pens set the perfect tone if you have any around).
2. Each of you look honestly at the person in the mirror—every detail from cute cowlick to linty little toes. If something isn't the way you wish it was, skip over that. Just concentrate on each tiny thing that is beautiful—and there's a lot in every female.
3. Write down each pretty piece—shiny hair, eyebrows that almost talk, teeth white as Chiclets—all of it.

Mini-Women

"My mom's pretty good with style but sometimes I just like something I like. A lot."

age 10

4. Smile at the girl in the mirror as if you want to be her best friend. Add new things to the list that appear when you do that.

5. Come back together and read your lists to each other.[4]

That may lead to the question: Isn't this conceited? My best answer? No. Being aware of your own loveliness so you can bring it out doesn't mean you think you're all that. Now, pointing it out to everyone in sight ("Do I not have *the* cutest freckles on my nose?") would be "stuck up," but that's not what you're doing. It is an honor to God to enjoy the beauty he's given you, just as it is to enjoy the splendor he's put into a rose, a black stallion, or a sunset over the Gulf of Mexico. Quietly appreciating what God has done for you is giving him the honor due his name.

In-between body

You can tell her in all honesty that she's going to grow and change shape a lot before she's fully mature, so she shouldn't get freaked out about the fact that she towers over all the boys. She might even believe you. But it's a lot more fun, and way more effective, to take her focus off of her current figure altogether and help her develop her personal style instead. We've already said she may be inclined to want to look like the identical twin of her BFFs, but even within those limitations she can find unique pieces of herself. Here is an activity that will help you guide her toward her own special look:

1. Go through a tween magazine like Discovery Girls *or a girls' clothing catalog or to a website.* As you chat, encourage her to make a wish list of the things she would pick out if money were no object and other people's opinions weren't a factor. Older tweens may argue that that's never going to happen, but most between eight and twelve eventually get into this. Your job is to listen, watch, and observe—not to say, "Well, you can just forget about that" or "I don't think that's you at all!" Nobody said you were going to buy anything—and this isn't about what you think, it's about what she thinks. As a sense of a style emerges, ask her to describe it. Multiple choice helps: sporty, romantic, creative, or classy, for instance.

Mini-Women

"When we're buying clothes, my mom always says, 'It's all about comfort!' That's because she always wears jeans and stuff. I want to buy some skirts or a dress. I'm just more girly than her."

age 10

Mini-Women

"When I was nine or ten, I used to want desperately to wear lots of jewelry and makeup and look like my mom. But now that I'm allowed to wear more makeup, I can tell I'm really not any more beautiful than I used to be! I'm so glad Mom didn't let me grow up that way too quickly."

age 14

2. Since you have pictures in front of you, help her make a collage of her style so she can dream on it. The tweens I do this with in workshops love to gaze at what they've come up with, and are amazed at how different theirs is from the BFF they've been cloning. What I love best is that the difference doesn't seem to matter.

3. Together make a small card she can carry with her the next time you shop together for clothes. On the card will be a list of her "requirements" for a piece of clothing to rock. Basics would be—

- helps me feel like I'm part of the group (not a loser).
- is my style (I don't feel like I'm wearing somebody else's shirt).
- brings out all my best qualities (instead of the ones I'm not so crazy about right now).
- isn't just cool to me because it comes from the right store.

On the back of her shopping card, you can write down *your* guidelines:

- Skirts can be _____ inches above the knee.
- Necklines can be _____ inches from the collarbone.
- Jeans can be _____ inches below the belly button and can only look tight enough to _____.

It's all right there. Debates in the dressing room are eliminated with a wave of the card.

Wanting to look like a teenager

It's tempting when she's eyeing your tube of lip gloss to say, "You want to grow up too fast. You need to stay a little girl." That's actually true—we do want them to enjoy what's appropriate to their age and not rush into places they're not ready for. But looking ahead is natural for all of us. While we're loving where we are, we're also preparing ourselves for what's ahead. When you were pregnant, I'm sure you read some how-to-take-care-of-baby books or suddenly took notice of how your girlfriends were mixing the formula for their infants. Right now, I'm definitely learning all I can about menopause! By sneaking a peek at *Seventeen* magazine or eavesdropping on her big sister's phone conversations, she isn't necessarily trying to rush into adolescence. She's just preparing herself. Which also means it isn't cause for you to give in and take her to the next Mary Kay party.

What could be more fun, actually, than playing around with the trappings of teendom without having to endure any of the angst? There are some healthy ways to do that.

One is to hold a "Makeup Madness" night at your house for your daughter and her BFFs. (This is described in detail on page 37 of *The Skin You're In*.) Basically all the girls bring stand-up mirrors and any makeup that can be put on with fingers or cotton swabs. You and your daughter supply tissue, washcloths, etc., and magazines with pix of girls in makeup. Anything goes as they do makeovers on each other, trying on different looks, telling each other they look gorgeous, taking pictures. Then they wash it all off, have a healthy snack, and go back to their natural selves with memories of fun and a glimpse of what they might look like when and if it *is* time for sophisticated makeup. Making it a party game keeps the wearing of makeup from being some mysterious and serious thing they have to do in order to feel grown up. Been there, done that for the time being. What's next? Wanna watch *Shrek* again?

God-respect

The older a tween gets, the more she's probably going to want to know why she can't wear shorts that say "Sweet Cheeks" across the seat—and I'm not sure that "Because Jesus doesn't want you look-ing like a hoochie mama!" is our most effective answer. It's true, of course, but you might get further with this approach—

Occasionally I'm asked to give a talk on modesty, and I always say I don't give presentations on the topic per se. Instead, I would rather discuss self-respect, or even better, God-respect. When a girl hon-ors the self she's been made by God to be—really made to be—she doesn't have to be told not to parade something that just isn't her. No girl just "is" happy to share her body with all takers. That comes from extra baggage that gets piled on through abuse and other ex-periences, including the culture. If she's being who she truly is, she won't even think about advertising what isn't for sale.

Mini-Women

"When I see other girls my age parading around looking like a newly painted Picasso, I feel really grateful I've been brought up by Mom in a way that has shown me that makeup is fine, but certainly not in excess."

age 14

So if she asks why, this is one time you can tell her that the mini-skirt that shows her buns when she leans over isn't her. That she's way better than the message that sends. No girl is going to say, "No, I am *not* better than that!" With all the work you're doing on helping her to be authentic and all the fun you're having together discovering her style, she probably won't even ask why she can't don "hooker wear."

Beauty bummers

Whether your daughter has an obvious physical challenge or a smaller anomaly that she's suddenly stressing over, or she's just adjusting to the wild changes in appearance that come with puberty, it's important for you as a mom to strike a balance between blowing off her discomfort ("Don't be silly—nobody even notices that") and pathologizing it ("We have to get those teeth straightened before she develops self-esteem problems that will plague her for the rest of her life"). Doesn't it seem like everything about raising a tween daughter requires some kind of balancing act?

This one isn't that hard to achieve, actually, if you teach *her* how to reach that balance. I advise the tweens I work with to apply the famous Serenity Prayer to their "Beauty Bummers."

God, please help me to know what can be changed and what can't.
Show me how to change what can be changed, even in a small way.
Teach me to accept what can't be changed, and maybe even make it work somehow.

Say she has what she considers to be the longest nose in the galaxy, and other kids (boys in particular) are calling her Pinocchio and she's ready to smack somebody. You can walk her through the questions and together come up with the answers:

- *Can you change your nose?* Not without plastic surgery. Besides, the rest of your face hasn't caught up with it yet. It could look totally different in a year. *Can you change Absurd Little Creep Boys?* Not a chance, so wrinkle that wonderful nose at them and walk away.

Mini-Women

"I didn't always understand it when I would ask my mom if she liked my outfit and she would say, 'That's pretty short ...' But now I guess I do. She just loves me and doesn't want to see me hurt."

age 13

- *How can you make it a little better?* Part your hair on the side and not too flat on top. Choose colors that bring out your eyes.
- *How can you accept it and make it work for you?* It's a family trait so be proud of it. Find another way to describe it besides "honkin' huge." Noble? Strong? Comical? Queenly? Call it that in your mind and it'll change the way you feel about it, especially when some ALC thinks he's being original and calls you Pinocchio for the forty-fifth time.

Suggestions for using the Serenity Prayer for glasses, braces (which have nowhere near the oh-no value that they used to have since they started coming in colors and became a status symbol; who knew?), being tall, being big, and skin issues are found in *The Skin You're In*. (I personally use it now for gray hair, crow's-feet, and the sagging of just about everything.)

Another way to help your daughter get "flaws" of any kind into perspective is to do this fun thing:

1. Roll out a big piece of paper and have her lie down on it.
2. Trace an outline of her onto the paper.
3. Load her up with non-black crayons, markers, or colored pencils and have her draw in all her features that she loves or that she hardly even thinks about or that, okay, at least nobody makes fun of. Encourage her to make it as colorful and beautiful as possible.
4. Give her a black marker or crayon and have her draw in anything she considers to be a flaw.
5. Look at the final picture together. You probably won't have to point out that there's a lot more color than black on there. There may be flaws, but they've got nothing on all that colorful beauty.

You may worry that all this attention to her flaws—perceived or real—will cause her to focus on them, but I have found the opposite to be true. This is big stuff to her and she wants to be taken seriously. If you drive this down someplace where she's not allowed to talk about it, it will continue to eat away at her, unresolved. If you can help her minimize or cope with it, while understanding how it's affecting her, she'll not only be able to move on to the more delightful aspects of being a girl, but she'll know how to do that for herself in the future—when those breasts seem out of control or she's struck with acne or she goes through a trip-over-everything phase. You won't be teaching her to be obsessive about her appearance. She will only be obsessive if she has to live with the teasing.

One more tidbit. If you see a change in her appearance that isn't all that attractive—an outbreak of pimples on her back, a mole on her shoulder, the first signs that she's going to have hips like your mother-in-law—and she either hasn't noticed it yet or doesn't seem to be bothered by it, by all means don't bring it to her attention. What, truly, is the point? If you have to—if that mole looks suspicious, for example—I suggest doing it quietly, in private, and as off-handedly as you can. ("Huh—you have a little mole there, hon. Let's have that checked out by the doctor, just to be on the safe side.")

Questions about taboos

Remembering that "What's wrong with tattoos anyway?" is just a question, not an indication that inked sleeves are in your daughter's immediate future, I think the first answer might be a practical one. Getting a tattoo or a lot of piercings puts a person at risk for infection or Hep C, for instance. The next answer might be interpersonal. Right or wrong, a person with major body art or so many rings on her ear it looks like a Slinky presents a particular first impression that puts some people off, especially teachers, and, later, possible employers, not to mention store owners, police, and other people's parents. That's a choice folks make when they go for the big-time tats, and it's a permanent one. The most important answer could be a discussion not of why *not* to get a tattoo, navel piercing, Ronald McDonald dye job, but why *do* get one. Together you could actually ask some people who've gone that route, or want to, and compile a list. It will probably include:

- I want to be different.
- It's my body and I have a right to do whatever I please with it.
- It's my way of expressing how sick I am of everybody telling me who to be.
- I like to weird people out, especially adults who control me.

- If people really want to know the real me, they have to get past the way I look. If they judge me by my appearance, I don't want to know them.
- I want people to notice me.

The potential for using that information in a discussion with your daughter is huge. It can lead to all kinds of mutually drawn conclusions about who her body really belongs to, what genuine uniqueness is, and how to work out issues in healthy ways instead of rebellious ones. You'll make the decision on whether there will be piercings and tattooings and dying-hair-purple on your watch, but you don't have to lay down the law like a drill sergeant right now. After all, she's just asking.

Basic beauty care

No matter where your daughter is hanging out on that bridge we've been talking about, someplace in the tween years it's time to instill some fundamental grooming habits. You've obviously emphasized hair brushing, frequent bathing, and clean clothes since she was a little bitty thing, and have probably had more luck with that in her case than with any sons you've been blessed with. Now that her body is changing—which we'll talk more about in the next section—new self-care tasks are becoming necessary. But teaching them to your tween doesn't have to become one more thing you have to nag her about. Again, skin care and nail filing may have become annoyances you have to squeeze in among the other thousand things you have to do, but they're new and potentially very cool to your daughter. Why not make it fun for her with a Beauty Chart?

On the blog, we entitled ours "Lookin' Good!" Yet again, details can be found in *The Skin You're In* (pp. 74–76). I include these categories down the left side of the chart, but you can tailor yours to your daughter's own needs and inclinations. These are the basics, but if you have a princess, she might want to add more primping tasks. The ones with *s, for instance, are optional. You may be surprised by my inclusion of moisturizers at this age, but with the sun's rays becoming more damaging and more toxins appearing in our air, protective skin care can't start too soon, not just for the sake of beauty but for health too.

At some point every day							
Wash body							
Wash hair							
*Use conditioner							
*Shave legs and pits							
Comb wet hair							
Use body lotion							
Clean under fingernails							
Drink four glasses of water							
Get thirty minutes of exercise							
Wash hands often							
Every morning							
Wash face							
Use moisturizer with sunscreen							
Brush hair							
*Style hair							
Every night							
Wash face							
Use moisturizer							
Brush hair							
Get nine to ten hours of sleep							
Weekly							
Soak feet							
*Remove old nail polish							
File nails							
Take care of cuticles							
Clean under toenails							
Clip toenails							
*Put on new polish							
Every Six Weeks							
Have hair trimmed							

Three things will allow this to work until she gets into a natural routine:

1. Let her decorate her chart however she wants, including stickers, stars, or cool pens to check things off.
2. Come up with the beauty basics together, rather than presenting her with a list. You'll obviously be making the suggestions and indicating which aren't optional, but you'll be surprised at what she actually wants to do. She'll feel grown up in the appropriate way, as opposed to making off with your eye shadow.
3. Start with the *very* basics and add things gradually.

I always tell the tweens that if they want to be more private, they can make a small chart in a notebook rather than something on poster board to hang on the wall. The more age-appropriate choices she has, the better.

Have fun with beauty

Again, if you're not having at least a little bit of fun with all of this, you're both missing out on making some memories that are sure to come up years from now when the two of you are cleaning up after a Thanksgiving dinner. A couple of suggestions might get you started.

Have a spa night. This is detailed in *The Skin You're In* too (pp. 35–36). Basically, the two of you—and her BFF and her mom too, if that works—will gather the beauty supplies in a space where you won't be interrupted by teasing brothers, curious fathers, etc. (Which may mean sending them out of the house completely. Or threatening them.) Candles, flowers, pretty towels, and fave music can set the scene. Give yourselves head-to-toe spa care (your own usual practices or those outlined in *The Skin You're In*). Follow up with a snack feast and, hopefully, the next step—

Take a girly shopping trip, even if you carve out fifteen minutes to go down the cosmetics and toiletries aisle in the grocery store without an entourage of brothers. It doesn't have to be a department store cosmetic counter or The Body Shop at this stage, unless you want to splurge (in which case, can I come along?). Pick out moisturizer, shampoo, body wash, nail polish (if that's her thing) that will be hers alone. If finances necessitate everybody using from the same source at your house (I know! That stuff is expensive!), get some travel-size containers and let her fill hers from there. She can keep them in a cosmetic bag or a special spot on a shelf in the bathroom closet. Anything that makes taking care of herself special. It's important, even if she isn't a girly girl.

Bridging the Gap

Almighty God, creator of all beauty and lover of all: I bless you for _____'s perfection that takes this mother's breath away. While I pass her body from my care to hers, please bridge the gap between the joy she needs to experience in emerging into her own womanly beauty and what I have within myself to show her that joy. In the name of your beloved Son, I pray.

Amen.

6

"But You're Beautiful on the Inside . . ."

Cultivate inner beauty, the gentle, gracious kind that God delights in.

1 Peter 3:4

"Sure, my mom's told me to look my best and stay clean and presentable, but she is always saying that people will think you're beautiful by the way you live, not by how much makeup you slather on."

age 12

I always tell tween girls they're my favorite brand of kid. Part of that is because they're so naturally precious—no matter how they're dressed or what state of neatness their ponytails are in. I've been to upper-middle-class suburbs where the ten-year-olds had highlighted hair and outfits more expensive than the one I was wearing. I've also been to rural boroughs with names like Possum Town where the girls had never seen the inside of a beauty shop, and hand-me-downs were worn as proudly as anything with a GapKids label. With their shining eyes and ready smiles and glowing skin, every one of them has been absolutely adorable.

Well, almost every one. There *was* the morning I walked into what was to be an all-day Girlz Only workshop where the room was set up so that one line of girls was seated directly facing the other line of girls. It took me about five seconds to see that there was no love lost between Group A — the chubbier, less coiffed, Kmart shoppers — and Group B — who seemed to have come directly from the Galleria, the nail salon, or the personal trainer. Group B was delivering disdainful, curled-lip looks to Group A, which was retaliating with bitter, slit-eyed glares that only barely covered their collective shame.

It was the ugliest group of young girls I'd ever seen. Bless their hearts.

I did bless their hearts, because neither group was picking up its respective attitude from, as my mother would have said, "anybody strange." The moms who had gathered in the chairs in the back of the room had also separated themselves into two well-defined groups, and while their contempt for each other was a bit more subtle than what was going on between their daughters, nobody was doing anything to stop the obvious exchange of hatred. I found that even more unattractive.

My job that day was to teach the girls and their moms about inner beauty. I definitely had my work cut out for me. It looked like everybody in that room was going to need a total makeover.

I did not, however, announce that developing inner beauty was what we were going to talk about in our workshop. Here's why:

For Group A, that would sound like a consolation prize. What they would hear through the filter already in place at age ten was, "You're nothing to look at, but you can always develop a nice personality and people might still like you." In their minds, being told they could have inner beauty would be like trying out for a role in a play and being given a job as an usher.

For Group B, it would be evidence that here was *another* adult who didn't know what she was talking about. In the first place, they knew very well there were no outwardly homely/inwardly beautiful girls in the Ruling Class. In the second place, "everybody" knows that inner beauty is what not-pretty girls and their mothers talk about to very pretty girls because they're jealous of their fabulous good looks.

Because we were in a church setting — yeah, that makes it even more disturbing, doesn't it? — both groups had been exposed to the misguided theology that outward appearance doesn't count at *all* (as we discussed previously). But that, they'd experienced firsthand, wasn't true. They all would have given *me* looks that said, "Lady, get away from me with that dog food."

We made some progress that day — especially after I rearranged the chairs into a circle so it would look less like they were mobilizing for Iwo Jima. But since then I have done some deep study into the "problem" of inner beauty, and I'm happy to share my conclusions with you. As always, read for interest, and take away what might be helpful to you with your own mini-woman.

Getting Clear: On Inner Beauty

I have discovered that the *way* inner beauty is talked about with girls has a profound effect on them.

The tween who knows she's not considered as cute as the other girls — and trust me, at some point she figures that out, or is informed of it outright by some RMG — is often told that it doesn't matter what she looks like, that she just needs to develop "character." At the same time, often nobody is helping her to be anything but unlovely on the outside, as if she's basically a lost beauty cause already. That approach doesn't build character; rather, it makes her angry, bitter, and ashamed, and fills her with self-loathing. That, in turn, makes her even less attractive.

Without any real, concrete guidance on exactly what "inner beauty" means, she's likely to draw the conclusion that since outer beauty doesn't matter and inner beauty does, then inner beauty must be the opposite of outer beauty. So therefore — in tween logic — girls who are pretty on the outside must be mean, snobby, and fake on the inside.

All those tween girls who are already drop-dead gorgeous are not, of course, mean-spirited, stuck-up, and synthetic. Unfortunately, though, some have been told since birth how perfect they are, with very little emphasis on anything else. It was easy to let them get away with whatever they wanted when they were little because they were such precious little dolls that even their crying was cute. (Daddies and grandfathers are often the perpetrators of that crime.) It's not quite as adorable when they hit their tweens, but by then much of the damage has been done, and holding them accountable now is like trying to restrain a wet Siamese cat. Easier to just let it go. Either that or Daddy simply says, with pride, "She's a pistol. I pity the poor guy she marries." Again, please know that I am *not* saying every exquisitely beautiful girl-child is a spoiled brat. They're just the most likely to be indulged, which can leave them thinking, "Why should I try to be all sweet and kind when I'm going to get what I want no matter how I act?"

The majority of tween girls actually fall somewhere in between. They aren't the ones who are easy targets for teasers nor are they preteen model material. Each one of them has her own special brand of pretty, but she either doesn't know it or it doesn't matter to her yet. She has friends who, as the tween so often puts it, "love me for who I am." She's healthy, happy, and on her way to blossoming into a beautiful woman someday. The term "inner beauty" isn't loaded for her. She probably thinks she already has her some of that (as we say in the South), and she probably does. But she's not totally safe from the dangers of her culture.

In the first place, she's aware of the in-crowd. She knows it isn't inner beauty that gets you in there. She doesn't need that group. But—if someone from the inside suddenly takes an interest in her, she's going to have to be pretty strong to resist the lure of ultimate belonging. The in-crowd isn't always like the movie stereotype, but entrance usually involves renouncing something from her old life and leaving it behind—i.e., the BFFs who loved her for who she was. Excuse me? Inner what?

Besides, unlike her peers in Group A and Group B, she doesn't discount inner beauty completely. But if she's told that it's the only thing that counts, that outward appearance doesn't amount to a hill of beans in God's eyes, she feels conflicted, even guilty, because she wants to be cute. Invariably when I ask a group of tweens to look in the mirror and tell what they like in their reflection, more than one will raise her hand to ask, "Isn't it, like, stuck up to think you're pretty?" The visual knockouts rarely ask that because even if it does mean you're stuck up, they don't think there's anything wrong with that. The girls who consider themselves ugly don't ask that because they don't think they're going to see anything attractive in that mirror.

All of this would be sad if they weren't so primed for change in their tweens. It's the perfect time to teach them four things that I consider to be vital to their happiness and their ability to serve God's world.

First, appearance does matter, but it's inner beauty that *makes* a woman beautiful on the outside. It isn't one or the other. It's always both, and every girl can have both. She was made to have both, and both are open to all, no matter what assets they were born with.

She also needs to know that developing inner beauty isn't an arduous, uphill battle that's only achieved through the sacrifice of everything delightful and exciting about being a girl. Getting there is, in fact, half the fun.

Possessing inner beauty—God's beauty—is the only guarantee that she will be truly, deep-down happy. Continuing to become more inwardly beautiful is the only assurance that she'll be able to make a difference in the world—and that is what her generation is all about. That is her true in-crowd.

From the Ultimate Parent

Whatever is true, whatever is noble, whatever is right, whatever is pure, whatever is lovely, whatever is admirable—if anything is excellent or praiseworthy—think about such things ... put it into practice. And the God of peace will be with you.

Philippians 4:8–9 NIV

Tweens of either gender don't respond well to abstractions. It's practically suicidal for a teacher to tell her students to "behave" and expect them to do it. They need a clear explanation that "behave" means stay in your seat, don't talk without raising your hand, don't put boogers on the kid next to you. Without it, they'll take over the classroom.

God knows (I mean that literally) tween girls need to have the abstract concept of "inner beauty" spelled out in concrete terms. If we're going to help instill such beauty in our daughters, we as mothers need a clear definition too. Given the popularity of the word *whatever* among tween girls, I'm delighted that Paul's letter to the Philippians is the Bible passage which draws the most complete picture of what we're talking about when we say "inner beauty."

"Whatever is true." No lies, fibs, creative manipulations of what really went down with her sister while you were out of the room. Beyond that—how to seek God's truth in such things as friend situations and conflicts on the soccer team.

"Whatever is noble." When to give up her turn, handle the insult without insulting back, volunteer to do the hard part. Beyond that—discerning when noble is noble and when it's just a way to make the right impression.

"Whatever is right." Even if it means being labeled a snitch, a traitor, or a goody-goody. Beyond that—avoiding becoming insufferably judgmental.

"Whatever is pure." Eschewing the crude movies, the disgusting song lyrics, the way-more-than-suggestive videos. Beyond that—filling the inner space with inspiring film, soul-moving music, heart-to-heart conversation.

"Whatever is lovely." In words that stir up love instead of hate, open lunch tables instead of closed doors, high hopes instead of low expectations. Beyond that—finding the lovely in everyone.

"Whatever is admirable." Inviting the "different" girl, volunteering on Saturday, giving her birthday money for her sister's mission trip. Beyond that—making sure the motivation is more than "to be admired."

"If anything is excellent or praiseworthy—think about such things." Doing her best in school. Giving her all for the team. Being a good citizen even when nobody's looking. Beyond that—doing it for love and not for praise.

It's a tall order for anyone, much less a nine-year-old. But we can reassure our mini-women they're not in this alone. Undergirding all the "whatevers" is the heart of the passage: *"The God of peace will be with you."* If we constantly assure them of that, share the disciplines that connect them with God, and show them the fruits in our own lives, the "whatever" becomes what is.

Yeah, I love that.

Test Your Own Waters

Relax. I'm not going to ask you to assess how you measure up to all of the above. Are you kidding? I'd have a panic attack if somebody asked me to do that. I don't even think *God* asks us to do that.

What I do think is that it's important for each of us to spot-check our basic *attitude* on a regular basis. We can talk to our daughters until their eyes glaze over—and the longer we talk the more likely that is—but what they really "hear" is the 'tude that shapes our behavior. It's worth some examination before we move forward.

Using your usual approach—or trying something different this time—look at it this way:

1. How do you respond to very beautiful women (even though, according to what we've said here, you yourself are one)? What goes through your mind? Does being around them affect your confidence at all? Change your behavior? Alter your mood? Threaten your religion? (JK!)
2. How do you respond to women who are what our older Southern ladies call "ill favored"? Ask yourself the same questions as in #1.
3. When you were a tween, did you fall into Group A, Group B, or somewhere in between? Did that have any lasting effect on your belief in the importance of inner beauty? Has it affected how you're raising your daughter?

If you have trouble getting a handle on this, just listen to yourself when you're talking to your girlfriends. Your answers will be there. At least, that's where I often find mine.

Going for It

Knowing what you long to instill in your daughter is, of course, only the beginning. That teacher who can list good behaviors on the board still has to show the kids how to do those things amid all the distractions that beckon like hands full of M&Ms. You face the same challenge, but it's very doable. I have some thoughts for you, which I offer according to the four vitals we talked about earlier.

Appearance does matter, but it's inner beauty that makes a woman beautiful on the outside.

I think the first step is to clarify the difference between "cute" or "pretty"—and truly "beautiful." That's important because we have to be realistic: while every girl has her own beauty, every girl is not going to be homecoming queen. We don't want our daughters to think we're trying to sell them the idea that everybody has the same shot at becoming Miss America, because they themselves know that's a lie. Saying, "You can be beautiful, both inside and out," which is true, is not the same as saying, "You can be on the cover of *Teen Vogue*," which may not be. The key is in showing them that homecoming queen, the Miss America title, and the cover shot are short-lived gigs that come to a few, while real beauty is available to everyone and lasts a lifetime. Be sure you're on the same page with her on that, or she's bound to get confused.

To show her how inner beauty affects outward appearance, have her look into a mirror and stare at her image poker-faced. (Be prepared—it's a tough task for an eight-year-old to do this without giggling.) Next have her smile like she's happy to see that face. Finally, ask her to glare as if she wishes that face would disappear. Talk about which expression was the most beautiful. The point is not to get her to go around grinning like Chuck E. Cheese all the time but to give her a visual she's likely to remember.

Ask her to pick out a few girls she knows who are considered pretty and have her watch them whenever she can. (This is a good time to introduce the word "unobtrusively" into her vocabulary.) If she sees one being rude, have her ask herself: "Is she still pretty? If someone caught her on camera at that moment, would a magazine put the picture on its cover?" (Only use this exercise if you know your daughter can resist the temptation to tell her BFFs, "She's not as pretty as you *think* she is.")

An alternative: give her a teen magazine (if you dare—some of them are basically a mini-*Cosmo*) and have her cut out all the pictures of the girls' faces—in both ads and articles. Then ask her to put them into two piles—girls she'd like to be friends with, and girls she would steer clear of. Talk about what the difference is. (To make this more fun, you yourself can do it simultaneously with a *Vogue* or *Ms.*)

Finally, talk about the women you both love. Seriously, are any of them ugly? Aren't they all just beautiful? Discuss what makes them that way. To prolong the joy, get them together and tell them. Bring Kleenex.

Developing inner beauty isn't an arduous, uphill battle. It is in fact part of the delight of being a girl.

Once your tween gets that the outside *shows* what's going on inside, the fun part is in finding more ways to reflect that. This draws on things we've already explored and which hopefully you're enjoying together on a continuing basis: her individual style — hair, clothes, accessories; how she takes care of herself — grooming, honoring her beauty; and her confidence — understanding who she is and having the freedom to be just that.

And it builds on those as you make her conscious of what's happening. For example, ask her how she wants people to describe her. Does she want her physical attributes to be the first thing that comes out of their mouths, or one of those things listed in the "whatevers"? Have her list Class Favorites titles (not the people who would win them, just the titles themselves), but instead of the usual Cutest, Most Popular, Best Dressed, have her use ones that reflect inner traits that make people her faves on the planet (Most Honest, for instance). For fun, you can both come up with the titles neither one of you would want to win — Most Rude, Most Likely to Betray Your Secrets.

Ah, the discussions you can have from that.

Bringing out the joy of finding inner beauty also involves focusing on the other things — besides painting toenails and curling hair — that make being a girl fun. I've listed some traditional ones that tweens often really get into when they're introduced to them:

Cooking — baking — sewing — knitting — costuming — room decorating — gardening — dancing just for joy — purely-for-fun sports like badminton, croquet, roller skating, ice skating, bike riding—having tea parties—flower arranging—picnicking—marathon talking—unexplainable giggling.

Use whatever *–ing* makes being female joyous for the two of you. Doing it will bring out the beauty. That's how joy works.

Possessing inner beauty—God's beauty—is the only guarantee that she will be truly, deep-down happy.

Winning the award, being voted team captain, or making the honor roll or first chair or the junior cheerleading squad can make a girl proud (in a good way!), sure of her abilities, and certain of some positive attention. But in the long run, they don't make her happy. We've all seen tween girls who achieve all that and more, and still bite their fingernails or chew their hair or have a weekly crying jag.

That applies as well to our girl who is so pretty she takes your breath away and has all of tweendom at her command, yet longs for more and becomes anxious when her throne is threatened because that's all she really has going. Her anxiety may come out in the form of girl bullying, which we'll discuss at length later.

My point: High-achieving girls and gorgeous girls and girls who are both can be happy. But not unless the beauty basics are also happening within. If a girl isn't happy, no amount of conditioner and Limited Too is going to make her beautiful. If she is genuinely happy, her beauty will bring tears to your eyes.

So how to coax out that inner, happy-making beauty? A few suggestions to get you started on your own approach with your daughter. Doubtless you're doing some or all of this already.

Know what's beautiful inside her and praise it appropriately.

You don't have to applaud every time she refrains from screaming at her brother even though he probably deserves it. But when she sits down beside him after his team loses the championship and tells him he was the best thing out on the field, that deserves a hug and a thanks and a brownie later. Don't be afraid that you're going to make her full of herself by paying attention to her virtues. You're going to make her want to use them even more, until the mere act of doing good is enough for her.

Get to the bottom of any acting out she does, instead of immediately punishing it.

That doesn't mean let her get away with grand theft auto; consequences are certainly a part of learning. But understanding the impetus for any not-so-beautiful behavior will help you to know how to heal it. Most of the time tween-girl misbehavior has one of these behind it: *the need for attention*, *the need for acceptance*, *the need for more trust and responsibility* (she has an ironic way of showing that one, doesn't she?), *the need for more privacy*. The lack thereof could be happening at home, but it's just as likely that it's coming up at school or in her circle of friends or at the site of her activities, and you're just the one she's taking her fear and frustration out on. After all, you still have to love her even when she's slamming doors and yelling at her siblings and talking back to you.

It always worked for me to say to Marijean, "This isn't like you. What's really going on here?" Most times if I really thought about it, I already knew. I'd been out several evenings that week and hadn't been there to have our bedtime talk. She needed attention so she got it by arguing (and the girl could hold a debate over a ham sandwich). Or she was coming home from school with her sweatshirt sleeves pulled over her hands and her hair hanging in her face, ready to pinch my head off. I knew Heidi and the Heinous Ones were at it again, and it took only a few questions to get it out of her: Heidi had made a huge production out of asking Marijean if she had any mirrors at her house.

One time, when Marijean blatantly broke the no-arguing-about-things-inside-the-box rule, we had a serious Come-to-Jesus about tone. Once she was sufficiently contrite, we discussed taking a few items out of the box and making them negotiable. After that, tone was seldom an issue.

Help her deal with negative emotions in positive ways.

No one can be happy—and therefore inwardly beautiful—when she's struggling with negative stuff, and no one can hold an interior wrestling match like a tween girl. She doesn't know how to referee that kind of thing yet so she just keeps punching until she's bruised and miserable. Possibly everyone else around her is, as well, depending on whether she's an internalizer (it's all my fault) or an externalizer (it's all *your* fault). It's up to Mom to help her express the hard, snarly feelings in healthy, even creative ways. You'll know which of these might work with your daughter:

- Buy her a journal and show her how to vent in it. Guarantee her privacy.
- Provide some art supplies and let her paint, draw, or scribble whatever's currently messing with her little mind. No evaluating or psychoanalyzing. Just let her have at it. These works of art don't go on the refrigerator.
- Give her some clay to abuse or shape. Again this is not for firing in the kiln. Just a way to give form to something that's not making sense. Yet.

The idea is to allow her to get the uglies out where she can look at them. Whatever she comes up with may give you a way to start a conversation. Or she may just feel better, which is wonderful. How many times have you chewed on an issue until your jaws ached, dug in the petunia bed (or something!) for an hour, and forgot what it was you were so worked up about? That can happen for even the youngest woman.

Let her play!

Much happiness, and therefore beauty, is found in playing. I've probably harped enough on the drawbacks of nonstop structured activity in tweens' lives so I won't go there again. Let me just add another brushstroke to that picture by saying that free play—as in acting out Robin Hood with her BFFs in the backyard or getting up a pick-up game with a soccer ball and a gang of cousins—provides the canvas for practicing the virtues we've been extolling—fairness, compassionate give-and-take, mercy, and more.

Time and space to dream of who she wants to be is absolutely essential too. That's when God gives her the images, albeit unconscious ones, of how she's to live and move and have her being. She may dream now of being a missionary and declare she's going to Africa, even though she has yet to complete the fifth grade. Alas, she may never have a ministry in Botswana, but if she has "seen" herself bringing food and medicine and the good news to orphan children, she will also "see" herself into unselfish giving and a willingness to sacrifice, no matter what her life's work is. If she does *not* dream it, however, the development of those marvelous qualities will be delayed. Why deprive her of that so she can take yet another Something Lesson?

Okay. I'll leave it alone now.

Continuing to become more inwardly beautiful is the only assurance that she'll be able to make a difference in the world.

Even pundits who insist on continuing to be critical of "youth culture" have to admit that the Millennials are far more interested in volunteering, mission trips, and fund-raising for causes than previous generations. They love words like *team*, *community*, and *posse*. In general they think less about "making a lot of money" than about "making a difference." (Granted, they expect to have all the same goodies they have now while they're out there changing the world, but that's an entirely different topic!)

The desire is there, and it's genuine, especially among the girls I've met who are being raised in the church. Moms are in the perfect position to foster that altruism in the tween years and bring out the beauty within.

Provide opportunities for her to give and serve.

The closer she can get to the people she's helping, the more effective the experience will be. If she's helping you bake cookies for the nursing home, why not have her help deliver them as well? If there is self-sacrifice involved in giving, so much the better. Is she using some of her allowance to buy Angel Tree gifts at Christmas? Spreading mustard on bread for sandwiches for Habitat for Humanity volunteers when she could be on the computer with her friends? Turning down a birthday party invitation because she's already signed up to help at Special Olympics? Taken out of herself and put into a situation that needs what she can give, she will show her true—and beautiful—colors.

Help her find her own connection with God.

One of the most exciting things about the tween years is the growing sense that there's a lot more to loving God than singing "Jesus Loves Me" and praying, "God bless Mommy and Daddy and Grandpa and Nanny." Somewhere between eight and twelve she sees the concrete evidence that loving God and talking to God and doing as God says makes a person different somehow. And developmentally she's ready to explore that on her own: she can read, organize her thoughts, and translate experiences into ideas. It is remarkable to watch a tween girl take off in her relationship with her God, but she usually needs some help to get it started. I receive emails weekly from tweens saying, "I want to be closer to God but I don't know how." The desire is there. You're in the best possible place to help. This is what I tell the girls—some of which is detailed in *The Beauty Book.* Suggestions for encouragement are in parentheses:

- Have a quiet time with God every day. You can ask God any questions you want, present God with the things you and the people you love need, and even just listen. (The most important thing you can give her to foster quiet time is space and privacy. She'll take care of the rest.)
- Read God's Word and think about how it applies to you, right that very moment. (Provide her with a Bible that has helps designed for her age group. I, of course, am partial to the *Faith-Girlz Bible.* Special tween devotional books, such as *That Is SO Me,* suggest what to read and give further guidance.)
- Write about your God thoughts in a journal. In the Lily books, Lily has a "Talking to God Journal," and you can make one too, and use it to work through problems the way she does. (If she doesn't stare at you as if you've just arrived from Planet Weird for suggesting such a thing—not all tweens enjoy taking pen in hand—take her journal shopping or provide tools for making her own. On the tween blog this summer, I had the girls email me pictures of the ones they created. Look out, Hallmark—they were great.)

- Surround yourself with other beautiful Christians as friends. (While you're hosting the Sunday school class sleepovers or forming a FaithGirlz Club, be careful not to give her the impression that girls who aren't being raised in Christian homes aren't worth being friends with. You'd be amazed how many Christian tween girls think they aren't supposed to talk to the "unchurched" and look down on them the way they would a shoplifter. Then they can't figure out why the non-Christian kids don't want to listen to them witness about the Lord.)[1]

- Pray. A lot. At certain times during the day. In little quick breaths all day. Even just saying "Please!" or "Thank you!" whenever God comes to your mind. Most of the time, nobody even knows you're doing it. (The most effective way to foster this is to model it, although it doesn't have to be a steady stream of "Lord, please give us a parking place. Oh, yes, Lord, thank you. Right in front." Unless that's natural for you. Just saying, "You know, I was praying about it this morning, and I'm getting the sense that I was too quick to say no about the field trip. Let's talk about it some more" is a meaningful indication to her that you and God are in conversation, and that it affects her life.

You may be wondering, is that enough? You know this is the single most important relationship your daughter will ever have, and that can make you so anxious for her. You just want it to be right. Yet you can't force this delicate, sacred thing. What you can do is everything possible to *allow* that relationship to grow without pushing it. A few thoughts on how:

- Make sure she has a church home where she feels like part of the family. The tweens I know who love church are helping out in the nursery or the preschool class, singing in the youth choir, running around with their BFFs at potluck suppers. Beware that the sense of belonging is more of a challenge at a mega church, though not impossible if she's involved in small-group activities.

- Allow her to have doubts and questions about her faith. If she doesn't have any, she's not paying attention! Rather than show disapproval or fear, talk her through them, and find out what prompted the question. Just as when she asks about tattoos and piercings, it's usually just a question. Give her the information she's missing and steer her toward the right answer. Telling her it's wrong for her to question God will drive her underground, where there are no answers.

- When she's making a decision, ask her what she thinks God wants her to do. Together see if it lines up with the Bible.

- Try not to preach at her. It's always more effective to share your own story. "I had a big fight with my brother one day when I was ten, and later that night he was hurt in a car accident. That's when I figured out why God says don't let the sun go down on your anger. I mean, what if he hadn't made it? So—do you want to reconsider what you just said to your brother?"

- Emphasize God's love and grace, rather than rules and restrictions that actually aren't part of the gospel at all. Have rules at your house, of course, but don't make God the heavy when it comes to enforcing them. Learning to do what's right because God loves you is not the same as "the wages of sin is death." No nine-year-old responds to that in a healthy way. It sure isn't going to bring out her inner beauty. Her inner pointy-nosed hall monitor, maybe, but not her godly beauty.

- For older tweens, special sacred practices can be good ways to help her concentrate on God. More and more youth groups for teens are in fact introducing candle lighting, labyrinth walking, and other simple rituals that bring teenagers into godly focus.[2] We can find video screens and rock bands anywhere, teens are saying, but a room lit only by candlelight where a Gregorian chant is playing—that sets us apart from the world for an hour so we can hear God. They carry the images with them back into the world, where they're going to need them.

This may be hard to wrap your mind around if you don't come from a liturgical tradition, so just know that a ritual is not *necessary* for coming into the presence of God. It's a reminder that you are always there. For a tween girl it might be as simple as lighting a candle to start her quiet time (depending on her level of responsibility) or setting up a sacred space in the corner of her room. Again, that doesn't mean that's the only place she *can* pray, but it's a place where she knows she *will pray.*

If you're still put off by the term "sacred practice," think about the spiritual rituals you participate in. Do you fast? Raise your hands in the air during praise and worship? Attend baptisms and weddings and funerals? These sacraments are outward and visible signs of inward and spiritual grace. God's grace.[3] Your daughter may respond beautifully to God by using spiritual practices.

- Be sure your own relationship with God is healthy. We've already established that daughters learn most from what mothers do themselves. If you're concerned for your daughter to experience God, you're already doing a lot.

- And, of course, most important of all, pray for her. If you can do nothing else, this is enough. It is, in fact, more than just enough, because your prayers put you in a working relationship with her third parent, her heavenly Father.

Are you prepared for the beauty you're going to see emanating from your daughter in the months and years to come? The only way I know to describe it is "delicious." You work with her, you play with her, you pray for her, you laugh with her—and you get to taste of the fruit of your labor of love. It is luscious. Please, please—savor it.

Bridging the Gap

Father of all goodness, thank you for the seeds of loveliness you've planted in _____. Knowing how hard it is for those seeds to grow in this world, I pray that you will bridge the gap between what she needs in order to see her inner beauty and what I have in me to help her nurture it. Through Jesus Christ our Lord. Amen.

PART 3

Who Are You, and What Have You Done with My Little Girl?

What It Looks Like

She comes home from the sleepover Saturday morning with a scowl that's obviously the result of something more than just lack of sleep. Snapping at her brother for looking at her a millisecond too long is evidence of that. So are the near tears because you're out of Froot Loops, and the length of time she's been holed up in her room.

You give her a few more minutes, in the hope that she'll emerge sunny-faced, as she so often does lately after an emotional thunderstorm. When she doesn't, you gain entrance by announcing outside the bedroom that you found a backup box of Froot Loops. She doesn't want them anymore, but she lets you in anyway, taking elaborate care to close the door behind you. Her eyes are puffy from crying—zero percent chance of sunshine there—and she retreats to her bed where she has apparently been alternately hugging her teddy bear and beating the stuffing out of a pillow. Your suspicions were correct: All is not well in Tweenland.

Your first attempt to find out—"What's wrong, honey?"—is met with a stony "Nothing," followed by a sideways glance which indicates her hope that you'll continue to pursue this line of questioning.

Your next query—"Did something happen at the sleepover that upset you?"—gets you a "No." And then, "Yes!" And then it all floods out.

At the sleepover, Anna said periods were painful—except SHE still isn't actually sure what a "period" even is except the dot at the end of a sentence—and Sydney's started wearing a bra—but SHE hadn't even noticed Sydney needed one—and Kayla's been shaving her legs and armpits—which really *does* sound painful—and nobody wanted to tell ghost stories like they used to—all they could do was talk about boys and going on a diet—and SHE spent the evening sorting the Peanut M&M's by color.

Still wailing, she reveals that she has just checked out her own body in the mirror, and Mom, she has hair in weird places and her hips are big and when she took a sniff at her armpit—ewww!

"I don't even look like me anymore!" she cries.

There has never been a truer statement.

————

You wouldn't have been faced with a situation like this a hundred years ago, at least not when your daughter was a mere tween. In the early 1900s, the average age for the onset of *puberty* (not even periods) was fourteen.[1] But moms have to deal with puberty and all its issues much earlier now, often long before they're ready. Today the average age for the hormones to begin their dance is nine, with periods usually starting within two years. That's a full year earlier than in 1960,[2] when *I* was nine years old. A study of more than 17,000 girls in the US found that 1 percent of Caucasian girls and 3 percent of African American girls showed signs of puberty by age three. By age eight, roughly half of African American girls and 15 percent of Caucasian girls show clear signs of sexual development.[3]

The reasons for the shift are still unclear, but the point in presenting these statistics is to show that the time to talk about puberty arrives sooner than many moms think. You and your daughter will fare best if you're informed and prepared, and, more importantly, if you use this time to talk about womanhood in ways that open your daughter up to a lifetime of loving that temple of a body.

That's how I want to help in this section. During puberty, a girl experiences more physical growth and change than at any other time in her life except for the span from birth to one year. It can be confusing, awkward, embarrassing, humiliating, and the time most likely to make her cringe even twenty years later. Or it can be interesting, exciting, confidence building, bonding, and the time remembered as a celebration of becoming a woman. Your daughter's experience can be the latter, because once again you are the single most important influence on this phase of her development—and you are the one best equipped to walk her through it with intelligence, humor, compassion, and empathy.

You can do this. What I think you'll need are the following:

- Information on what to expect
- Suggestions for talking to her about the various aspects of her changing body
- A plan for helping her shape her beliefs about what it means, physically, to be a woman
- Preparation for the practical side

A tween recently sent me a one-line email: *I wish my mom knew I am growing up*.

You can be the mom who knows—really knows—and the one who can make it the best time she's ever had.

7

The Biggest Deal Since
Potty Training

Learn to appreciate and give dignity to your body.

1 Thessalonians 4:4

"When I had questions about puberty and growing up and all that, I was afraid to come to my mom because she never invited me to tell her everything. Even now I have trouble being open with her and telling her my problems."

age 15

One day when I was about ten—just a few weeks after I got my first bra—I came home from school to find a pamphlet on my dresser. The cover was plain and uninviting, but being the kind of child who read everything from Nancy Drew to the back of the cereal box, I immediately snatched it up. Within minutes, my little heart was pounding, and I could feel my face sizzling with embarrassment, even though there was no one else in the room. I had just been introduced to menstruation.

Not a word was spoken on the subject until two years later when, while at the circus with my grandfather, I went to the restroom and found blood on my underwear. I went home after the grand finale, crawled into bed, and cried until my mother came in to investigate. Pads and a belt were produced, and we returned to our silence on the matter of womanhood.

That was 1964. Fast forward to 1989. Marijean, age ten, and I were hanging out on the couch after watching a movie when she suddenly pulled up her shirt and said, "Look, I'm getting breasts—only one of them's bigger than the other one. Is that weird?"

That wasn't the first of our discussions about what was happening to her body, or the last. Those talks were funny, unpredictable, and sometimes awkward (for me, not for her!), but I was glad we'd had them when two and a half years later, at almost thirteen, she strolled casually out of the bathroom and said, "Well, we knew it was going to happen soon, and it finally has." When I offered to help her with a pad, she looked at me blankly and said, "I'm already wearing it." There was only one thing to do then. We had a celebration. There was much chocolate.

I'm not saying that I was a better mom to Marijean than mine was to me. My mother was born in 1916, when I don't think "sanitary napkins" had even been invented. For her to talk to me about anything even remotely related to—shhhh—sex would have shattered the silence she was raised in like a soprano shrieking a glass into bits. And as an ultrasensitive, easily mortified tween, I probably would have required psychiatric care if she'd launched into an explanation of where babies came from. Although I had a vague idea of what went on—and knew that a girl getting pregnant in high school was not good—I didn't get the details until my college roommate filled me in. I'm serious.

When I had a daughter of my own, however, I was determined not to follow the family tradition of being closemouthed about all things womanly. I didn't do such a great job with potty training, and when it came to teaching Marijean how to keep her room neat, I was a complete failure, but this was one area where I wanted to do right by her. By then, in my late thirties, I had come to appreciate my own sexuality and was emerging from anorexia with a deeper love for the body God had given me. I didn't want my daughter to view the natural, beautiful workings of her female self as something to be ashamed of and frightened by. If I did nothing else right as a mother, by the grace of God, I was going to teach her to love being a woman.

Fast forward to today. Marijean is happily married, ready to start a family. Two years ago, I held her hand as she was going into the OR with cervical dysplasia, a precancerous condition. Three months ago I held all of her in my arms when she was told she was having a miscarriage. Her husband was there both times, and her dad and friends and cousins were at the ready to comfort her. Yet the bond she and I forged at the first sign of those little breast buds was the bond she reached for in the darker hours of her womanhood. I hope it will be the one she relies on when she does indeed bring home a child of her own to raise.

What I didn't get right I learned from, and I've intentionally learned more in order to write three books for girls about puberty and to work with them and their moms through workshops and blogging and individual mentoring. I'm not an expert, but I now know some things that can be helpful to you in guiding your own mini-woman.

Getting Clear: On Puberty

Let's start with what you can expect from puberty. Since most of this happens before a girl actually begins having periods, the signs give you plenty of time to get her ready for the big event—and judging from the emails I get from tweens, Getting Your Period is right up there with either Getting Your Driver's License or Having an Appendectomy, depending on how she's being prepared.

The most obvious signs of puberty are:

- Breast buds that seem to suddenly pop from a flat chest and then go through the stages of developing at various rates.
- New hair under the arms and in the pubic area, starting straight, light colored, and fine; ethnic background will have an effect here.
- Thicker, coarser hair elsewhere, especially on her legs, which may lead to a sudden interest in your razor.
- Sweat that has a less-than-lovely odor, a development you will probably notice before she does.
- A thicker waist and wider hips as her pelvic bones grow and normal fat gathers around them. This isn't as noticeable in the little waif body type until you go to shop for jeans and discover she's slightly changed shape.

- A growth spurt (in some girls more like a long, steady stream) in which she puts on weight and grows taller at a faster rate (as much as four inches a year) than before (two inches a year on average); this slows down by the time she has her first period, at which point she's probably grown about nine inches since she started puberty.
- A thick, clear discharge on her underwear, the sign you're least likely to know about, since she's probably not going to bring it up over lunch.
- Changes in her face. The lower portion usually gets longer, her chin juts out more, and her forehead gets wider as she begins to look slightly adult-ish. You get your first real glimpse of her as a grown-up.
- A sudden increase in shoe size, because the bones in her feet start to grow before the others — which means her feet will reach their adult size before the rest of her does (Marijean was in a size 10 at age twelve!) This accounts for some of those unexplained six-point landings in the middle of the kitchen floor.
- Changing moods, often giving one the image of a theme park ride gone out of control. Hormones bounce moods around to varying degrees in different girls, depending somewhat on their natural temperament.

As for exactly when each of these signs will appear, that I can't tell you precisely. In fact, the part of puberty that seems to cause the girls I work with the most distress is why SHE has breasts/pit hair/her period and I DON'T. They're often convinced that something is terribly wrong with them. One eleven-year-old wrote to me recently, asking if I thought maybe she wouldn't be able to have children, since she hadn't started her period yet and all her sisters got theirs when they were ten. Even the age at which you started yours isn't a guaranteed predictor for when she'll have hers.

Whenever estrogen kicks in, the changes it causes are a lot to cope with in a relatively short time. Add the progesterone and, as a result, new monthly periods to that, and life becomes a delicate balance for a while. Just as in any woman, clear signs that menstruation is imminent appear in a tween too. Some may include:

- puffy, bloated abdomen
- tender, swollen breasts
- an attack of the munchies, especially if sugar is involved
- lower backache
- more than the usual crankiness or tears for reasons even she can't name
- outbreak of pimples (precipitating said crankiness or tears)
- fatigue and a recent morphing into a couch potato

Basically she'll experience what one mom I know calls Baby PMS. Cramps, bloating, and the urge to rip everyone's lips off is hard enough for us even when we know what it's all about. If she doesn't have a clue, the whole experience can be pretty miserable.

Especially because she has even more going on. One confusing issue on her mind is yet another natural pubescent development: a change in her attitude about boys. Where once she was convinced they were all possessed by demons, or at the very least had cooties, she now finds herself wanting to look cute for them. Or she secretly enjoys it when the one least likely to actually *have* cooties unties her tennis shoe for the forty-third time. All of the following is completely *normal* for a girl who's entered puberty (although if she expresses none of these, that's normal too):

- Commenting that a certain boy is "cute"; she may even use the word *hot*, just because she's heard it, not because she necessarily comprehends what it implies.
- Having a friend who's a boy and remarking that she likes him because he doesn't gossip or get jealous of her other friends, the way girlfriends do.
- Having a crush on a boy her age, daydreaming about him, wondering what it would be like to be his girlfriend, especially after he's just looked at her or said hi for the first time.
- Having a crush on an older or famous guy, experiencing fluttery feelings about a handsome male teacher or a youth

director, daydreaming about meeting the Jonas Brothers or Taylor Lautner or some other luscious celebrity whose name will go up in lights before we can get this book into print.

- Saying she's "going out" with a boy, indicating that she and a same-age boy have agreed that they are boyfriend and girlfriend, which means exchanging texts and smiles until they "break up," usually within a twenty-four-hour period because they have exhausted everything that "going out" can entail at their age.

All of that is perfectly and delightfully normal, and it just as normally leads to wondering about sex. Not because she's planning to have it, for Pete's sake, but largely because she wonders what the connection is between the hand-holding and starry-eyed gazing she's beginning to envision for herself and the fuss being made over this mysterious Thing everybody's trying to keep her away from. Her questions about sex—spoken or kept hidden—arise quite normally from what she needs to know as her body turns her into a woman. These are the kinds of questions I hear from tween girls in emails weekly:

- "Why don't my parents want me to watch PG-13 movies? What's in them that's so bad?" (age 10)
- "I have my period now. Does that mean if I kiss a boy I could get pregnant?" (age 12)
- "I know this might be a strange question, and I'm not sure if we should be thinking about this ... but I was wondering if it is a sin to be excited about, well ... umm ... having sex with your husband (the right one), when I get married of course (I would NEVER do it when I am not married, and I am waiting for the right one). Please, I am just wondering." That one was signed "Homeschoolchick, age 13."

The innocence and trust bring me to tears every time. How precious is that timid awakening into what will become such an important part of who she is? I'm always honored to be asked, and yet I struggle with how to answer. I always want to say, "Sweetie, where is your mother? Why aren't you going to her with your questions?"

It is absolutely vital that your tween daughter have total access to her most reliable resource—you. She has to know she can come to you with any question pertaining to the complex process of growing into womanhood. But there are a number of reasons why she may *not* come to you willingly and confidently. Girls tell me they're afraid their moms are going to "put them down" for asking about sex. They're embarrassed to go to them with questions about their periods because "we never talk about personal things in our house." They don't want to broach the subject of boys because they know their moms will "freak out." Some girls are just shy or private by nature, and even though they want to talk, they can't imagine how to start. All of those reasons make it much easier and less threatening for them to email *me*, a person they think they can trust but whom they have never met and probably never will. (How embarrassing would *that* be? Yikes!)

That means that if dialogue about all things pubescent is going to take place between you and your daughter, you're probably going to be the one who starts it. And start it you must, for what I see as four extremely important reasons.

Reason #1: Her fundamental view of her womanhood starts here.

Please indulge me while I reiterate. It's hard to see your ten-year-old, who still sleeps with a stuffed animal, as a sexual being, but that part of herself is already stirring within her. Without even being able to name it, much less understand it, she knows something is happening to her. You know what it is, and you know that it's going to be a force within her for the rest of her life, just as it has been for you. I love the way Elium and Elium urge mothers to pay attention:

> Not to recognize that such a powerful, cyclical force wields tremendous impact on a female and all those around her is to stand in the middle of a cyclone and not notice the wind is blowing.[1]

Reason #2: She's up against a highly sexualized culture.

We've mentioned before that the so-called "youth culture" is the creation of non-youth who don't have the best interests of our kids at heart.

Mini-Women

"I wish my mom knew that sometimes my sister and I are afraid to ask a certain question because we feel embarrassed or stupid. I just wish she knew that."

age 12

(Their spending money, on the other hand, they're interested in.) But it's there, nevertheless, and we do our daughters a disservice if we don't talk to them about how they're going to deal with it. The good news is that the older members of their generation—the teenagers—are paving the way for them *to* deal with it. An article in *Newsweek* reports, "The culture at large may seem debased—sexualizing singers, actors, and models at a younger and younger age—but teens themselves appear to be thinking harder than ever about the potentially grave consequences of sex, namely unwanted pregnancies, disease, and death."[2]

As well they should. According to the Centers for Disease Control and Prevention, the overall rate of occurrence of common STDs (sexually transmitted diseases) among girls in the US ages fourteen to nineteen is 25 percent.[3] That doesn't include the rarer diseases such as HIV/AIDS, syphilis, and gonorrhea, which would drive that rate even higher. While the rate of teen pregnancy has steadily dropped since its peak in 1990, one in three teen girls in the United States is still estimated to get pregnant at least once before age twenty.[4]

The appropriate response from you in the face of all of this is not to put your daughter into protective custody—literally or figuratively—until you can find her a husband, nor is it to inundate her with warnings and statistics that convince her being a woman is the most frightening role a person could ever be saddled with. Now is the time to lay the groundwork so that she will respect her body and the God who made it. In order for that to happen, she has to know it and what it's capable of. If you talk to her about that now—in a way that is upbeat and accepting, emphasizing the potential joy of protecting her sexuality rather than the dangers of even acknowledging it—she will be prepared for the choices she's going to have to make in her teen years. Not to put too fine a point on it, but it's hard to "just say no" to something you don't even see coming.

Reason #3: There is sexual harassment even in her world.

Tween boys are going through their own changes—which you know well if you've ever raised one or are in the midst of that now. Part of *their* confusion arises from what seems to be happening to the girls around them. Their newly surging hormones tell them they ought to be doing something about that, but they haven't a clue what—but the same media blitz the girls are subjected to gives them plenty of suggestions. What used to manifest itself in pigtail pulling now appears in the upper elementary and middle school world as:

- bra snapping (to see who's "wearing" and how freaked out you can make her because of it)
- suggestive name-calling (even if they're not entirely clear on what a "ho" is)
- comment muttering (remarks like "nice boobs" out of the earshot of adults)
- drive-by touching (a pinch on the rear at recess, an "accidental" brush against the budding breast in the lunch line)
- "just kidding" (which is funny to no one but them and their cronies when it consists of dirty jokes and embarrassing pranks)

It doesn't happen in every school situation, although don't think that the private Christian school always rises above, because many of my complaints from tweens and young teens express horror that harassment goes on "right in Bible class!" But when it does occur it's a violation that no girl deserves at any age, especially in a place she's required by law to go to every day.[5]

You won't know about a situation that is demeaning, humiliating, and a threat to your daughter's self-esteem if she doesn't tell you about it, and she isn't going to tell you if she isn't able to talk to you about the other hard things, like periods and body odor. And if you haven't talked openly with her about how boys are different from girls, she's going to think she has done something small and dirty to deserve that kind of treatment at school or, I'm sorry to say, even church. The stories some middle school girls tell me about the goings-on at youth group prompt an immediate reply from me telling them to go directly to their parents with that information—without passing Go.

Reason #4: If you can talk about all of this together, you can talk about anything.

And you will want to. The older she gets, the deeper the issues will be and the more serious the natural consequences if she doesn't make good choices. Establishing great communication now insures that your daughter will always be willing to come to you for advice and guidance, everything from what to do about a BFF problem today, to how to know she's in love seven or eight years down the road. And it's not only the tough stuff you'll hear about. Being the mom who listens, helps her process, shows her the bottom line, and doesn't go ballistic will also make you the mom who gets to know about her first crush, share the joy of a repaired relationship, celebrate a victory over algebra. Right now, you will often have to be the one who initiates conversations about growing from girl to woman. But once you've established that you're her go-to gal, the door will swing both ways.

From the Ultimate Parent

God created man in his own image, in the image of God he created him; male and female he created them.

Genesis 1:27 NIV

It seems to me that moms, particularly highly committed Christian moms who want so much for their daughters to be pure (and rightly so), tend to think of God at one end of the life spectrum and matters related to the body—particularly sex—at the other end. That often translates into a parenting philosophy of "If I keep her focused on the Lord, she won't care about boys and sex." I've had more than one twelve-year-old tell me that whenever she starts thinking about a boy she likes, she goes straight to her Bible as soon as she can because she should be thinking about God, not boys.

I always want to say, "Let me get this straight. God created men and women as gorgeous images of himself, and made them different from each other in amazing, creative ways so they could be partners to each other and have babies who will grow into more God-filled men and women. But when you're focusing on God, you're not supposed to think about how any of that applies to you?"

I don't say that to them—at least not that way!—but I am saying it to you. At some point in our history, we Christians got off track and turned sex and anything surrounding it into a specter that's always waiting on the horizon to grab us and drag us into sin. That has led us to think of God as being the opposite of the body and its functions, instead of the Creator and Preserver of them.

I do ask girls when we talk about periods and so forth to think about the divine care that went into the designing of a woman's body. I point out that puberty alone boggles the mind with all its details and the way everything works together to turn a tween girl into a woman.[6]

As a mom who longs for sexual purity for her daughter, you can tell her the same thing. God gave her exactly the body she's supposed to have. She has to love it the way God does. She's responsible for taking care of it. You can tell her that your job is to show her how to do that, by giving her the information she needs and setting an example and helping her make the right choices. You can tell her that the two of you will work together under God's love and guidance and grace to make everything about her young womanhood a beautiful thing, so that she will be ready very soon to make good decisions concerning her body on her own, with God.

You can tell her that, because *that* is what is true.

Test Your Own Waters

I've got some questions for you to consider. As always, handle any or all of them however you like. The object is not to make you feel like Loser Mom—which you SO are not—but to help you discover where any misgivings you have might've come from.

- How are you about your periods, your breasts, your hairy armpits? Is it all a royal pain? A necessary annoyance? A continuing source of amazement? Something in between?
- Have you had experiences that have shaped your body 'tude? The way your mom handled your puberty? Your sexual history? Childbearing?
- What would you change or replicate about the way you "came of age" (learned about periods, got your first one, discovered how babies came to be)?

Going for It

It's really pretty instinctive when you think about it. I'm saying that the best way to guide your tween daughter through puberty is to *talk* with her. And, for heaven's sake, what do we women do better than *talk*?

So, we need to talk to our daughters. We can totally do that. The question is *how*, especially when it comes to this hotbed of discussion topics. I'm offering a few principles for you, some of which can be applied to any mother-daughter dialogue and some of which pertain to particular topics. All of them should be passed through the filter of your own personality, and your daughter's. Using something in a way that feels forced to you will send both of you running back to hide under your respective covers.

If your daughter comes to you with a question related to womanhood, make sure you know what she's really asking you.

We've talked about this before so I'll just touch on it briefly. Most tween girls don't inquire about what's going to happen in the future much beyond this week. They want to know what's going to affect them now. If your daughter asks if it's okay to "go out with a boy," she probably doesn't want to know when she can actually date, get engaged, and plan a wedding. If you think about her life this very minute, you can relax because she more than likely just wants to know if she can call some eleven-year-old her boyfriend. To be sure, start with, "Define 'going out.'"

By the same token, if she does express interest in a topic that is way beyond her realm of experience—does it really hurt that much to have a baby, for instance—she's not hinting that she or any of her BFFs is currently pregnant. She's curious in a detached kind of way about something that may or may not happen to her someday. A simple "Yes," or "It hurts some, but you forget about it as soon as you hold your baby in your arms" is probably sufficient. She's not really asking for a full rendition of your labor and delivery experience.

If her question is specific, borders on the bizarre, or seems to come out of nowhere—Can you get a disease from kissing somebody? Can a boy really tell you're having your period by the way your breath smells? If I got pregnant before I got married would I go to hell? — you can bet that came out of something she heard somewhere that didn't ring true, and you can thank the Lord she came to *you* for clarification. Which, by the way, is all she really wants. Again, she's not necessarily indicating that she's already kissed some boy and is now worried about her health.

In any of those cases, I think it's best to say, "Interesting question, Kate. Why do you ask?" She's far too young to be good at dissembling. If she says, "Just curious," that's what she means. It will either save you from a long dissertation she's not even asking for, or give you time to form an answer you hadn't expected to give just yet.

This is key: If she asks a question, always give her an honest answer to what she really wants to know. "You're too young to be asking that yet" or "We don't talk about things like that in this house" are going to close a door you'll be hard-pressed to pry open again. You get to decide how much you're going to explain, but explain you must.

Stay aware of what's going on with her physically, without invading her privacy.

That's often just a matter of noticing that breast buds are nosing at that T-shirt she's almost grown out of, or keeping general track of her mood swings to see if there's a pattern, or realizing she could braid the hair on her legs right now. We'll discuss what to actually do about that in the next chapter. For now you're just noticing, without commenting, unless she brings it up. "Sara, you stink, girl! Go use some of my deodorant" is not "noticing," and it's definitely not the kind of "talking" I'm describing here. More on that in a moment.

The more difficult thing is to be aware of changes such as vaginal discharge and pubic hair. Since there are so many other visible signs, you don't technically have to know about the more private ones. By not asking you are actually showing her respect and allowing her to make some basic decisions on what she shares about her body. One of the most disturbing emails I've received recently was from a girl of almost twelve who hadn't had her period yet and all the other females in the family had started by age ten. She said every time she came out of the bathroom her mother asked her if she'd started yet. I suspect that when she does, she's going to be reluctant to tell her.

If you stay in the loop and respect your daughter's privacy, she will come to you with changes she's concerned about. If you drill her with a puberty checklist in hand, you'll send her the message that her body is not her own.

View all variations from everybody else as normal.

Because they are. The moment she complains that "everybody else" has gotten their period and she hasn't, rather than asking if she has actually taken a poll of the girls in her grade (that might work with other topics but not this one), tell her, every time it comes up, that no two girls experience puberty at the same time in their lives or in exactly the same way, and that she is exactly where she's supposed to be right now, at this moment in time. There are three things that will help you do that without losing it and saying, "How many times do I have to tell you this—you're fine! Be grateful you don't have to put up with any of that mess yet." I don't have to explain why *that* response would be disastrous.

To keep from going there, understand that there may be teasing going on among the girls she associates with. Such comments as, "You need a bra about as much as you need dentures" are not unheard of, and are especially hurtful when they come from a BFF.

You also need to know that these days, completing the "steps" in puberty often becomes a competition among tweens. Who's going to get their period first? Who'll get a bra ahead of everybody else? Whose mom is going to cave on letting her shave her legs before the others? As more of them get up those steps, a subtle club is formed, one she knows she can't belong to until she too is wearing a bra and a pad. She may not even be excluded from anything else among her friends, but she's aware that she's still more of a little kid than they are somehow.

Just be sure *you* accept that variations of the imagined "norm" are, indeed, normal. If you don't, she's going to sense it and begin to anxiously wonder. Anxiety leads to more crying out for reassurance—"Why haven't I ..."—which brings out the exasperated Wicked Witch in you. If you're really concerned that your daughter is "behind," take that poll yourself among the other moms, or talk to your gynecologist. He or she will probably tell you to ask again if your daughter turns fifteen and still shows no signs.

If your tween isn't convinced by you, you might want to pick up a copy of *Body Talk* for the two of you to read and discuss together. Pages 12 – 14 and 24 – 25 apply specifically to this challenge.

Be especially sensitive if she's an early bloomer.

I don't hear much from tween girls who've been wearing a bra since they were nine or started their periods while they were still dressing Barbies. That isn't because they're fine with looking fifteen at age eleven. It's because their early blossoming sets them apart in a way that's so painful for them, they often don't even want to talk about it.

I see it when full-figured tween girls come to events. Too often they have their arms crossed over their chests and their shoulders curved in. If they're tall, they slump. If they weigh more than the skinny-minis around them, they hide in big shirts. Hair hangs over faces. Smiles are guarded. It's the rare physically precocious tween who breezes in looking confident that she'll fit in with the wispy-waisted girls in training bras. In her mind, how can she? She can't wear the cutesy little fashions her smaller counterparts have on. She isn't having the same dance-cheerleading-soccer experiences they're having. And she's been teased so much she would have a hard time trusting anyone who extended a welcome to her anyway.

The only thing she thinks she has going for her at an all-girl occasion is that there are no boys there. In most situations she is fair game for tween males who, bless their hearts, are freaked out by what constant exposure to this woman-look-alike does to their hormones. They feel compelled to embarrass her to hide the fact that they feel completely inadequate around her. Faced with constant ALC "humor" about her breasts, her hips, her height, and her understandable disdain for *them*, is it any wonder she's afraid to even try to enjoy her tween years the way she has every right to do?

This is especially troubling for a girl if she virtually blossoms overnight. Marijean was always one of the shorter, less physically developed girls in her age group until the summer she was twelve.

In two months she grew to a statuesque five-foot-eight, slipped into a size ten shoe, and caught up with me in cup size. She was suddenly going through my closet for possible options and looking almost womanly in her favorite flowered shorts. She was pretty pleased with the way she looked, and it showed in her level of confidence. She informed us that she was going to make straight A's from now on and was primed for middle school. Until she was met there with "Dude, you're an Amazon!" "Hey, the breast fairy finally came!" and "You think you're better than everybody else, don't you?" Tears after school became a common occurrence, and then a certain bitterness crept into her worldview. All boys were stupid. All popular girls were worse. And she herself—the worst of all.

I wasn't having it. I wanted to declare open season on every boy in the seventh grade, but I knew if she didn't work this through, she would continue to feel powerless. She couldn't do it alone, however. So we talked—

- about the fact that boys don't mature as fast as girls do and need to largely be ignored for the time being.
- about the very real possibility that they and her girlfriends were intimidated by her sudden leap ahead.
- about the realization that the same girls who'd teased her in elementary school (Heidi and the Heinous Ones) were trying to hold their own as the Ruling Class and not having that much success; they hadn't been put in the accelerated classes, and it was the "smart kids" (like Mj) who were taking the reins in middle school.
- about the confidence she'd found, that it was hers to keep, and that she could use it to attain the things she really wanted—a place in the school chorus, membership in Shakespeare Club, closeness to some girls she'd found commonalities with during the summer.
- about how to respond to teasing (which I'll go into in detail in section four).

If you have an early or overnight bloomer, let your heart go out to her. Listen to her pain. Don't discount it or try to soothe it away. Just tell her the truth, and help her deal with it. Before she finally embraces her vibrant, robust beauty, there will be times when you are the only one who can possibly understand what she's going through. Be there, not with support for wallowing, but with guidance for forming a plan, for answering the question, "So—what am I going to do about it?"

Help her prepare for her period on every level.

First, talk about what's going to happen. Whether you go through a book like *Body Talk* together or you have your own approach, *you* need to be the one who shares the details about this major development in her life. Even if she gets the news from a presentation at school or a church girls' group, you should follow with a discussion of your own. She'll then know what you want her to know, and you'll know what she knows. This is far too important to leave entirely to anyone else. Both of you will benefit from the bonding that occurs.

On this level, keep it simple. Does she really need instruction on how the hormones change during pregnancy, or what the risks are for breast cancer? Let what you say be on a need-to-know basis. Use humor if you can. This is not an upcoming trauma you're talking about, so share your funny first-time experiences. Admit to the parts that really are annoying but that can be handled with wit and a grin. Just let it be about the beauty of joining the company of women. She gets to have babies if she wants someday. She'll experience a rhythm she can depend on. She'll be cleansed month after month, allowed to start anew in a symbolic way.

Next talk about what she'll need to do. Show her the pads. Discuss how she'll dispose of them, how often she'll need to change them, what she can do in case of a spillover. Offer to let her wear one to see what it feels like or to be reassured that it isn't going to show. Make a plan for what she'll do if she starts at school or home alone with Dad or in the middle of a soccer field. Shop together for supplies. Answer every question she has. But, of course, don't feel like you have to do all of this in one session. If you start soon enough, you'll have plenty of time to stretch it out.

Mini-Women

"My mom's so good when it comes to the growing-up thing. She never acts like I'm younger than I really am, and she helps me with all the girl stuff — you know, respecting the fact that I hide bras under things when I'm in the store. I can't stand anyone seeing them except me!"

age 12

Finally, model what a great body 'tude can be. You can give her all the right information and get her prepared for every possible period-starting scenario, but the attitude *you* have about "feminine hygiene" will have the most profound effect on whether her experience is rich and satisfying or just a huge pain in the neck—and not just now but perhaps for always. There are some things to consider before you begin.

One is how you name things. Do you refer to your period as "the curse" or speak of "that time of the month" like an upcoming root canal? My mother and older sister called it "falling off the roof." What the Sam Hill was *that* about? "My friend" is a little better, but why not dignify it with its true name, "menstrual cycle"? The rhythmic, natural sound of it implies that it is exactly that. As for breasts, I would definitely stick to that quite lovely name. "Boobies" and "tits" are used in such demeaning ways these days, I'm not sure you want your daughter applying them to herself. I know women who refer to their breasts as "the girls"; that's kind of fun—makes them sound like ever-present companions.

Be aware of your general view. Is menstrual blood disgusting to you? Do you think of the whole business as something unclean, rather than the actual cleansing process that it is? Do you think breasts ought to be kept under cover because they're ugly, rather than as a matter of personal dignity? Whether you actually say any of that to your daughter or not, it will seep into your tone if you're not aware. If someone once instilled a negative view of feminine body functions in you, this would be a great time to heal that and stop the legacy with your daughter. You have that choice.

Probably most important of all, consider how your periods affect your life. Some women seem to just breeze through their menstrual cycles. (I was fortunate enough to do that.) Others welcome it all as a rich reminder of their womanhood. (That's my daughter's MO.) Still others have to suffer through cramps and headaches and low back pain that make the cycle anything *but* "rich." And then there are those whose mood darkens so much they just feel lucky to get through it without committing a homicide. All are valid and understandable. Your task is to decide how much of that you're going to discuss with your daughter before you know what periods are going to be like for her. To say "Be prepared for major cramps because I always get them and you probably will too" might not be necessary if it turns out she takes after the women on her father's side and never has to touch a Midol. Whatever you choose to tell, consider doing it with a "It could be this way, but we'll find a way to make it easier" approach.

Talk about moods, rather than simply chalking them up to hormones.

If you're like me, you hate it when people—men in particular—call any emotional response other than smiling agreement "PMS." That annoys the daylights out of me not because PMS isn't real, but because it isn't at the root of every mood a woman has. The premenstrual shift in hormones may intensify those moods, but the everyday events of life cause them in the first place. (And might I add that men do their share to bring out the cranky ones?)

So even though roller-coaster moods are a part of puberty for many tween girls, we really shouldn't excuse any out-of-control expression of them. In other words, your daughter shouldn't get away with shoving her brother out of her room while screaming that he's lucky she isn't pushing him out the second-story window instead, just because she's about to start her period. Otherwise, you run the risk of her taking the entire household down with her. "Our home was so peaceful," one caller told me on my radio spot, "until Emily turned nine and the hormones kicked in." I think this is another one of those opportunities to instill a true lesson in living. A few suggestions to get you started:

- Be sympathetic to the fact that the new intensity of her emotions is confusing and hard to control. In other words, don't tell her she's turned into a witch and she'd better just get off her broom and straighten up.
- But set limits on how she expresses them. She may leave the upsetting situation and go to her room to get calmed down, but she can't slam the door when she gets there. (We had to add "No muttering under your breath on the way" for Marijean.) She is certainly free to cry, but she may not try to use

tears to get her way (especially with Daddy). You know she gets angry so she can go ahead and vent, but name-calling, swearing, spitting, and projectile throwing are not allowed.

• Suggest healthy ways to express emotions rather than taking them out on people or stuffing them away to fester. We talked about creative outlets earlier. Others might include shooting baskets, hitting a tennis ball, walking the dog, or playing a mean "Chopsticks" on the piano. Any nonviolent way to expend some of that extra emotional energy is okay.

• Show her how to say what she feels in a manner that might actually change the situation for the better. If she's screaming at her sister for wearing her fave T-shirt without asking and spilling grape Kool-Aid on it, call her on her inappropriate shrieking, but also give her an alternative approach with her sister: "Here's what you did that ticked me off and here's what I'm asking you to do about it." (You'll of course deal with the sister and *her* issues as well … pure joy this motherhood thing, huh?)

The goal is to help your tween gain personal power over her emotions without denying them. If you explain that PMS is a sign that her cycle is moving, it also makes sense to tell her to treat herself to a little TLC. Curl up with your favorite book, you might suggest. Make yourself a smoothie. Ask for a hug. That will go a long way toward heading off the moods before they even start. (And never underestimate the power of chocolate.)

Let the boy-thing be the boy-thing.

I think we're already established that, like it or not, boys are going to be part of the picture at some point, and refusing to let your daughter talk about them or telling her it's wrong for her to be giving them a thought is probably a mistake. If you won't discuss boy stuff with her, she'll find someone else to talk to, somebody who's likely to give her misinformation—you know, like her BFF, who knows even less about the male gender than she does. If you tell her she shouldn't even be thinking about boys yet, she won't stop thinking about them.

She'll just feel guilty for thinking about them, and become secretive. All that boy stuff may grow far bigger in her mind than it would have if you'd just said, "Of course you're noticing boys. You're growing up. So—tell me about it."

I get why you're reluctant, I really do. If you admit that she's starting to be interested in the opposite sex, you have to admit that she isn't totally a little girl anymore. It's a loss for you. And you're afraid she's going to grow up too fast. If she "likes" a boy now, at eleven, does that mean she's going to want to date at twelve, have sex at thirteen? If she starts her "romantic" life as a tween, how can you be assured that she'll remain pure until she's married? It seems like the general acceptance that teens have sex is more widespread than ever, and you just don't want her to buy into that. Keeping her away from boys, convincing her that thoughts of them will only lead her away from God—that seems like the only way to protect her. Besides, you just don't need the drama.

The inclination to stifle the whole thing is especially strong if your daughter shows signs of being "boy crazy," babbling nonstop about the boys in her class, wanting to call them, text them, email them, chase them around the church parking lot. If you engage in that for even a moment, won't that encourage her to go completely out of control? Your concern is very real—you're afraid all her decisions are going to be made on the basis of what will impress a guy. All the more reason then to hear what she's saying. Only then can you guide her toward a more balanced perspective.

When a tween girl is nuts over anything in a ball cap, there's usually something going on with her. Not enough attention from Dad? Lack of confidence in any ability aside from her talent for flirting? A recent loss that's made her want to grab for something new to fill the hole? The only way you're going to find out is to talk until you discover it. Telling her she's "sinning" by craving male attention won't bring you closer to that. Teaching her to respect herself will.

Yet again, find out what she's really talking about when she brings up the subject of boys. As she's discovering that those Absurd Little Creeps may not be so creepy after all, she may just be interested in one as a friend. At this age, a buddy relationship really is completely platonic. Many things about the way boys think can be explained to her by this reliable source while they're climbing trees or shooting baskets together. If you deny her all contact with boys, they become mysterious creatures she won't know how to deal with at all when the time comes.

Don't approach "the talk" with dread—but by all means approach it.

The obvious first question is when to tell your daughter about sex. My feeling on that is—tell her when she asks either outright or with a hint. Her asking, "When did your mom tell you about babies and stuff?" might be one indicator that she's ready. Asking you to explain a joke she's heard is another. As always, be sure you know that's what she's really asking you. Then—talk.

How do you do that? You do it in whatever way you've prepared beforehand, because that's the first thing you need to do. I don't mean type up a script and whip it out when she shows a spark of interest. I'm just saying think through what you want her to know, and what feeling about the beauty and wonder of a committed, marital sexual relationship you want her to come away with. Imagine yourself sharing that with her.

I think we've all envisioned walking through a field of flowers and butterflies as we impart our wisdom with our daughters, or talking over hot chocolate by a fire, or strolling along a beach with her at dawn, but really, it doesn't usually happen that way. You may be thinking that on her thirteenth birthday you'll pack everybody else off for the day and have a tea party for the two of you at which you'll give your well-prayed-over "talk." That is a beautiful thing and if that truly works for you and your daughter, that's the way it should be. If you're more inclined toward talking when the topic arises, even if you have to bring it up as you sense she wants to, that's perfectly fine too. The thing has the potential to be awkward enough without you suddenly behaving like somebody else!

What do you say? What truly is in your heart—not what comes from fear or shame or a set of rules. God created sex for our joy and for procreation, in the context of a committed marital relationship. It is only its misuse by human beings that can twist it into anything ugly or wrong. If you use that beauty as your foundation, then whatever information and guidance you want to give will come from the love in your soul. Anything you say to scare her or guilt her away from what lies within her will deny her joy, even if she remains a virgin until her wedding day.

If you're concerned about other influences besides yours, continue to do the things you're already doing. Be vigilant about the media she's exposed to. Limit and monitor television viewing. Preview movies she wants to see. Listen to her music (if you can stomach it!). Point out the sexual fallacies you see in advertising.

Doing this now, and telling her why you're doing it, and gradually giving her more options will not only protect her from damaging sexual images, but it will insure that she'll be able to make those determinations for herself when she's a teenager.

With all this talking, eyes may begin to glaze over (yours as well as your daughter's!). That's the time to bring in the fun stuff. Who said this whole puberty thing has to be a completely serious business? Here are a few suggestions of things to do to reinforce all of the above.

Celebrate Woman's Day.

I wish I could take credit for this one, but I actually saw it on *The Cosby Show* years ago. When Rudy started her period for the first time, Claire asked her what she wanted to do for "Woman's Day" to celebrate this important transition in her life. Rudy didn't see what there was to be happy about, which was exactly her mom's point. You can get bogged down by the mechanics of using a pad and the worry over whether there's going to be spillage right there in Language Arts and forget what the happening itself means in a girl's life. Whether you plan ahead or let it be spontaneous, go out for high tea or share a bowl of popcorn at home, it can be a tender time for both of you and allow her first period to be less anxiety producing. Needless to say, you won't want to announce to her brothers that Hannah has started her period so you're taking her to Baskin Robbins.

Have a myth-busting session.

Sleepovers are veritable smorgasbords of misinformation about puberty. Can't you remember hearing over a bowl of Skittles that a dentist can tell if you're on your period or that a tampon can get lost up in your body? When girls gather in groups with the lights out and the parents out of earshot, they're obviously going to go straight to what's on their minds. But where on *earth* do they get this stuff? The problem is that they take everything their BFFs say as gospel, and it's up to you to set them straight.

Rather than tell your daughter that she—and her BFF—don't know what they're talking about, sit down with her sometime when the two of you are alone, grab snacks and pen and paper, and together make a list of all the things she's heard about puberty and periods that didn't come from you. You can make a game out of busting the ones that are myths or just laugh over them. ("A boy can tell you're on your period by your breath? Are you kidding? In the first place, he would have to get past his own breath to even smell yours, and besides that . . ." You get the idea.)

Have a menstrual memories session.

If your daughter has other adult women in her life that both you and she trust—grandmothers, aunts, grown cousins, family friends—you might get two or three of them together with your daughter over tea and share menstrual memories. Their most embarrassing period moments. What their moms told them about girl stuff. What advice they have for her about changing into a young woman. You know whether this would work for your daughter or plunge her into a pit of embarrassment. Obviously you'll want to ask her beforehand if this sounds good to her. If it's done right, most tween girls love the idea of officially becoming One of the Women.

Encourage a sisterhood.

When Marijean was in her tweens, she developed a friendship with two sisters who, like her, loved dreaming and imagining and creating and being authentic in ways they felt they couldn't be in front of Heidi and the Heinous Ones. Their bond was formed while making masks and pots and hats at their house (the chances of that happening under *my* roof were practically nil!) and writing plays and producing, directing, and starring in them at ours.

When the oldest of the three started her period, the bond took on a deeper, richer feel, as they marked every new development—getting bras, shaving legs, wearing deodorant—and helped each other over the inevitable bumps—comfort for cramps, rescue from being padless when somebody's period started in PE, a united front in the face of teasing over Mairin's well-developed breasts and Marijean's height and Chamaea's precocious maturity. Their sisterhood carried them through middle school and high school, and later through marriages, pregnancies, miscarriages, and cancer scares. Today, in their late twenties and early thirties, they continue to make their way into the fullness of their beings, with each other to hold them up, coax them forward, and celebrate the progress.

The sisterhood took on a life of its own that neither their mother nor I predicted. But once we saw in the beginning how in tune they were with each other, she and I did all we could to foster the threesome. You can do the same by calling your daughter's healthy relationship with her circle of friends a sisterhood and encouraging them to share the experiences and anxieties and joys of going through puberty.

Suggest ground rules—no spreading each other's personal information around, no teasing, no comparing to each other. Ask them if they've decided how they're going to deal with teasing from other people, especially boys, or if they have a plan for helping each other if somebody's period starts at school, or if they've made a formal promise to be there for each other when things get confusing or scary.

We need relationships with other women to keep *us* from becoming isolated with our hang-ups and our anxieties, and we're adults. Still-fragile tween girls need them just as much, if not more. Since we are the ones with the influence, not to mention the wheels, I think we have a responsibility to help get them there and suggest ways to solidify the sisterhood for the adventures to come.

Introduce the Boy Manifesto.

One of the most important things a sisterhood can decide is how they're going to behave around boys. You can set them up for that by providing your daughter and her friends with a time and a space (devoid of young males and other curious onlookers) for creating a Boy Manifesto. Have your daughter tell her BFFs to come with advice they've gathered on the subject from wise people (especially dads). Once they've assembled, they can make a list of situations they could run into with the male of the species (such as, "a boy teasing you to be mean," "a boy teasing you for fun" — there's a complete list on page 106 of *Body Talk*). Using the advice they've brought with them, the Bible, and other reliable sources, they can discuss how they'll handle each situation and write it down as part of a manifesto. "If a boy teases me just for fun and it doesn't annoy me, I'll tease back." "If a boy teases me to be mean, I will first remember he isn't telling the truth about me." And so forth. You're around on the periphery in case an issue comes up they don't have an answer for, with art supplies so everyone can make a creative copy to keep. You can also tell them that now that they have a plan, they won't be caught by surprise and can relax and enjoy friendships with boys, knowing that they are mini-women who make good choices. Prayer is a fitting end to that session (and don't forget to pray for those precious boys, who wouldn't write a Girl Manifesto even if you threatened them with house arrest!).

Bridging the Gap

Dear God, Father of our bodies as well as our souls, thank you for the gift of womanhood you've given to me and to _____.
In the midst of the confusion and the worry and the excitement and the joy and the doubt she's experiencing, please bridge the gap between the wisdom I have to share and the wisdom she needs to hear. I ask this in the name of your Son, who gave *his* body for us. Amen.

8

The Care and Feeding of a Tween

[The one] who has clean hands and a pure heart ... will receive blessing from the Lord.

Psalm 24:4 – 5 NIV

"I finally got the nerve to ask my mom about deodorant, and she said not until I'm older. I don't think I can fight back, but I really need it. I stink!"

age 11

There were times when Marijean was eight and nine when I would look at her and think, *Do people who don't know me wonder if she even has a mother?* The straggly hair with the knot in the back, the baggy sweatshirts, and the raggedy fingernails would make anyone consider the possibility that she might be an orphan. Those were also the days when Jim and I were so involved in our new theatrical ventures, meals were always catch-as-catch-can, her homework was often done backstage during a dress rehearsal, and we were setting a pretty poor example of rest, balance, and control over stress. Still, she seemed to be doing fine.

But then her fourth grade teacher told us—quite diplomatically, so I really have to hand it to her—that Marijean could be doing far better than she was academically and socially if, perhaps, she had a bit more "normal" schedule. I took a good long look at my child— and couldn't understand why no one had called social services.

Okay, so that's an exaggeration. She wasn't neglected, and to this day she says some of the happiest moments of her childhood were spent sleeping in costume bins and eating Happy Meals in the scene shop. But her dad and I both realized that while we were attentive to her emotional and spiritual needs, we tended to let some of the physical basics slide. There weren't enough veggies in her diet. She didn't always get to bed at a decent hour. She definitely wasn't getting enough exercise. And "Didn't you just wear that shirt yesterday?" was a question too often asked as she was dashing out the door for school.

We focused on remedying that, with fairly good success, though we never could get her to quit biting her fingernails, and as for neatness in her room . . . we just closed the door and called for all dishes when we could no longer set the table. But I have often pondered what would have happened if that astute teacher hadn't called it to our attention that our daughter needed better care and feeding.

Even if you aren't caught up in a career that makes you forget to do the laundry or get fiber into your daughter's diet, it's easy to let the basics slide. For one thing, we tend to think of tween-age kids as being somewhat self-feeding and self-cleaning. They can make a sandwich. You no longer have to stand over them in the bathtub for fear they'll drown. Most of them stay fairly healthy during these years. It certainly isn't like when they were babies and you had to be all about the vitamins and the regular feedings and the constant washing of the pacifier so they wouldn't suck up germs. And with all the puberty issues to focus on, it's easy to forget that your daughter's still a child and needs a bedtime, a daily bath, and a balanced diet—and that she isn't going to get all of that on her own.

Fortunately, this is one of the easier parts of raising a tween daughter—I mean, compared to talking about periods and comforting her when she doesn't know who she is and you don't either. It may also be one that benefits your whole family, as it did us. I know I took better care of myself when I started taking better care of my daughter. Let's look at the areas of most importance for your healthy, vibrant, world-at-her-fingertips tween girl.

Getting Clear

My talks with pediatricians and child development specialists, as well as my own experience, have brought four main tween needs to the surface. You'll see that they're actually things every body needs, but I've tried to pinpoint how they apply specifically to an eight- to twelve-year-old girl.

She needs to be clean.

Those hormones of puberty change not only the way her body looks and functions, but the way it smells too. General body odor, the less-than-delightful aroma of the underarms, and stinky feet can all become issues. Female hormones increase the amount of sweat a tween girl produces, and with millions of those little glands in her body, that can be a lot of perspiration when she's hot, active, or nervous—all of which she probably *is* a large percentage of the time. The sweat glands in her underarms and between her legs become active for the first time during puberty, although it isn't the sweat itself that causes the not-so-lovely scent, but the bacteria living on her skin in those warm, dark places that break down the sweat and cause odor.

Feet can have their own special brand of yuckiness, especially if a girl spends most of her day in tennis shoes and socks. Foot fungus may also make its first appearance during this time, athletes being at particular risk.

And then there's the breath. There was nothing sweeter than that baby-girlfriend breath she used to have, even when she first woke up. Now the foods she eats—which contain onions and garlic and other things that weren't in her preschool diet—combined with bacteria can make mouthwash a serious option now.

Finally—and this I didn't know until I consulted a stylist for tween beauty tips—"The glands in their little scalps also sweat now. That can cause a sour smell if they don't wash their hair almost every day."[1]

While nowhere in the Bible does it actually say that cleanliness is next to godliness, we'd have to have olfactory damage not to know that it's at least socially challenging to go around smelling like dirty laundry. Sweat is a good thing because when it evaporates, the skin cools down and it removes toxins from the body. But other kids aren't thinking about that when they curl their lips and wrinkle their noses in the middle of the vocabulary test and say, "Who smells? Is it you? It is you! Gross me out and make me icky!"

At the same time that the sweat glands are going into high gear, so are the ones that produce oil. In some girls they really get going, causing clogs of dead cells and oil that become infected and—presto—pimples. Although a tween doesn't break out because she's "dirty," a skin care regime helps—and a face full of acne does *not* when she's already self-conscious about her appearance. Again, her peers may not be kind, and the nickname "Pizza Face" cuts to the heart.

The oil glands going to town on her skin can also pump up in her scalp, making her hair look greasy even if she skips one day of shampooing. Two days and it's matted to her head. Few things make her feel less attractive and "gross," unless it's the teasing about being a "Grease Ball." I'm telling you, it gets ugly out there in Tweenland.

She needs to be active.

You're already aware of the benefits of physical exercise for adults, and I'm sure you know the same is true for tweens. Exercise gives them energy and staying power, helps them sleep, makes their muscles stronger and more flexible, gets their eyes sparkling and their skin glowing, lessens their chance of becoming overweight, and evens out their moods. (That last one alone is enough to make you want to buy her a gym membership . . .) Girls need to move around for other reasons as well. Developing physical competence boosts their self-esteem, giving them a healthy can-do attitude and warding off peer abuse. Team sports teach important lessons about community, adversity, and respect for rules and officials, and forge friendships among girls working toward a common goal.

However, while 25 percent of girls between the ages of eight and sixteen participate in an organized sports program during the year,[2] and millions participate in phys. ed classes and noncompetitive athletic activities like swimming, skating, skiing, and hiking, many still get very little exercise at all. They may be constantly "busy," on the go from breakfast to bedtime, but they aren't physically active. Fewer and fewer tween-age girls spend time playing run-around games or riding their bikes or hanging from the playground equipment.

In 2000 sociologists did a study of a cross-section of families which showed that for American children between six and twelve, the average time spent outdoors in unstructured play per week was thirty minutes. The follow-up study done six years later found that fewer than one in five children spent *any* unstructured time at all playing outdoors.[3] Time, space, safety, and other attractive options (such as computer games and cable TV) have become factors in the prevention of free play, and some of those reasons are completely understandable. But experts say that the lack of an adequate amount of exercise children used to get naturally from playing is a major reason why obesity in children has increased by four times over the past forty years,[4] putting them at risk for Type 2 diabetes, high blood pressure, and high cholesterol, even as children.

On the other hand, sports doctors warn that physical exercise of the wrong kind or practiced incorrectly can also be a danger. I give you what Gloria Beim, physician to the US National Track Cycling Team, says on the subject:

> Girls are not little women. There are marked differences between the two in terms of coordination, strength, and stamina. In girls, bone-tendon-muscle units, growth areas within bones, and ligaments experience uneven growth patterns, which leaves them susceptible to injury. What might be a bruise or sprain in a woman can be a potentially serious growth-plate injury for a girl.[5]

That is *not* to say that girls shouldn't play sports, or that you need to bite your nails to the quick worrying that your daughter's going to give herself a growth-plate injury. Just know that young female athletes—with those between the ages of eleven and twelve being the most vulnerable—have special needs because their bodies are growing, and they require different coaching and conditioning than more mature athletes, which they don't always get.[6] Tween girls who take up a sport early on and play that and only that, year round, in their elementary and middle school years, can be at risk for fractures and inflammatory conditions of the growth plates (such as Osgood-Schlatter "disease") caused by chronic stress and overuse. Early specialization and the trend toward viewing her sport as a means to a scholarship or a career, when the player is only eleven years old, can actually prevent her from developing overall balance and strength and well-rounded coordination. While learning to dribble, pass, and shoot, she might not have learned how to hop, skip, or jump. Without those basic skills, she's susceptible to injury.

By the way, to help you get sports-as-a-means-to-an-end into perspective: Only about 5 percent of high school athletes continue to play competitively in college. No more than 1 percent of high school athletes get full scholarships.[7] That sounds like a great reason to put just-for-fun back into the game.

Are you going to find me and smack me if I say one more time that overstructuring is hazardous to both physical and emotional tween health? It does apply very directly to sports and physical activity, so I'm going to let sports sociologist Nancy Theberge say it for me:

> Exercise and sports are not the same thing. It's a false argument to advocate competitive sports for health reasons. The best examples of physical activity for health are kids involved in regular, non-extreme physical activity in a noncompetitive environment.[8]

She needs to be well-fed.

We are one of the richest, most advanced countries in the world, but you'd never know it by the eating habits of the average American. We are not a healthy nation in terms of our nutrition, and that is especially worrisome for our kids during the years when they're rapidly growing. Even if you're the exception, it doesn't hurt to keep some things in mind as you grocery shop or take the family out to eat.

As we've said, your daughter is growing more between the ages of eight and twelve than in almost any other period of her life, which means she needs more and better fuel than she ever has before. "Better fuel" is harder to come by in a culture that consumes so much fast food, junk snacks, and processed fare. An average of one out of four meals consumed by Americans is prepared in a commercial setting,[9] a statistic that hasn't changed with the current economic downturn. When they do want to cook at home, they find that the healthiest foods, such as fresh fruits and vegetables, are among the most expensive items in the supermarket. The price of organic produce? For*get* about it.

Even when families are determined to eat healthy, they're often thwarted by busy schedules that mean dinner is served from a drive-through window and eaten in the backseat of the car or is popped out of a box and into the microwave at home. Whatever nutritional value might be in there is smothered under salt, chemicals, and saturated fat.

School lunches aren't the healthiest affairs either, and even those mother-packed with carrot sticks and apples may go uneaten if somebody at the cafeteria table is sharing a bag of Starbursts.

It's puzzling that a culture which eats such unhealthy food has such a thing about weight. We — as a society — offer girls huge portions of super-processed, fat-filled, low-fiber, high-fructose food, and then tell them they need to look like ninety-pound supermodels. The emphasis on being thin starts young, as I pointed out earlier, and its effect on tween girls is not limited to the later development of eating disorders. The fifth grader who throws away half her lunch every day because she's afraid she's going to get fat already thinks of her body as an enemy she always has to control. She can't even enjoy an ice cream cone at the fair because she's not as skinny as the candidates for Miss County. At the time when she should be increasing (the right) caloric intake, she's skipping breakfast, picking at her lunch, and feeling guilty because she wants to consume the entire contents of the refrigerator when she gets home from school. Thinking she's not going to be good enough unless she's a rail cuts her off from appreciating who she is and prevents her from seeing her choices realistically. The same thing happens when she thinks, "I'll never look like that so what difference does it make what I eat? Bring on the Krispy Kreme."

Mini-Women

"I wish my mother would understand how hard it is to talk about some things that I really want to talk about. Like, sometimes I'm worried about if I'm eating right, but I rarely get up the courage to talk to her."

age 11

She needs to be balanced.

You know where I stand on the subject of tween time. A girl's mom needs to help her strike a balance between her propensity to be active and busy—to be a doer—and her need for leisure time she can fill however her creative self wants to. Just like every other human being who has ever lived.

She needs her sleep.

Tweens should get at least nine (count them!) hours of sleep every night, but according to a study reported in *Newsweek*, only about 15 percent get that much. "A full quarter get less than six."[10] What possible reasons could there be for that? Girls tell me it's due to too much homework to do after the afternoon's activities, too much going on in the evenings at home (noise, activity, general familial chaos!), not winding down before going to bed, and stressing over things while trying to fall asleep. Yikes. That sounds like half the *adults* I know.

She needs downtime.

Breaks during a tween's day are practically unheard of. School requires nonstop concentration. After-school time is packed, and when she does get home she has to get right to her homework and possibly even chores. Adults in the workplace would picket if they had to give up their coffee break, but we expect our kids to work all day, as if we're afraid a moment without something specific to do will lead them into trouble or allow them some boredom. Can't have that. Seriously, downtime is essential, especially for a girl grappling with her menstrual cycle, her changing body, and her all-consuming relationships. Basically, she needs a break. A lot of breaks.

Watch out for stress.

Stress is the new S-word. And for tween girls, who are ultra-aware of everything that goes on with the people around them, the big S is very apparent. Even without anyone telling them, they know when their parents aren't getting along, when money is a problem, when job security is threatened, or when something bad's going down in the extended family. They pick up tension the way a black dress picks up lint, and they carry it around with them, on top of all the other things they're worried about, age appropriate or not. A tween girl doesn't yet have the inner resources or the practice in coping with that kind of stress, so it may show itself in sleep problems, mood changes, dropping grades, and differences in appetite. Since some of those things can also be attributed to just plain puberty, it's easy for a mom to miss that her daughter's stressing out.

Be aware of the "body bullies" that lurk out there.

As if it weren't hard enough just being a kid, today's tween girl has to learn about things that frankly even most adults have trouble wrapping their minds around. Illegal drugs. Alcohol. Tobacco use. In many schools, alcohol and tobacco are easy for eleven- and twelve-year-olds to get their hands on. Many kids first experiment with drinking and smoking in fifth and sixth grades. One in every ten children ages ten through twelve tries drugs (usually marijuana). Girls are equal in number to boys when it comes to becoming addicted.

The average tween girl sees 40,000 commercials a year on TV; that's 666 hours worth, and 466 of those hours show people looking and acting sexy over things like cars, deodorant, and frozen dinners.[11] It's a no-brainer that that can affect her thinking about her own body.

Then there's the sexual predators and Internet stalkers. It's very hard for some tween girls to keep perspective and enjoy the rest of their childhoods without constantly wondering if that boy in her class who seems nice but dresses a little dark is going to bully her online, or whether she's ever supposed to trust an adult male without seeing a complete dossier. The job of boundary keeper is yours until she learns how to maintain her own safety zone. Some girls freak out at all the evil out there, and need help in getting their confidence and equilibrium, while other girls act as if there's no danger at all, and need to learn balanced wariness. You'll want to know where your daughter is on that continuum, and respond accordingly.

———————

Did I say earlier that the physical care of your child was one of the easier parts of raising a tween daughter? Silly me. Truly, though, the principles for the care and feeding of your daughter really are simple. Perhaps not easy, but simple. Let's start, as always, with the wisdom of our Father.

From the Ultimate Parent

"Make yourselves holy for I am holy.... I am God who brought you up out of the land of Egypt. Be holy because I am holy."

Leviticus 11:44 – 45

You won't find me quoting Leviticus very often. Really—"When a woman has her regular flow of blood ... anyone who touches her will be unclean till evening" (15:19 NIV)? Wow.

But I have to admit, nothing was left to chance in terms of health and wellness for the children of Israel. Six chapters of Leviticus are dedicated to what is "clean" and "unclean." All of chapter 11 describes in minute detail which foods are to be eaten and which must be "detested" lest the person be "unclean until evening," or, in the case of eating blood, cut off from the people (17:4). Chapter 12 explains how a woman is to be purified after having a baby. In chapters 13 and 14, they could find everything they ever wanted to know about skin diseases and mildew. If they needed to look into unclean discharges, the information was in chapter 15. (Yes, I'm aware that the Scriptures weren't divided into chapters back then!)

While most of us aren't going to give up lobster (11:10–11) or force people with psoriasis to cry out "Unclean! Unclean!" and live alone outside of town (13:45–46), we can appreciate the fact that God wanted his people—and us—to live long and healthy lives, free of sickness and disease. I think we can also agree that the precise instructions (11:4–8 being a prime example) reflect God's desire for us to be mindful of the divine presence and influence in every detail of our lives. I don't see that as restrictive or punitive—"Don't touch that Twinkie or you're sinning against the Lord"—but as an urging toward joy.

Washing, cleansing, coming out pure and shining—that is a beautiful process.

Eating wisely and well and savoring every bite—that is a foretaste of heaven.

Stretching and strengthening and becoming vigorous—that is a reflection of God's own energy.

Resting, breathing deeply, succumbing to the softness of sleep—that is reminiscent of the first satisfying Seventh Day.

Taking pleasure in the care and feeding of our bodies is a tribute to the God who made it. So why not teach your daughter that washing her hair and munching on a fresh-picked apple instead of an Oreo and skipping just to skip is the glorious, godly stuff of real living?

"If you live by my decrees and obediently keep my commandments," we read in Leviticus 26, "you'll be able to go to sleep at night without fear. I'll get rid of the wild beasts ... You will chase out your enemies and defeat them ... I'll give you my full attention ... I am God, your personal God."

The commandments are to be clean, to eat well, to exercise and rest and sleep, all in godly balance. The reward: freedom.

I think I like Leviticus after all.

Test Your Own Waters

Something a little different this time. Before you check out ways to improve the care and feeding of your tween daughter, it would be a good idea to look at how *you* take care of *you.*

To do that, keep track for a twenty-four-hour period of how you feed, exercise, rest, cleanse, and balance your body—and how you don't. This is going to be most effective if you jot notes to yourself throughout the day and evening and then go over them and assess.

As you look at the things you do and don't do for your health and well-being, for heaven's sake don't rake yourself over the coals about any of it. This is just a way to see what you might be modeling for your daughter—positive as well as could-use-some-improvement. Do I need to say again—she's watching you, Mom!

Going for It

So—*how* do you keep your tween daughter clean, active, well-fed, and balanced, especially when she's spending more and more time away from you, and when the world is constantly pointing her toward unhealthy options? Rather than tell you exactly what to feed her for breakfast (though should you need advice there I do name some resources for you), I think it will help you more to have some guiding principles that you can apply to your tween and your family situation. I offer you four.

Make health and wellness a priority, ahead of many others.

Ahead of a sparkling clean house. Ahead of the soccer championship. Ahead of straight A's. Even ahead of being at the church for absolutely every event. Put it right up there with her spiritual life and her authenticity and her acceptance of her beauty and her adjusting to the changes of puberty. There are several ways that can be done with your tween daughter.

First, the old USDA Food Pyramid for a healthy diet that we used to go by has been refined. Now you can go to www.MyPyramid.gov and personalize a plan for your daughter according to her age and level of regular exercise. It's perfect for fifteen minutes of mother-daughter time at the computer and will give her a stake in her own nutrition.

The two "food groups" not included on the Pyramid Plan are fat and sugar, but the guidelines for tweens are simple: no more than sixty grams of fat and no more than ten teaspoons of sugar a day. If you have a you're-gonna-have-to-show-me daughter, have her measure eighteen teaspoons of sugar into a glass of water and ask her if she would drink that (even a tween with a sweet tooth the size of Montana won't do it!). Then tell her that's how much sugar there is in a twenty-ounce bottle of soda. Ewwww. A convenient rule of thumb is not to eat anything with more than four grams of sugar per serving. (She's likely to become an avid label reader. Sorry about that.) Just be sure to emphasize that her Pyramid Plan is for feeling great, not for getting as skinny as her BFF.

Consider not having some or any of these in the house: soda, any processed foods with sugar as the first ingredient listed on the package, crackers and chips containing hydrogenated oil, snacks and cereal made with corn, and store-bought cookies. If that cleans out your entire pantry, start small, eliminating one source of empty calories and replacing it with something healthy and just as yummy. For item-by-item alternatives, check out page 77 of *Body Talk* — with your daughter, of course.

If she sets up a howl because you're tossing out the junk food, observe her over a few days to determine whether she munches when she's nervous, upset, or unhappy. Since saying, "You're just snacking because you failed your math quiz — give me those chips" is going to drive her hand back into the bag, try simply using your tried-and-true talk technique for finding out what might be going on with her. You could be saving her from a future of feeding the things she buries alive.[12]

It's not only the right food that makes good nutrition attractive. It's the environment it's eaten in. Sitting down together on the floor around the coffee table in the family room with vegetable soup and whole grain bread is every bit as good as gathering in semiformal dress in the dining room for roast chicken and organic asparagus. The only necessary environmental ingredients are family and focus. No TV, no movie in the DVD player. If a media-obsessed group starts into withdrawal when you turn off Nickelodeon and serve the chili, try an around-the-table fun thing. Everyone tells their high and low of the day. Each person answers the question of the evening — what did you see today that was purple? What made you LOL today? Did you witness somebody going out of their way to do the right thing?

Sharing a meal together can take on a spiritual feel, probably because the Supper has such a central place in our worshipping lives. Eugene Peterson, translator of *The Message* and devoted family man, writes, "Given the prominence of meals in the Jesus work of salvation, it is surprising how little notice is given among us to the relationship between the Meal and our meals."[13] Coming together, the way Jesus did with his discipled family, to share conversation and good food and yourselves is to open all of you up to the unhurried, unforced rhythms of grace. Who isn't going to thrive with that in the house? Can the schedule be adjusted to invite that in at least a few times a week?

Taking your daughter grocery shopping for the family meal brings her closer to owning her nutritional health, especially if she helps plan the menus. If, as she's cruising up and down the aisles with you, she asks for the cereal with the marshmallows in it, you can ask her, with a grin, where *that* fits on the Pyramid, and let her make a better choice that does. When you get home, invite her to help with the preparation, which is a great time for some of those talks in the last chapter. I know—all of this is going to slow you down, and you have things to do. But since you're looking at rearranging the priorities … Again, even if you make this happen just a few times a week, that's healthy progress.

Make sure she's drinking enough liquid, which is about 64 ounces a day depending on weather and how much she's exerting herself. You can try having her drink a glass of H_2O before she has that juice she's reaching for. When she hollers she's hungry, give her water as an appetizer, since hunger pangs are just as often a sign that she's thirsty as that she actually needs something to eat. Tell her that her body is 90 percent water; tweens love facts they can spout at the next gathering of the BFFs.

Insist that she get enough sleep—no matter what. "Enough" means she's wide awake and alert within fifteen to thirty minutes after getting up, even if she isn't a morning person. Going to bed and getting out of it at the same times every day will help her settle into a natural rhythm—and the more routine a mini-woman has in an unpredictable world, the better. Help her establish an unwinding routine before she climbs into bed so that she can fall asleep within a half hour—be it a hot bath, a protein snack, or writing in a journal. Bedtime prayers and then some music and she'll probably nod off long before that half-hour mark.

Falling asleep to the TV is not a good idea. In fact, any disturbing media within two hours of her head hitting the pillow can lead to disturbed sleep. Exercise just before she turns in will keep her from sleeping at all until her body settles down. If she lies awake for longer than a half hour every night or is plagued with frequent nightmares, it's time for another gentle what's-going-on probe.

Be attentive if her level of activity slows way down in her tween years. If she spends more than two hours a day playing video games, sitting in front of the computer, watching TV or movies, or reading, she's more sedentary than is healthy for her age. She already sits for a lot of her day in school, riding in the car, and doing homework.

Much more than that and she's not burning enough calories to keep her body running in good condition. If she wants to curl up with a book, have her walk the dog first. Let her watch TV—while she's resting up from a wild game of hide-and-seek.

Remember that even if she's an athlete, she's still a child.

In terms of health, that comes into play most directly if your daughter is involved in organized sports. As we've pointed out, sports can be unnecessarily hard on her little body. The upside is that with the kind of information found in this chapter, you're equipped to monitor her involvement and step in when you see that something isn't good for your child. While you can explain your decision to her, this is a situation where you are completely in charge of the choice. Modeling how you make it and carry it out will teach her more than you'll probably know for some time. In addition to what we've already touched on, consider a few more things.

A girl should be seven or eight before you enroll her in organized team sports; girls under seven aren't usually physically ready for contact sports or perhaps emotionally prepared for winning and losing on that level.[14] Long-distance running—more than half to three-quarters of a mile at a time—should be put off until her teen years.[15] If she's passionate about a sport—and some tween girls truly are—be sure she's being coached by someone who knows that girls run, jump, and land very differently than boys and need to be taught how to do those things safely; any sport that involves changing direction quickly—like soccer or basketball—puts her at risk for ACL injuries in her teen years if she doesn't learn proper techniques now, particularly if she plays that same sport year round. In fact, it isn't safe for her to play back-to-back seasons of one sport without a break and without pursuing other kinds of exercise as well. Overuse injuries in the teen years usually follow repetitive use in the tween years.

No matter how much or how little she plays, put safety before winning. Don't let a coach push her to buck up and get back into the game when she's hurt or overly fatigued. Taking a hit for the team shouldn't involve endangering her body—she's not playing NFL football for millions of dollars a year.

As a matter of fact, put safety before anything in sports. Be sure she warms up before she starts practice, even if the coach doesn't require it. If she's practicing her sport on her own, insist she wear the same protective gear as when she's playing, including high-top shoes for basketball. If she's biking, inline skating, or skateboarding, make a helmet and knee pads a requirement. Safety in sports and physical activities is always inside the Box.

Never (and note that you haven't heard me say "never" very often in this book) tell her she needs to exercise to lose weight. Unless she is medically obese, health and strength are the goals, not some ideal number on the scale. She's going through puberty, so you really don't know that any extra fluffiness she has going on is totally the result of inactivity anyway. Just get her up and moving for fun and to feel great and enjoy everything she does in her daily round. If she's chubby, she probably gets enough grief about it from other kids. From you she needs encouragement to be healthy and whole.

If your daughter isn't athletic and you're concerned that she isn't getting enough exercise, don't push her into sports. Aside from the fact that organized sports aren't equivalent to exercise anyway, if being on a field or a court with a ball and a bunch of people depending on her performance isn't her, it isn't her. The benefit of self-esteem that sports can have for athletically inclined girls is reversed if a less sporty girl has to do something she's bad at three or four times a week. Help her find an activity she enjoys that will increase her heart rate for twenty minutes, suit her personality, and fit into the family's schedule and lifestyle. Together make a brainstorming list of all the things she could do, scribble through the ones that don't jive with those three qualifications, and then let her choose one. Then do what you can to facilitate it. The goal-oriented tween can try the personal fitness plan on pages 62–64 of *Body Talk*.

Deal delicately with the special health and hygiene challenges of puberty.

If you're a busy mom with multiple offspring and an overwhelming to-do list, it's going to be hard for you to stop and address each tween issue that comes up right then and there. It's good for a girl to learn to handle reasonable waiting, and she can do that if she knows that some undivided attention is forthcoming. You can actually even lessen the intensity of those issues by making your quick responses sensitive ones. Choose the gentlest way to address body issues. Rather than pointing out that it smells like something died in her tennis shoes and she needs to get them the heck out of the laundry room before they stink up the whole house, you could whisper for her to take her shoes outside and you'll explain why later—especially if fellow siblings are in hearing range.

Avoid bringing up what you know are embarrassing topics for her in front of other people. Just because the ride from school to dance class with all her friends in the car seems to you like your only opportunity to ask her if those pimples on her chest have cleared up, it won't seem like that to her. There has to be a better time, doesn't there?

Try not to invalidate how huge this is to her, even if you only have a second to address the issue. "Honey, I promise we'll talk about this tonight before you go to bed, but we really have to get going now" doesn't take any longer than, "It is just so not that big of a deal that some boy said you were fat. He's an idiot. Now get your cleats or we're going to be late for practice."

Don't expect her to instinctively think about all that *you* have going on instead of what *she* has going on. You can *teach* her to consider that, and she'll learn it, but she doesn't automatically *know* to do it yet. She's a kid. So "Can you not see that I am completely stressed out? Why are you bringing this up now?" won't teach her. "I wish I could stop right now and talk to you about that—I really do. We will absolutely do it later—but for future reference, if I'm already screaming at everybody, that's not a good time to ask"—that will.

Take the initiative to deal with matters of odor and hygiene when you do have some (relatively) uninterrupted time to give her. Then you can talk about daily bathing, clean clothes, deodorant, and baking soda in those tennis shoes. Like everything else we've talked about, approach it with a sense of fun and as part of the something-new-all-the-time path to womanhood. For example, you can suggest that she set up her underwear drawer with a pretty (or hip) paper liner and a sachet to celebrate those new bras. Get out the candles and the music for her first attempt at leg shaving (with you in attendance, of course). *Body Talk* provides a "That Is SO Me!" checklist on page 94 which lists all the pubescent hygiene areas. You can help her accomplish one small thing—and cheer the results together. No matter how busy your life, you always have time to smile at that little girl who won't be a little girl much longer.

Help her learn to pay attention to what her body needs.

The end goal is for your daughter to take care of herself in healthy, happy ways. Developmentally, she won't be able to do that completely for some years, but you can gradually move her toward that not only by the care and feeding you give her, but by the questions you ask her before *you* tell her what she needs. The better she gets at answering, the less you'll have to tell her.

- *If she's cranky, try one or more (but not all!) of these:* What do you think is going on? How long has it been since you've eaten something? Did you sleep okay last night? Do you need some alone time?
- *If she's tired in the middle of the day:* What's up with the dragging around, hon? Do you feel okay? How did you sleep last night? Do you think you might be doing too much?
- *If her appetite drops off at mealtime:* I wonder what snacks you had earlier—do you remember? Why do you think you're not hungry right now?

As long as you don't shoot down her answers—"Why would you think *that?*"—or go after her for her unwise choices—"Well, see, no wonder you can't eat! What were you thinking, having that right before dinner?"—she's going to feel increasingly confident about assessing her physical needs and taking care of them. "How's that donut going to make you feel a half hour from now?" may pave the way for a lifetime of healthy choices.

Bridging the Gap

Dear loving and caring God, who feeds us everything we need, thank you for my healthy, growing daughter, _____. I so want her always to be full of life, so please bridge the gap between the care I can give her and what she needs to know to someday take care of herself. And who knows, God, maybe even me. Amen.

PART 4

Why Can't They Just Get Along?

What It Looks Like

She comes home crying again. It seems that the girl drama has reached global proportions. From what you can distinguish amid the tears and the unintelligible monologue and the stuff running out of her nose, it went down like this today:

Her used-to-be-Best-Friend-until-last-Monday, who has been ignoring her for a week, has now formed an alliance with Popular Girl—the very one they both used to make fun of because Popular Girl thought she was all that. You know about Popular Girl. You've been hearing about her all year. How she got an iPhone—"An *iPhone*, Mom! Do you know how much those things *cost*?" You've told her you do. How she acted all flirty and mature (you're not sure how those two things coexist but you don't question her logic) when the D.A.R.E. officer was there and made him think she was all wonderful when she's SO not (a fact which apparently everyone knows except P.G. herself. And her P.G. friends. And, of course, the D.A.R.E. officer). How she rolls her eyes and curls her lip—"She has lip gloss on, like, all the time, Mom, in *fifth* grade!"—whenever Daughter tries to be nice and tell her she likes her outfit or something—"It's like how *dare* I even look at her? What*ever*." She has been the course of much hilarious disgust for Daughter and her BFF, which has reassured you that she isn't interested in being like P.G. so she can be included in the inner circle. This is a good thing.

But now, ex-BFF and Popular Girl are whispering together everywhere, all the time, and when they see Daughter looking at them they laugh and turn away and act like she has H1N1 and they can't be around her. And when she finally did get ex-BFF alone today, she was told they weren't friends anymore, and that BFF doesn't remember now why they were ever BFFs in the first place. Bottom line: Daughter is never going back to that school, so can she please be homeschooled so she doesn't have to see any of them ever again?

Her tween world has been shattered, and for that matter, so has yours. As flashbacks from your own tween-years girlfriend crises rush into your mind, you can feel her pain. You have to do something to fix this, don't you? But what? Tell her this is just normal girl stuff and she'll get over it—like you ... didn't? March to the school and demand instant peer mediation? Call ex-Best-Friend's mother and become *her* ex-Best Friend?

As you fold your arms around her heartbroken little self and lamely offer her a cookie, you decide that dealing with puberty was a cakewalk compared to this.

———

Been there? Then you know how painful it is to watch your daughter agonize in varying degrees over her relationships with other girls. This can in fact be the most challenging part of parenting a tween girl because it's the part of her life that you have the least control over. That's scary when you realize how those relationships will affect her for the rest of her life.

Think about it. You may not remember the name of your fourth grade teacher or in which year you learned fractions or Roman numerals, but you can probably name your BFF from that year—if not your whole circle of BFFs—and, maybe even more clearly, the name and face of the girl who was mean to you. I can definitely see myself running out onto the playground to giggle at the fence with Beth Anne O'Toole—and crying in the corner at the sleepover at Ruthie's house because that Linda girl with the red hair called me a "pill." As for the Roman numerals, I still can't get past XXIV.

Even if you can't remember the names or recall the faces, the messages you internalized influenced your later relationships. After your BFF totally betrayed you in sixth grade, you were either reluctant to trust a girlfriend with a secret thereafter, or you were determined to pick more trustworthy friends. Once you were kicked out of the circle at age twelve, you either made it a point after that to always be the kicker rather than the kickee, or you avoided tight-knit groups, or you selected friends with no history of booting people out of their lives. For good or for ill, what happens in Tweenland doesn't stay in Tweenland when it comes to BFFs, RMGs, PGs—all the players involved in the confusing realm of girl politics.

I've placed this as the last section in our book because everything else we've talked about comes into play in this arena. And that's good news. Because of the other three major things going on at home—the move toward authenticity, the emergence into beauty, the acceptance of body changes—your tween daughter is better equipped to handle what goes on "out there," wherever she spends time with other girls her age. Without you there to watch over her and tell her what to do next. Matter of fact, she wouldn't have you there if you paid her. This is her turf, and well it should be.

Having said that, let me assure you that you are not completely out of this loop of friends, cliques, and really mean chicks. As always, you have a profound influence. So let's go in and find out just what that is.

9

The Gospel according to Friends

Jesus said, " 'Love the Lord your God with all your passion and prayer and intelligence.' This is the most important, the first on any list. But there is a second to set alongside it: 'Love others as well as you love yourself.' These two commands are pegs; everything in God's Law and the Prophets hangs from them."

Matthew 22:37–40

"There are two things that are important to me that my mom doesn't understand and I wish she would—and that's skinny jeans and friends."

age 12

Standing on an intermediate school playground during recess is an education in itself.

The tween boys bolt out of the building already yelling—about what, no one knows—and immediately become involved in some activity that involves throwing something, climbing on something, jumping from something, or concocting something. Punching each other for no apparent reason will also be part of that. If they stop moving and start talking, it's either to plan the next throwing-climbing-jumping-concocting-punching thing, or to agree on how to get the most squealing out of the girls with their throwing-climbing-jumping, etc. I love tween boys. They can be so wonderfully predictable. Seriously. If a disagreement arises, they solve it with a shove or a shout, and five minutes later (if it even takes that long) they're back to throwing-climbing-jumping as if nothing ever happened.

And then you have the tween girls.

A trifle more sedate than the boys at this age, they stroll out of the building, sometimes arm in arm, already chattering—about what, *everyone* knows because they do it nonstop, whether you want to hear it or not—and immediately busy themselves with getting into groups. One group settles against the fence. Another gathers around the playground equipment that nobody actually plays on anymore because that would not be cool. Still another hangs out by the water fountain, because the boys all end up needing a drink of water at some point after all that throwing-climbing-jumping-concocting-and-punching, and even though they're absurd little creeps, there's something fascinating about them. A few girls don't seem to have a group, but rather than band together and form their own, they wander wistfully at the fringes of the others, some quite obviously longing to be invited in, others pretending, just as obviously, that they don't care that they're alone.

Once the groups have been established, some activities might begin. That group gets up a game of jump rope or practices cheers. That one sits in a circle and does ... something that periodically makes them erupt into shrieks. And that group by the water fountain spends the period rolling eyes and flipping hair and hoping some boy will reveal something about the boy world that they can write notes to each other about for the rest of the day.

When the bell rings, they all return to class, boys and girls, to practice long division and use vocabulary words in a sentence. But one of the most important parts of their education has already taken place out there among the swings and the slides.

The boys are learning how to stand out, prove themselves, become independent, and still be okay in the group—because who are you going to throw-climb-jump-concoct-and-punch with if you don't have friends?

And the girls? The girls are learning to connect, give and take, care and be cared for—because how will you know who you are and how to behave if you don't have friends? Close friends. *Best* friends.

If you're raising a tween daughter, this is no surprise to you. What may be news is how difficult it can be to understand it even though you were a girl once. A look at the big tween friendship picture may help you remember why friendships are, in her mind, a matter of life or no life.

Getting Clear

As I see it there are four things you need to know about the tween friendship realm.

1. Why friends are so important to tween girls

The first reason, surprisingly, is hormonal. I'm not joking. Elium and Elium are once again my reliable sources:

> Although our daughters will develop their own unique expressions, estrogen and progesterone influence females to create, to be aware of the whole, to communicate, and to be in relationship.[1]

Your daughter may be an introvert, content with just a few friends she doesn't even want to be with 24/7, but let one of them move away and see what happens. The need to connect in a deep way is as natural to the tween years as puberty itself.

As your daughter has grown from babyhood, her circle of people to relate to has grown wider, and now it's also growing deeper. She is at the center of that circle, which doesn't mean she's *self*-centered or has to run the entire show (though some certainly do!). She simply feels safe when her "significant others" are around her. To become separate and autonomous is not where her natural psychological development is taking her.[2] By nature of her gender, her personality is defined and toned and brought into focus in her relationships, in how she connects with people, especially other girls her own age. The interactions she has with them now are more complex than they were when everybody played on the swings together and then went home. She's learning who she is, as we saw in section one, and she has to discover how that works when she's out in her world, where all the other girls are trying to do that too. This is her first step, her first circle, and if the response is positive, she's assured that the self she's discovering is okay. No wonder she clings to her circle of friends like it's a life preserver. It is.

She's doing more than just "hanging out" with her friends. She's learning some major life skills from them, and they from her. How to get along with people. What kind of people she wants to have in her life. How she responds to and handles conflict. How to trust and be trusted. To be honest. To show respect. To share and be supportive. She, of course, wouldn't put it that way. For her, you have BFFs so you can:

- giggle together until you can't breathe.
- have a whole conversation from opposite sides of the room without saying a word.
- finish each other's sentences.
- speak your own language.
- tell things you wouldn't share with anybody else.
- stand up for each other when the world is mean.
- be absolutely yourself when you're together.[3]

Just writing that makes me want to stop and call one of my own BFFs for a latte.

2. What's normal in a tween friend relationship

Everything on the above list is normal. Anything that brings happiness and a healthy connection is normal. Having that absolutely every minute of the friendship is not normal. These are people we're talking about—very young people—so issues and conflicts are bound to arise. The challenge for you as a mom is to know which disruptions are to be expected and which are a sign that something unhealthy is going on.

This is how I introduce that concept to tween girls themselves:

"Certain stuff happens in most groups of friends. Raise your hand if you've ever experienced these:

- A girl gets left out.

- You used to be friends with a girl, but it just sort of ended and it was okay.
- Sometimes you fight and break up and then start being friends again.
- Somebody's feelings get hurt even though nobody meant for it to happen (like maybe name-calling for fun went too far).
- You get irritated with each other.
- A girl doesn't fit in so she finds another group and that's okay.
- You know you have to break off a friendship for good (like if your old friend got into stuff that wasn't right)."[4]

There's never been a girl in a workshop room who hasn't raised her hand at least once. The admissions are made with knowing nods and even the significant exchange of glances with their BFFs, because, as is almost always the case, the normal funkiness of occasional jealousy and hurt feelings and minor annoyances is quickly repaired or fades with the moment. Sometimes friendships even end with a minimum of distress as girls develop new interests, wind up in different classes, or simply drift apart. If the circumstances require little more from you than a sympathetic ear and some microwave popcorn, they were the normal, to-be-expected stuff of tween friendships.

One of the biggest concerns I hear from mothers about all this is: "How do I know her little circle of friends isn't a clique? I remember how mean those little snotty groups could be when I was her age." Judging from the way the nostrils flare when they're asking me that, I'm convinced they do remember, and their concern is well-founded. To discern whether that's what's going on in your tween's girl group, take a look at the difference between a clique and a peer group.

A *peer group* is a gaggle of three to probably five girls who are together because they share common interests, beyond what everybody's wearing and how much their dads make, and who are open to new friends who find those same things delightful. There are no requirements for belonging except a willingness to be authentic and accept everybody else's uniqueness too. In the *Sophie's World* series of fiction books I wrote for tweens, those girls are called the Corn

Flakes; others may see them as corny and flakey, but they are all about keeping the power they have to be themselves.

A *clique* is a knot of three or four—seldom more at this age— who are together because the leader decided they would be. This is the same leader who also decides who gets in and who goes out. Those who are kicked out or who never get in are excluded from all activities of the clique. Those who want to get in must meet certain requirements, which are usually based on where they live, what they wear, and what they own. Those who are already in have to work hard to stay there, because membership status is subject to change at the whim of the leader. Individuality is not encouraged; a member bases her worth on her acceptance by the clique. While there are closed groups on the fringes of tween society, most cliques at this age are the Popular Girls. (It may expand to include boys in late middle school.) In *Sophie's World*, these are the Corn Pops, a group which shrinks out of existence over the course of twelve books under the positive influence of the Flakes—in the hope that readers can duplicate that in the nonfictional world. Lest we Christian moms

Mini-Women

"When I was in elementary school my best friend was in a different class than I was so I never saw her. Instead I was kind of part of a clique, which was really mean to one girl in particular. I would come home upset all the time about what was happening because I knew it was going on but I didn't stop it. It was extremely stressful.

My mom was the smart one. She told me to get out of the situation and that those girls were catty, but I couldn't comprehend not being one of the popular girls. When I finally got to middle school I think I under-stood. I wish I had listened to my mom back then. I would have saved myself a lot of trouble."

age 14

become too smug, cliques are common in Christian schools and large intermediate Sunday school programs. The potential for stirring up hate and discontent is high in any tween venue, a subject we'll talk about in chapter 10.

With that in mind, all it takes is listening (while pretending not to be listening) to the conversations your daughter has with her friends to determine whether her circle is a clique or a peer group. If you want to probe a little further, you can have her take the "That Is SO Me" quiz on pages 28–29 of *Girl Politics*.

However, just because the girls all talk alike or seem to be sharing a brain doesn't mean their group is an exclusive club. "Group think" is common among tweens and is not always unhealthy. All having the same taste in music, the same opinion of boys, the same slang vocabulary is part of the fun of belonging. But when a girl accepts that whatever the group considers acceptable is what she has to do to stay in, "group think" is a concern.

3. What the challenges are

Because tween girls are still socially immature in the grand scheme of things, though not necessarily for their age, they're bound to make a lot of mistakes, particularly since their relationships are so intense and carry so much significance. The time-honored female tradition of gossip, exclusion, and verbal manipulation shows no sign of dying out among tweens (and that's with their friends!). When it gets ugly, verbal aggression is still the weapon of choice among girls. That actually makes sense since in utero, the jawbone of the female fetus develops and begins to move before the jawbone of the male. I mean, how fun is that!

However, just because the nasty stuff commonly happens doesn't mean it's acceptable or should be allowed to go on as part of "girls just doing their girl thing." Girls doing this kind of thing become women who do this kind of thing:

- mean-spirited, behind-the-back gossip
- lies and rumors
- confidences betrayed

- control of one person over the friendship
- stifling of honest feelings
- jealousy
- harsh, hurtful teasing
- exclusion and shunning
- possessiveness
- constant drama

And we call *boys* absurd little creeps!

None of that happens because tween girls are evil in their souls. Slitted eyes and curled upper lips notwithstanding, they aren't inherently mean. There is always a reason why they sometimes treat their friends like bitter opponents, or allow themselves to be treated that way. Some possibilities include:

- They're struggling to maintain connection while still developing an individual self.[5] ("Will they still like me if they know who I am?")
- They don't understand give-and-take yet, so they either always give to others at the expense of their own needs, or equate being loved with always being given their way. ("If I don't give in she'll dump me." "If she's really my friend, she'll do what I want.")
- They're not sure exactly how to ask directly for what they want from the relationship so they manipulate. ("If I give her the silent treatment she'll stop talking to that other girl and ask me what's wrong.")
- They're afraid if they're too nice someone will take advantage, so they protect themselves. ("If I let her have her way this time she's gonna walk all over me next time.")
- They need constant reassurance that the BFF is still the BFF, and they don't know how to get that except to require proof. ("I'll tell her she can't be friends with me if she's friends with her. If she's really my friend, she'll pick me. Especially since I have a swimming pool at my house. And Wii. And DDR.")

It's hard enough when all of that goes on within a friendship. But at least there *is* a friendship. An even bigger heartbreak for a tween

Mini-Women

"My friend was being extremely selfish and mean and just dumping me and going off with her other friends. If my mom and me could have mother-daughter time just to talk about it, that would help."

age 11

girl—and her mom—is when the friendship breaks up, or there aren't any friends in the picture at all. She's just moved to a new school or a different class where she knows no one. Her old friends have made new ones. Or she just never has been able to connect well with people. The loneliness and the emptiness and the fear make it hard to go to school, where all the "friend slots" have been filled and she doesn't seem to fit in anywhere. Quite frankly, the thought of being there *now* stirs up the anxiety in my stomach.

4. When to be concerned

There are certain situations that should raise more than an eyebrow. They require your attention if not your involvement or intervention. We'll talk about what action you can take in the pages ahead. Take note if:

- She only hangs out with boys. Boys make great friends for tween girls, but if she isn't making any connections with girls her age too, it's worth looking into.
- All her friends are much older than she is, say by more than two years. An older girl or two in her life who she can look up to like a big sister will enrich her life, as long as you see them

Mini-Women

"My mom was a great help in encouraging me to write to my friends when we moved, and a great comforter when I didn't receive letters back. When I got the letters I had sent to them back in the mail, she helped me remember that, hey, maybe I can't communicate with them anymore, but I can still send long-distance love that doesn't need stamp, stationery, or envelope. I still love them and pray for them and hope we'll meet again someday. Without Mom, I'm not sure I would've done that."

age 12

as good role models. But if the only girls she spends time with are out of her age group, she'll have to act older to keep up, and she'll miss important steps in her development.

- She spends all her time alone. It isn't healthy for a boy to be a complete loner, but it borders on pathological for a girl to play that role. She may say it's by choice, but you probably shouldn't believe it. Something is keeping her from seeking out the company of her same-age peers, and that needs to be followed up on.

- She shows signs of depression: change in appetite and sleep habits, drop in grades, loss of interest in activities she generally enjoys, anger, or withdrawal. That sounds a little bit like the effects of puberty, but over two weeks, without any lift in mood or symptoms, it means something more than crazy hormones is going on. While there are other situational causes for childhood depression, troubled relationships are at the top of the list.

- She's being bullied. Deliberate attacks on her by her peers — verbally, physically, mentally — are a serious situation. So much so that I've devoted a full chapter to bullying of all kinds. If you know this is happening to your daughter, you might want to skip to chapter 10 right now — it's that important.

From the Ultimate Parent

In Girl Politics workshops, I often take tweens through 1 Corinthians 13:4 – 7. When we substitute "true friendship" for "love," the comprehension is visible in their body language.

"True friendship doesn't want what it doesn't have." *Gulp*.

"True friendship doesn't keep score of the sins of others." *Squirm*.

"True friendship doesn't revel when others grovel." *Blush*.

I'm quick to assure them that if 1 Corinthians 13 doesn't describe their friendships right now, they are not losers. It's the perfect time to say, "Okay, Mini-women, this is some of the hardest stuff you'll ever face, but it's going to be SO worth it when you get some skills down."

Help with those skills, I tell them, is right there in the gospel. Jesus talks constantly about relationships.

"You're blessed when you care," he says in the Beatitudes. "At the moment of being 'care-full,' you find yourselves cared for" (Matthew 5:7).

Later in that sermon, he instructs them: "If you enter your place of worship and, about to make an offering, you suddenly remember a grudge a friend has against you, abandon your offering, leave immediately, go to this friend and make things right" (Matthew 5:23–24).

I've always wondered if Jesus gave us the following snippet because he knew if we remembered nothing else we might take this away: "Ask yourself what you want people to do for you, then ... do it for *them*" (Matthew 7:12, emphasis mine).

Those being but a few of the passages Jesus offers, I think it's appropriate to say that the Bible is a guide to all the stuff that goes on with girls (any of us, actually). As the tweens and I dig in, I give them the summary of the law—quoted at the beginning of this chapter—as a foundation:

- Love God.
- Love your neighbor.
- Love yourself.

You're already following that, I assure them.

You may be going to church and Sunday school and reading the Bible and having your own quiet time, which means you're getting to know GOD better—even if the sermons are too long or your mom makes you wear something lame to the worship service.

Having friends is, like, the most important thing in life right now, and you spend a lot of time on the phone and giggling in corners and going to sleepovers, which means you're getting to know OTHER PEOPLE (AKA your neighbor) better.

You're finding out whether you would rather play soccer or take dance or paint your dad's toenails while he's asleep, which means you're getting to know YOURSELF better.

See? You know what this is all about, I explain—while they're settling back down after the "dad's toenails" comment. You don't have to memorize 1 Corinthians 13:4–7 like a checklist of friendship rules. "When you love others," we read in Romans (13:8–10), "you complete what the law has been after all along.... You can't go wrong when you love others."

So when you're about to make a friend decision, I tell them, just ask yourself this: *Does this show love for God, for the other person, AND for my true, honest self?*

That's what I tell them. If you tell them that too, perhaps they really can change the world the way they dream of doing.

Test Your Own Waters

You can hear it comin', can't cha? You know I'm going to suggest that you look at the way you model friendship skills for your daughter through your dealings with *your* BFFs. But, hey, remember that (a) this shouldn't come in the form of self-flagellation and (b) it always turns out you're doing a much better job than you've given yourself credit for. Realizing what you're doing *right* will insure that you'll do it even more.

Let's make it easier with some specific questions. Shall we start with your hubby?

- Can you and he differ in opinion without losing connection?
- Can you make a mistake without fear of losing his respect?
- Can you agree to disagree—no grudges or silence?

How about the aftermath of friendships that have caused you pain? (Do I need to mention that your tween hasn't missed that?)

- Do you suffer "well"?
- Do you harbor resentment?
- Find it hard to let things go?
- Bad-mouth people who've hurt you—forever and ever amen?

And with your current BFFs? You might want to do the self-assessment the girls take in the "Talking Trash or Talking Treasure?" workshop:

Have you ever said—

- "I don't mean to talk about her, but ..."

- "Let me just tell you what she said to *me!*"
- "And she goes no, and I'm all, *what?*" (or some facsimile thereof).
- "She's such a _____." (The name doesn't have to be obscene to be "trash.")
- "If I wasn't a Christian, what I would have said to her was _____."
- "I'm not entirely sure this is true, but I don't doubt it . . ."

None of us is a perfect friend. It's the *intention* to get close that makes for great relationships. Go in that direction, and your daughter will be right behind you.

Going for It

"I have had two really horrible happenings when friends were really really horrible. My mom helped meget through it. She comforted me and loved me and helped me act like Jesus."

That statement by one of my twelve-year-old blogging buddies pretty much sums it up. A mom's job is to provide emotional safety for her daughter in the midst of girl politics—not to make them go away. Eliminate her chances to sort through and work out and ponder over, and you make off with her learning opportunities. The learning, however, can be painful, and helping her benefit from the pain is where you come in.

Your role can be anything from helping her come up with detailed plans for approaching a problem to simply saying, "You look a little bummed. Wanna talk about it?" In fact, your first step is to ask your tween daughter how much she wants you involved. You might not even have to ask if you already know that she's been I-want-to-do-it-myself independent since she could crawl, or if she tends to be uncertain and hold back. Still, I'd give her a chance to say, "I could really use your help with this," or "I think I want to do this on my own." No matter what, at the very least you are her safety net, her sounding board, her provider of a shoulder and a hug and that infallible comforter, the cup of tea. (This is the perfect time for her to learn its benefits, with lots of milk and a teaspoon of honey.)

The chances are good that your tween will want you to do or say *something*, so I thought you could use a few Do's and Don'ts, to be implemented according to her—and your—style.

Do

- Know her friends and, whenever possible, their parents. You can be a lot more understanding if you know the people she's dealing with. Have you ever met a girl she's been complaining about and think to yourself, *Oh, I get it now?*
- Make your home a place where your daughter and her friends can be themselves, have an appropriate degree of privacy, and enjoy being girls, but set boundaries in terms of both space and time that work for you, the boss of the house. You don't have to have wall-to-wall pink sleeping bags every weekend—unless, of course, you're nutty that way—in order to know what's going on without prying, but you'll know very little if your house is never the gathering place.
- Listen to her woes all the way through before you respond. Use duct tape if necessary (on yourself, not her!). Sometimes just

Mini-Women

"I know it sounds weird, but my mom has helped me pick out my invitation list for birthday parties! She's really helped me know who to have over more often, and who might be offended if I don't spend as much time with her, and who has invited me to HER house recently, and who really wouldn't care, and who I shouldn't hang out with, and if I've hurt anyone and how to fix it ... the list goes on and on."

                                                                    age 11

her saying it out loud is enough for her to clear her head so she can figure out what to do herself. This is definitely the case if she's an extrovert. She probably wants somebody to hear her just as much as she wants advice, if not more.

- Empathize. A quick (emphasis on the "quick") story about your own experience with infuriating past friends can be validating, after she's told her story. Example: "I think I know what you're going through, because almost exactly that same thing happened to me when I was in fifth grade." Pause for an invitation to tell it. If you get one, hit the highlights. Otherwise, skip that part. (Needless to say, you won't want to regale her with details of your popularity in middle school at this point.)
- Encourage her to be honest with her friends, expressing her feelings in a positive way without fear. You can do that in a number of ways, from a simple, "Just say what you feel, babe. You have the perfect right to do that as long as you aren't ugly about it" to a role play so she can practice.
- Paint a picture for her (figuratively speaking) of what a good friendship should look like, so she can see what hers might need. You won't have to point out where hers "goes wrong." She'll see it once she has the big picture.
- Help her see that if this one falls apart, there will be other friendships waiting in the wings. That doesn't mean saying, "Are you kidding? You can have any friend you want. Forget her!" It does mean the two of you wrapped in afghans, drinking hot chocolate, and agreeing that lost love is a bummer.

Don't

- Minimize her pain. Yeah, you want her to feel better, but the only way out, as they say, is through. The healing is on the other side of the hurt. The comfort is in validation that this truly does stink.
- Tell her exactly what to do. In the first place, you might not even know. Some of that girl drama is so complicated Dr. Phil couldn't figure it out. And seriously, the solution needs to

---

Mini-Women

"I wish my mom would understand that I need to be with just my friends sometimes — you know, without her around. I love her, but — really — "

age 12

be hers. You can help her come to it, but she'll be much better equipped next time (and there will be a next time) if she knows she's capable of solving problems herself—albeit with guidance.

- Suggest cutting out as her first option. Some friendships really are a lost cause, but most deserve a solid try. Walking away at the first sign of trouble isn't a good pattern to form, for obvious reasons.

- Tell her she's a quitter if she does decide to give up a friendship after a good attempt at reconciliation. Everybody needs to learn how to know when to hold 'em, and when to fold 'em. That's a far more important skill than how to put a nice face on a relationship that's toxic. Whether the friendship makes it or not, you have the perfect opening here to talk about forgiveness—what it is (letting go of I-wish-you-were-dead feelings) and what it isn't (what you did is okay and I'm going to let you do it to me again).

- Intervene and try to solve the problem for her. No calling the other moms whose daughters are involved. No insisting that the teacher fix it. The only exception is if bullying is taking place that hasn't stopped via other means, which we'll talk about in chapter 10.

That's it in general. In terms of specific friend situations that commonly come up, it might help both of you to know the direction to suggest if she really wants your advice. In Girl Politics workshops, we call this "Friendship Flubs and How to Fix Them."

The rumor tumor

From "I heard, from somebody who really knows, that she . . ." to "she" sobbing in the restroom (where all broken hearts end up) usually takes less time than a good manicure. But the repercussions can last an entire school year. To help her put a stop to her own part in this malignancy, take her through these steps:

1. Find out if it's true, by going straight to the source or using common sense.

Mini Women

"My mom always said that, like, not all girls really know how to be friends, but you should be the best friend you can be to them."

age 11

2. If the answer is no, simply stop it right here. Refuse to pass it on. Change the subject.

3. If the rumor is true, ask yourself if it will help the person it's about to tell someone else.

4. If the answer is no, stop it right there.

5. If the answer is yes, go to the person who can help, usually an adult, and never the entire sixth-grade class.

A visual diagram of the above is found on page 45 of *Girl Politics*. Some other words of wisdom from you could include:

- If people gossip TO you, they'll probably gossip ABOUT you.
- A person who gossips CAN'T keep a secret.
- Don't be the person who can't be trusted.

Notice that none of those tells her directly what to do. She can—and will—get that, and she'll build confidence in her integrity at the same time.

The boots and the doormat

One friend always gets her way (in our house we called that B.O.S.S.Y., although why we spelled it out, I'm not sure . . .), while the other consistently gives in. If your daughter is the doormat, saying, "You have to stop letting her walk all over you" isn't going to help. If she could do that, she would have by now. It's time to teach her about being *assertive*—saying what she needs, wants, or thinks in a firm, polite way, so she and the boots can make decisions together.

The clique trick

If your daughter is feeling left out of THE clique described earlier, invite her to really look at the group she thinks she wants to be in and see if it fits that big picture of a good friendship that you painted together. It probably won't, in which case you can ask how you can help her find girls she can trust and enjoy.

If she's part of the popular group and you sense that it's unhealthily exclusive, introduce her to the word *inclusive*. Point out the good qualities in everybody who comes up in conversation, without saying, "Do you see what I'm trying to teach you here?"

This whole thing gets muddy when, truly, there are girls your daughter just doesn't want to hang out with, because nobody can be best friends with absolutely everyone. If you can show her that there is a kind way to *set boundaries*, that will help her avoid the temptation to be snitty. She can be coached to say, "This seat's taken right now, but I'll see you in class later. We could talk then?" rather than, "You can't sit here—this is, like, private." A girl may wail that her crowd will dump her if she associates with someone she considers to be a loser. If you can hardly keep from blurting out, "Then they aren't nice girls and you shouldn't be hanging out with them," try, "It sounds like they're taking away your power to make up your own mind. Do you really want to let them do that?" In any case, it's never okay to be hateful to other people. If you witness her doing that, call her on that behavior at your very next alone moment with her. She has lowered herself; please don't let her continue to do that.

The mind-reading game

Need I say more than, "If you don't know, I'm certainly not going to tell you"? Most of the time when a girl expects her friend to know what she wants or feels, she's just afraid to ask. The answer might be no and she'll feel rejected. Since that's an expectation no one should have, this is the teachable moment for *honesty* and *trust*. "What's stopping you from telling her how you feel?" you may ask. "If she won't tell you what's wrong, could you promise her you won't freak out if she tells you? Can you do that?"

The drama queen

Although there's a degree of the dramatic in just about every tween girl, some friends are more Academy Award-worthy than others. If your daughter is tired of a BFF who makes a production out of every little thing, advise her to wait until her BFF isn't in the middle of a tragic performance and ask her to simply talk to her the next time she feels a soap-operatic moment coming on. Not participating in the drama or even being an audience for it works too—along with "I like it a lot better when we're not always running to the restroom in crisis." If your daughter is the drama queen, some help with *choos-*

ing battles, more appropriate ways to get needed attention, and dealing with boredom (one of the chief causes of keeping things stirred up) is in order.

The green-eyed monster

Nothing wreaks havoc on a relationship like jealousy, and yet as insecure as fragile tween girls can be, it's no wonder it rears its ugly head so often. If your daughter is the jealous type, help her admit it and shine some light on the damage it's doing. Usually, jealousy comes out of "not feeling as good as ...," so remind her of her great individual qualities and stunning talents. Demonstrate how to turn "I wish that happened to me" into a *compliment*, a congratulations, if not even a celebration. "I really wanted that, but if I couldn't have it, I'm glad you got it because you're totally the best."

If it's attention being paid to other girls that's the problem, coach her in being honest and in *asking for what she needs*. "I get kinda nervous when I see you hanging out with other kids because I'm afraid you'll like them better and it won't be the same with us. Is that lame?" Should the BFF be the green-eyed one, helping your daughter see where she might be coming from will lead her to the obvious: "I really like that new girl, but that doesn't mean you and I are not still Best Friends FOREVER!"

Cloning

We talked before about how natural it is for tween girls to want to look, talk, walk, laugh, and snort just like their friends—all part of the necessity of belonging. When that goes too far—a phone call every morning to find out what "they" are wearing—it can be incredibly annoying for the copied one, leading to snapping or an outright "You are just a *copycat*!" in the middle of science class. Cloners can be urged to compliment verbally rather than dress identically and to find their uniqueness. Clone-ees can point out how much they *love the differences* between them. If that doesn't stop the identity theft, she can try a kind, honest "When you always copy me, I get annoyed. I love you, but yikes! We need a different plan."

Mini-Women

"When my friends were trying to make me choose between them, my mom gave me suggestions on how to handle the situations when they happened and sympathized with me when I went through a downtime afterwards. Mostly she helped me understand why we all did what we did."

age 11

Worthless words

This one covers a lot of territory:

- unkept promises
- betrayed secrets
- 24/7 complaining
- exaggerations of the truth (to make a better story)
- saying more than needs to be said
- just plain lying

It's hard sometimes to figure out who's the guilty party here since it takes two to pull most of them off. I love to see girls make a written pledge to each other to be careful with their words, listing specific things from the list that they particularly need to work on. They also like having a physical mouth-stopper, like slapping their hand over their own lips when they feel tempted to spill a secret or make a critical remark (even though saying it is guaranteed to get a laugh). If your daughter really is on the innocent end of a relationship in which a friend consistently lies or breaks promises, ask her if that's a friend she needs to keep.

Dealing with rejection

Somewhere in the mix of fun and growth and pure satisfaction, there is bound to be some rejection in your tween daughter's relationship experiences. That can be anything from not getting invited to that one birthday party, to constantly being left out of everything. Your importance as Mom is never more important than at those times. Again, you can't take away the pain. Nor can you turn it immediately into "Okay, you've learned something. Now you can move on." In between is that thing almost no one but you can provide: unconditional love and absolute acceptance. No small thing, since that is exactly what she's lost, at least temporarily, out there in Tweenland. What does that love look like?

If she's lost a friend or a group, whether by their choice or hers, let her grieve for a while. Depending on the girl, that can be a few hours or a week. If mourning goes on for longer than two weeks, she needs more help from you in getting things into perspective. Once she's

Mini-Women

"I know probably all moms say this, but it really stuck with me when mine taught me: If you don't have something nice to say, say nothing at all. Whenever I find myself in a bad situation, it just seems to help."

age 12

past the I'll-never-have-friends-again point, you can talk about what might have gone wrong, focusing on improving the flubs she might have committed rather than on how heinous those little wenches are. Pray together, so she knows that God is there for her in this traumatic-to-her time. Don't let her give up or avoid things because her former friend is there. Help her take back the power to be herself. Tell her she's brave and worth being friends with. She might roll her eyes, but she's hearing you, and eventually she'll believe you. If you don't see her making new friends within a few weeks, go on to the next paragraph.

If she doesn't seem to be able to make friends, keep it positive, avoiding both what she's doing "wrong" (or she would have friends) and what everybody else is doing "wrong" (or they wouldn't be missing how utterly cool she is, which you as her mother can plainly see). Ask her what she wants in a friend. Have her make a list of people she'd actually like to have friendships with (as opposed to just being "in"). Ponder together how she could start a conversation with one of them, in a way that's real (see page 76, *Girl Politics*, for specific suggestions).

If you get "I already tried that! They all hate me!" ask her exactly what kind of reaction she gets when she tries to talk to someone. That may give you information on what's really going on—she's a little pushy, she gets nervous and clams up, she's picked out the biggest RMG in the class to start with. Just don't say, "Well, there's your trouble!" Most of those things are the result of anxiety. When she gets more comfortable with herself—which you can help her do using section one—the fear will dissipate and she won't be obnoxious or timid. It's so hard for you to admit to those things in your child; think how much harder it would be for that to be brought to *her* attention.

If there really are no other girls in her realm of experience that she can be friends with, try widening the experience. Is she participating in outside activities she's really interested in? There will be other girls there who share the same passion, and common interest is a great starting place for tween relationships. Be careful that she doesn't isolate herself just to keep from being hurt some more. Above all, keep your own fear out of it. If she senses that you're stressing that oh-my-gosh-what-if-she-never-makes-a-friend, she'll take that on, making her even less likely to relax with her fellow tweens. If you are truly worried about her, talk to her teacher and other adults who observe her with her peers and see what insights you might gain.

The girl who's doing fine!

You might have skimmed down the page to this point if your daughter seems perfectly well-adjusted socially and is, in fact, the leader in her circle of friends or a part of the group everybody envies. It's hard not to be kind of proud of that, and you should be—if you know she's living out "love God/love your neighbor/love yourself." Just because she's popular doesn't mean she's clique-y. It just means that her temptations and issues are different from those of the tween who struggles to be accepted. She is the one those girls want to be accepted *by*—and *she* needs her mom's wisdom too.

So—check to see that your sought-after daughter's circle of friends is a peer group, not a clique. If you're surprised to find that she and her BFFs are exclusive and careless with people's feelings just because they can get away with it (because they're pretty, smart, well dressed, and strong willed), observe her more closely to determine, honestly, what's driving her. Under all that "leadership" is there some lurking insecurity? Is attention her real motive? Are things out of her control elsewhere and she needs to find it someplace in her life? (There's a divorce in the works? Another sibling in trouble and exhausting the family's emotional reserves?)

Or—and this one's a toughie for you—has she been given her own way so much, she only feels normal when she's the boss of everything? In some cases she's been told all her little life how wonderful she is, and she holds in contempt anyone who doesn't see it that way. Bottom line: Even if she knows intellectually and even deep in her heart that the way she treats her peers is wrong, to do otherwise now might cost her something that feels pretty good—and which keeps her from being the girl who's mistreated. You may be the only person who can convince her otherwise—because you're the one who's going to love her if she falls from grace in Tweenland.

Are you exhausted just thinking about all this? Unplug for a minute (or fifteen) and touch bases with yourself. Because when her friend-ships flub—and they will—you're the one she'll come running to. Be ready.

Bridging the Gap

Loving God, Creator of connections and the joy they bring, thank you for all that makes _____ loveable. In these often-troubling years as she's learning how to love all whom you have made, please bridge the gap between what I know about people loving people and what she needs to make a part of her very self. I ask this in the name of our only pure example, your Son our Savior. Amen.

10

When It Gets Ugly

I shudder at the mean voice.
  quail before the evil eye,
As they pile on the guilt,
  stockpile angry slander.

Psalm 55:3

*She is having such a difficult time with girls at school. I just
don't remember girls being that mean when I was her age.*

Mother of a tween

Evidently, the following are tween crimes that need to be
punished:

- being new
- not having enough self-confidence
- having too much self-confidence
- being something-other-than-white
- being white
- being something-other-than-Christian
- being too Christian
- having a physical challenge
- speaking your mind
- being smart
- being "dumb"

- having a hobby
- not having a cell phone
- using big words
- using the wrong words
- being shy
- being loud
- having red hair . . .

The list goes on. So does the punishment. If a tween girl commits any of the above—and who *doesn't* at some point during tweenhood?—she's subject to sentencing by somebody—or a group of somebodies—who considers those behaviors "not normal." Those somebodies are the RMGs. The Really Mean Girls. The Bullies.

The tween girl-bully has a precise job description: (1) set your sights on a girl who's sensitive, "different," unsure, independent, unique, or in any way doesn't fit what you have decided is acceptable; (2) take that girl down; take away her power to be herself, deliberately using whatever social, verbal, emotional, mental, or physical techniques you can get away with.

Ask any tween girl, and she can tell you what those techniques are—

- She does things just to make other people feel less than she is; she has to be on top at all times.
- She shows open dislike for people she thinks are beneath her.
- She tries to get other people to shun her target, leaving the bullied girl isolated and alone.
- She can act like she cares but only uses that to get what she wants.
- She usually has a group of "friends" working with her (or *for* her).
- She refuses to accept responsibility when she hurts people; you will never hear her say she's sorry, probably because she isn't.
- She does her dirty work when adults aren't around; teachers often think she's perfectly lovely.

And what does that dirty work look like?

- Threatening her target's other friendships, if not ripping them away completely.

- Spreading vicious rumors (not just gossip).
- Taunting (not just teasing).
- Using threatening looks and gestures.
- Intimidating her target via phone calls, texts, or the Internet.
- Threatening her with physical harm.
- Actually causing physical harm (hitting, biting, kicking, spitting).
- Damaging or destroying her target's belongings.
- Using offensive names or code names in her presence.
- Writing graffiti about her in common areas (the stalls in the girls' restroom being a favorite).
- "Rating" girls and putting her at the bottom.
- Building an alliance against her.

If you compare the list of "crimes" with the list of techniques and dirty work (the punishments), the results are more than a little disturbing, don't you think? A girl chews with her mouth open or comes from a mixed-race family or memorizes poems—so she has to put up with rumors and name-calling and threats against the very core of who she is? Most people would agree that is absolutely heinous. And those same people can tell you about the bullying they received, participated in, or witnessed back in the day. It's been a part of the youth scene since Cain clobbered Abel over the head, they say. They're right. Where they go wrong is when they insert the word *normal.* "Bullying's bad, but it's a 'normal' part of growing up."

Just because something happens consistently doesn't make it acceptable. Illegal drug use goes on all the time too, but it isn't "normal," "okay," or "just part of growing up." Peer abuse leaves emotional scars that significantly shape the way a young person thinks about relationships—and what is more important to a tween girl than her friendships with her peers? What, in fact, is her tweenhood about if not the building of skills for getting along with people and forming bonds? It doesn't take much to see how bullying behavior can distort a girl's view of people for the rest of her life. It's not just momentary pride that's hurt, but long-range trust. Security. Self-esteem. Beyond all of that, if it's happening to your own daughter, if she's involved in deliberate meanness in any way, it's impossible for you as her mother to see it as "normal."

If she hasn't been unfortunate enough to be at the pointy end of girl cruelty, the chances are good that she'll at least witness it before she enters high school. The *Journal of Pediatrics* published a study in which 25 percent of the children surveyed said bullying was a significant problem for them.[1] Many of them felt they had to avoid situations they might otherwise have participated in, such as sports, to avoid potential abuse. In that same study 45 percent of tween girls said they had been cyber bullied, which is the use of any electronic device to intimidate another person.

Things have also gotten physical. CDC (Centers for Disease Control) data shows that during a school year 8.5 percent of female students are involved in a physical fight on school property.[2] We aren't just talking about inner city or alternative schools for "at risk" kids. All of our kids are at risk for bullying.

These statistics are about real soccer-playing, school-attending tween girls whose worst problem should be little brothers reading their diaries. Not a week goes by that I don't receive an email from a precious child whose heart has been shattered by a pack of RMGs.

- She was the only girl in her class who wasn't invited to the sleepover—and the night of the party, all the girls sneaked out in their pjs and wrote LOSER on her driveway in chalk.
- She got fifty emails in one day, telling her she'd better watch her back.
- She tried to join in the game at her youth group, but everyone turned on her, throwing ice and food. Her mom is thinking about changing churches.

Every week. From mini-women who just want to go to school or church or dance class without being humiliated.

Bullying is rampant, but it doesn't have to happen, and it shouldn't. Do I even have to point out that the moms of tween daughters have a huge responsibility not only to help their girls deal with this travesty, but to enable them to stop it entirely? You can do this, and I think I can help.

Getting Clear: The Who, Why, and What of Bullying

You probably remember fights erupting among the little girls when your daughter was preschool age. "She took my toy. She took my cookie. She took my friend." You probably also remember how easy it was to restore peace and get everybody playing nice again. "Give her back her toy. There are plenty of cookies to go around. You can *all* be friends." If some Really Mean Mini-Girl didn't get that, a short time-out usually did the trick, or "we" just didn't set up play dates with her anymore. Sigh. Would that tween altercations could be remedied that easily.

Even if you tried that early childhood approach now (to the accompaniment of "Mo-om, you're em*bar*rassing me!"), it wouldn't work because (A) you're not there with your daughter every minute of every day anymore, so you may not even know bullying is occurring until she begs you not to make her go back to school ever again, and (B) it's important for her to be empowered to deal with peer abuse herself—up to a certain point, of course, which we'll talk about further on. You are, as always, the guide and the ally. Here's what you'll need to know going in.

The dangers to the bullied

Bullying is seldom a one-time attack. When a bully gets the response she wants—cringing, crying, crumpling—she feels in charge and in control. But tears dry and the resilient tween target regroups. If our bully is going to stay on top of things, she has to continue her bullying, creating a threat that doesn't go away and probably gets worse. She knows she can create a hamster wheel for her targets—

Each time this occurs, the target loses more of her power to simply be who she is. That makes her easier and easier to bully, until she feels hopeless. From first attack to that feeling that there is no hope of ever getting off the wheel, a number of things can happen, none of them good.

- She becomes convinced she's everything the bully says she is; her real personality is smothered as she comes to believe she's a loser.

- She turns the anger she feels toward her aggressor on herself, often giving her an "angry edge" so that she always looks like she's about to "flip out." That makes it hard for her to develop relationships even with non-bullies.[3]
- If the abuse is physical she may suffer injuries; if she's at the end of her rope with the verbal abuse, she may lose control and start the punching herself (for which we almost can't blame her).
- She becomes depressed; her grades drop off or she makes up excuses not to go to school; the joy goes out of activities she once enjoyed.
- In cases of ongoing abuse, she may come to believe she deserves to be hurt and turn to self-punishment in the form of cutting or anorexia; older tweens in seriously abusive situations have been known to contemplate suicide.
- She becomes physically ill with headaches or stomach problems that can become chronic.
- She may try to get back at the bullies and become one herself; her wonderful God-given personality is twisted into something it was never meant to be.
- She eventually thinks nobody can be trusted, especially if the bully is a former friend; for a long time she hesitates to believe in real friendship.
- Her self-esteem and confidence in social situations erodes to nothing; she carries that self-doubt into adulthood, long after the bully is out of the picture; there will, in fact, always be bullies, and she will be easily cowed by them; most tragic of all, her perpetrator may be her spouse.

The additional dangers of cyber bullying

Again, this is anything cruel or harmful that's sent through an email, website, blog, chat room, Facebook, text, or cell phone call. While it would seem that that sort of faceless intimidation would be less threatening than name-calling in the cafeteria, it can, in fact, be more so. If a girl gets a ton of emails telling her to watch herself at lunch tomorrow, she may not be able to tell who to be afraid of and avoid. Everybody becomes a potential stalker. If she receives a half dozen texts from various unknown numbers, calling her names they would never risk saying out loud, she doesn't know who it is that hates her. Going from class to class is like dead man walking. If somebody spreads a rumor about her on a blog comment, hundreds of people could read it. She doesn't know who to defend herself to. Who's seen it? Who believes this nasty thing about her? Every time she turns on her computer, she's terrified she'll see another hideous picture of herself somebody has doctored up, a picture which lies more convincingly than any RMG could do before a fascinated crowd in the girls' restroom.

All the things that are true about in-person bullying apply to cyber bullying, but in some ways abuse in cyberspace has even more power to hurt.

- It can be extremely difficult to find out who the RMG is, and most tween girls don't have the technological knowledge required to do so.
- The abuser may be someone she least suspects, since a girl doesn't have to be the leader of the mean clique — or any clique for that matter — to bully online or over the phone. The bully can hide behind her computer and say whatever she wants. If she herself has trouble feeling significant, this can become an addictive boost for her "self-esteem."
- The abuse happens in the victim's personal space, usually her own home and maybe even her bedroom. It can feel as if there is no getting away from it. If she has a cell phone, she might even wake up in the morning to an attacking text message.
- Being able to read and reread what someone has said can actually cut deeper — and more often — than just hearing it once.
- It can happen without adults even suspecting that anything is going on.
- Other girls are more willing to join in and gang up because no one knows who they are.[4]

Thus, the dangerous reactions listed above are even more likely for a girl who's experiencing abuse that has no face. Of course, not all of those things happen to every girl who's bullied. Some find the courage to walk away, to grow from the experience. They all might be able to if they had the right kind of help. The problem is that the damage is often done before they've had more than they can stand and reach out in desperation.

Why girls don't tell that they're suffering from peer abuse

The reasons for keeping this to themselves depend on a tween girl's personality, as well as the reason she's being attacked (not that "reason" has anything to do with it). These are the most common.

- At first she doesn't realize that what she's experiencing is bullying. She just thinks it's girl stuff she should be able to handle.
- Once she catches on, she's ashamed about being a target. As far as she can tell, only the ugly, stupid, uncool people get bullied, so if she admits she's being attacked, she has to admit she's one of the misfits. Better to suffer in silence. She's unaware that girls who are too independent, too smart, and too gifted can also bear the brunt.
- She's down on herself because she can't do anything to stop the bullying. She's convinced that if she wasn't such a wimp, she could get this girl to leave her alone. She thinks maybe she deserves it.
- She's afraid that if she tells anyone, especially a grown-up, the bully will do something even worse to get back at her. She may even have seen that happen to other girls, and she thinks that if she just puts up with it, it won't escalate. She is, of course, wrong.
- She doesn't think anybody can help. She knows other girls have seen the abuse going on and they haven't come to her aid. That must mean they either can't help her, or they just don't want to.
- She's sure no grown-ups will believe her because the RMG has made it a point to be the favorite of teachers, counselors, coaches, and maybe even our target's own mother.
- She doesn't want to be branded as the girl who will "rat you out."

Why bullying happens

I can almost hear you saying, "What possible reason could there *be* for this kind of behavior? These girls are just plain mean!" I'd be inclined to agree if psychologist Dr. Dale McElhinney hadn't explained to me that every kind of behavior has a reason behind it, a premise that makes sense if only to the person herself. "Even serial killers operate under a basic life premise," he says. "It's a false one, but it's the frame of reference for their choices every bit as much as our faith provides the basis for our more sane decisions."[5] I'm obviously not suggesting that tween-age bullies are destined to become sociopaths—at all. But they do have reasons for tearing their fellow tweens' hearts to pieces, reasons we need to know about, not to excuse their actions, but so that we can treat and heal bullying from every side.

So, what possible premises could there be?

Yelling and belittling are just what you do.

A girl is likely to treat people the way she herself has been treated. If she's constantly screamed at and put down at home, what else does she know how to do? It's either that or be a victim everywhere else like she is in her own house. A certain personality won't let that happen.

The only way to get attention is to grab it.

If a girl has a naturally extroverted, gotta-be-in-the-spotlight personality (not necessarily a bad thing in itself) and gets zero attention at home, she not only craves that attention, she's angry that she isn't getting it from the people who are supposed to give it to her. She's absolutely right. Where she goes wrong is in taking out both her buried rage and her hunger to be at the center of attention on a girl who has nothing to do with any of that—even a girl who might actually give our bully some positive attention if she weren't being hunted down and humiliated by her. The irony is heartbreaking.

If you don't get on top, you'll end up at the bottom, getting squashed.

Girls often buy into this when they've been bullied in a previous situation and have a chance to start fresh elsewhere. It seems like a good idea to her to rise to the top in her new place before anybody gets any ideas about doing that to her again.

You can't let anybody see your weakness.

It sounds strange to say that a "mean girl" would be frightened, but it is often the case that a bully-girl is so afraid her "weakness" (a learning disability, a bad family situation, her basic insecurity) is going to be found out, she has to constantly show how powerful she really is.

Everybody's out to get you.

At home she's absorbed the idea that people only want to take advantage of you and hurt you, so why not hurt them first before they have a chance to kick you in the teeth?

I run my house; why shouldn't I run my class?

It's shocking when I meet the parents of an RMG and find out that they are lovely, decent, caring people who would do absolutely anything for their daughter. There's the problem. If a girl has been allowed to dominate the household, talk to her family members however she wants to, expect her every whim to be catered to — how can she be expected to give a flip about anybody else's needs beyond her front door? If any wish is denied, she's used to making life miserable until people come to their senses and give her what she wants. It doesn't matter if it's her parents, her "friends," or the unwashed masses who are annoying to her — if they cross her there's going to be trouble. This is the kind of bully a mom has the most difficulty recognizing.

I've learned from the women on TV and movies that I have to be powerful.

Physical aggression hasn't been presented in media entertainment as antisocial behavior for a long time, and the number of female role models in there kicking and shooting has increased. As for MTV, there is a positive correlation between the amount of exposure to their videos and physical fights among children of both genders.[6]

Our toxic culture's glorification of "hot, tough girls" gives ours extra encouragement to torment and hurt if they already tend to bully.

I'm a Christian and you're not.

I've seen it happen. Girls can take the whole concept of being "unsaved" to uninformed, tween extremes. They look down on girls who don't know Christ, harshly excluding them from their circle of "saved" friends, telling them God doesn't love them because they haven't accepted Jesus Christ as their Lord and Savior, spreading rumors that they're atheists or, hey, maybe even Satan worshipers. They missed the part where Jesus threw a fit right in the temple because religious cliques were doing those very things. A church following an us-versus-them theology often fosters this attitude.

How to know if your daughter is involved in bullying.

Actually, it's safe to say that she *is* involved, or will be at some point. To use the terminology of Barbara Coloroso, author of an in-depth book on peer abuse among both boys and girls, she has a strong chance of being either the bullied, the bully, or the bystander.[7] Wherever she falls, she may not share her status with you. It's important, then, for you to know the signs so you can help. She's going to need you.

Signs that she may be bullied:

- When she talks about the other girls, she expresses confusion, betrayal, hurt, sadness, or anger. Not just sometimes. Often.
- She stops participating in activities she once enjoyed.
- Where previously she was a good student, her schoolwork suffers.
- She seems withdrawn and listless—more than just pubescently moody.
- She suddenly seems to have no friends at all and may not give a reason why.
- She experiences anxiety symptoms when she has to go to school or activities involving other girls. Hyperventilating, unexplained crying, and freezing up are common.

- She develops mysterious physical symptoms, such as stomach pain, chronic headaches, constant nausea, all of which are real.
- She's missing belongings, such as jewelry, that were once dear to her. She may not be able to tell you what happened to them.
- She drifts off into her own world, even in the midst of family gatherings or crowds, so much so that it's hard to get her attention. When you do, she may not know what's been going on around her.
- She has nightmares or has trouble getting to sleep.
- She becomes over-the-top emotional over small issues at home, lashing out in inappropriate anger or crying uncontrollably — and you know this is not just PMS.
- She mentions thoughts of death, or you notice cuts, scratches, or bruises that she can't or won't explain.
- She stops wanting to eat, bathe, brush her hair — all the things a tween girl usually prides herself on doing on her own.

Signs that she may BE a bully:

- She uses put-down language when she talks about other girls — words like *loser, lame, stupid,* and *butt-ugly*.
- She isn't light-hearted with her friends — giggling, hugging, chattering. Their interactions are fraught with arguing and sulking.
- She has trouble following rules, or manipulates her way out of following them.
- She's either teacher's special pet or is always in trouble for defying authority.
- You get the occasional call from a mother, saying your daughter is mean to hers. When you confront her, your daughter isn't upset that someone would say that about her. She's more likely to respond with, "That girl is such a crybaby. She can't even take a joke."
- She doesn't cope well with stress. She blows up over small issues, and is easily frustrated when things don't fall into place.
- She's overly moody, sometimes showing signs of depression.

Interesting, isn't it, how the victim and her target exhibit so many of the same behaviors? They're both acting out of pain, it would seem. How absolutely sad is that?

Signs that she is a bystander (witnessing bullying on a regular basis):

- She may tell you about some of the bullying she's seeing, though she'll seldom do it in full detail.
- If you suggest that you need to intervene, she may backpedal, say it isn't that bad, and ask you please not to say anything.
- She may be unusually protective of her own circle of friends who talk about a girl or group they consciously stay away from.
- She's possibly defensive about why she looks the other way. "I don't want to be the next victim." "Even if I tell, nobody will do anything. All the grown-ups think she's perfect." "It doesn't do any good to turn her in. Her dad has, like, all this money. She gets away with everything."

If you're realizing right now that your daughter is probably being bullied, may *be* a bully, or is standing by while bullying goes on, this is not one of your happier moments of motherhood. It's the dark side of childhood, and no mom wants her daughter to have any part of it. But please take heart. You can be of great help to her, more so than anyone else in her life. There may, in fact, be nobody else who will. It requires careful guidance from you, and you in turn need guidance, beginning, of course, with your Father.

From the Ultimate Parent

I've come to think of Psalm 55 as the Psalm of the Bullied. It's really uncanny how it applies to our mini-women.

Psalm-writer David has obviously been bullied:

I shudder at the mean voice,
quail before the evil eye,

As they pile on the guilt,
*   stockpile angry slander.*

v. 3

He shows all the signs a bullied girl suffers from:

My insides are turned inside out;
*   specters of death have me down.*
I shake with fear,
*   I shudder from head to foot.*

vv. 4–5

But the bully isn't an enemy from an alien land (or, in our case, random strangers at the mall), but a personal peer.

This isn't the neighborhood bully
*   mocking me—I could take that.*
This isn't a foreign devil spitting
*   invective—I could tune that out.*
It's you! We grew up together!
*   You! My best friend!*

vv. 12–13, emphasis mine

David the Bullied One goes to the only hope for help that he has:

I call to God;
*   God will help me.*
At dusk, dawn, and noon I sigh
*   deep sighs—he hears, he rescues.*
My life is well and whole, secure
*   in the middle of danger*
Even while thousands
*   are lined up against me.*
God hears it all, and from his judge's bench
*   puts them in their place.*

vv. 16–18

Being the oh-so-human person that he is, David doesn't hold out a whole lot of hope that even God can stop the bullying.

But, set in their ways, they won't change;
  they pay him no mind.

v. 19

There is much venting. This is painful stuff that won't go away easily. It turns into an understandable desire to get back at that person who's tearing his life apart.

Come down hard, Lord—slit their tongues ... (v. 9)

Haul my betrayers off alive to hell—let them
  experience the horror. Let them
  feel every desolate detail of a damned life.

v. 15

Yikes. But that's no more vengeful than a tween girl who cries, "I wish all *her* friends would turn on her. I wish they would tease *her* till she wanted to throw up. Then she'd know what it feels like to be me."

Somewhere in the midst of all this understandable wailing and gnashing of teeth, David must feel God moving in his situation, because after the pause we so often see in the Psalms—that blank break between verses—he gives us a sound piece of advice:

Pile your troubles on GOD's shoulders—
  he'll carry your load, he'll help you out.
He'll never let good people
  topple into ruin.

v. 22

How does he come to that conclusion? Tell your daughter to pray about her bully, and she'll echo David in no uncertain terms: "She won't even listen to *God*, Mom!"

But David's sure God will intervene:

But you, God, will throw the others
  into a muddy bog,
Cut the lifespan of assassins
  and traitors in half.

v. 22

Not being a literalist myself, I wouldn't assure my bullied daughter that God was going to toss the RMG into the nearest swamp with the water moccasins and kill her off before she's thirty (which wouldn't be soon enough anyway, in her mind). But I would remind her that there are both natural and grown-up-made consequences for continued meanness. A girl with a reputation for peer abuse may have a following, but she's seldom well-liked. If she's caught, her "disciples" usually cut and run, disavowing any knowledge of her dealings. Her need for power is an addiction and addicts are not happy people. They always need more, and sooner or later that's going to catch up with them. An adult is going to see it up close and personal. Most schools have a Zero Tolerance policy; one discovered threat and she's suspended—no warnings, no second chances. She may be good at pretending, but nobody's so good she can keep abusive behavior under wraps forever—not at eleven or twelve years old. Again, when she returns to the fold, there is none, because nobody wants to go down with her. She may then act as if she doesn't care that no one wants to be around her, but social isolation is tantamount to being thrown in a muddy bog. Her lifespan as a ringleader has been cut off.

Here's the thing the mother of a bully needs to know: your Really Mean Girl isn't mean to the core. She just acts mean. She too needs to "pile her troubles on God's shoulders" and let him carry her load and help her out of this mess. She's in danger of living a life that bears no resemblance to her true self. If she calls to him, though, he won't let her "topple into ruin."

As for the timid bystander whom no one can blame for hunkering down and protecting herself and her friends—she too "shudders at the mean voice, quails before the evil eye"—and what's worse, she knows her shuddering and quailing is keeping her from showing her integrity and sense of justice. The guilt being "piled on" her comes from within, where she knows what's right to do but she just can't bring herself to do it. God will "hear and rescue" her as well, if she'll just call out.

I see the whole psalm as an outline for the bully, the bullied, and the bystander:

- Admit to your situation and own your part in it.
- Pour that out to God, in detail (shuddering, quailing, and innards turned inside out).
- Believe God hears you.
- Believe there will be fair consequences.
- Then trust, trust, trust, because your how-to answers will come.

If you have ever had trouble following that spiritual outline in your own life situations, you'll get a tenth of a sense of how hard this will be for a twelve-year-old girl to do, much less one who's eight or nine. She'll need you to walk her through it. She'll need for you to pray with and for her. And she'll need for you to constantly remind her of the following, no matter what her bullying status:

All you need to remember is that God will never let you down; he'll never let you be pushed past your limit; he'll always be there to help you come through it. (1 Corinthians 10:13)

Test Your Own Waters

Abuse by peers is not the sole property of the young. Bullies who weren't stopped in their tweens and teens usually go on to abuse people in their adult lives. Their behavior can be harder to name at first, until we realize our power to be ourselves is ebbing away. Bosses can be bullies. So can overbearing friends, coworkers, family members. The most painful experience of bullying occurs in abusive marriages, where a spouse who has vowed before God to love, honor, and cherish does nothing of the kind.

I bring this up for two reasons.

One: detecting bullying in our work or personal relationships reveals to us, sharply, the feelings involved. The anxiety, the knot in the stomach, the urge to stand up and scream, "Doesn't anybody else *see* this?" Those are the same visceral reactions our daughters have when they're caught up in daily meanness. Multiplied by a hundred, that is—because they have even less control over what's happening in their circumstances than you do in yours. Knowing that your child is suffering even a fraction of what you yourself have experienced in adulthood is enough to make you go in there swinging (which I don't advise that you do ... more on that shortly).

Two: I know I sound like a CD on repeat, but your daughter is aware of the way you handle your own difficult situations. If you come home from work venting about your tyrannical boss, she's listening. If you let your sister-in-law walk all over you, she's watching. If everybody in your household walks on eggshells around *you*, fearful of one of your blowups, she feels that. You can tell her how to stand up for herself or another kid with words even David would envy, but if you're not doing it yourself, your voice sounds to her like the parents on a Peanuts cartoon. *Wah-wah-wah-wah-wah-wah.* Do I even need to point out that your own bullying—even a little—is going to give her absolutely no motivation to stop her own?

So—an honest look at the peer abuse that could exist around you:

- Does a personal bullying situation immediately come to mind? A demanding supervisor? Domineering father-in-law? Rude bill collector using threats and intimidation when a simple past-due reminder would suffice?
- Or—is anything slowly dawning on you? How abrupt you are with the people who work under you? The feeling of power when you make decisions for people—and the anger when they don't appreciate it? The fact that you tiptoe around a friend because you're afraid she'll turn on you—and you've seen what she can do?
- Are you doing anything about it? Do you feel like you even can without dire consequences?
- Do you think going to God with it will change anything? Really—deep down—really?

No judgment. No guilt. Just a look at how hard this is. How important it is that all of us—the bullies, the bullied, and the bystanders—be healed. Let's move on to how.

Going for It

In this section you'll see this phrase used repeatedly: *take back the power to be yourself.* That's the goal, whether your daughter is being abused by her peers, or she's seeing it happen to other girls, or she's the one doing the abusing. She's not being truly herself in the situation—or it wouldn't be happening—and in fact she's lost sight of how to even be that. She's given up her God-given power, the only power any of us really has, and she doesn't know how to get it back.

It's easy to be puzzled by my use of the word *power* here, because it looks like the bully has all of it, and if her target takes that away, then she has it and she becomes the bully. Doesn't that just perpetuate the meanness by turning it into a power struggle?

It would if we equated *power* with *force.* The bully is using force to get her way. The bullied one doesn't want or need to do that in return. She needs the power, the innate ability, to walk away and return to herself. The bully has forced her to give up that power. She just wants it back. And the bully herself has given up her power to be who she truly is within. She doesn't even know it's in there, so taking it back is even harder for her. The girl who is watching all of this go on usually knows who she is, but she just can't be true to it. She too has lost power.

So as we talk about the ways girls can take back the power to be themselves, we're not talking about *might*, about who has control over whom. This is not, in fact, power *over* anything. It's a strong, gentle thing *within* that has the power to show itself without fear. I'm not giving you a plan to turn bullied girls and bystanders into bullies themselves, nor am I suggesting that bullies should become targets and get a dose of their own nasty medicine. I hope to help you equip your daughter to embrace her real mini-woman self, in a way that will not only remove her from bullying, but empower her to put an end to peer abuse in her community.

Helping your bullied daughter

Once you've determined that this is not just girl politics your daughter is embroiled in, that she's the victim of out-and-out abuse, you need to become involved in how she handles it. You can start by acknowledging that the problem is real and that you know she's suffering. Be clear that you're willing to listen and you want to help—but that you aren't going to march up to the school and make a scene. Do not say, "Just ignore them," "Don't take it so personally," or "You just need to stop letting people walk on you and stand up for yourself." If she could do any of that, she already would have. She may, in fact, have tried already, with bad results.

Of course, assess whether she's in physical danger from the bullies. If that's the case, all bets are off. She needs your immediate protection. Call the teacher, the coach, the principal—whomever—until somebody pays attention. Insist that the bully be kept away from your daughter, or anybody else she might hurt, for that matter. If it means a call to the school board, so be it. Do not assume that a twelve-year-old isn't going to carry out a threat to "kick your butt," "take you down," or "beat the snot out of you" (or variations thereof). Not convinced? Cruise YouTube. You can find over two thousand videos of girls pulling hair and knocking out teeth.

That's the extreme. If it hasn't come to that in your daughter's case, if it's her emotional and mental well-being that's being threatened rather than the physical, you can proceed to the next steps. The first is to learn all the details you can without doing a bare-bulb interrogation. Is the abuse happening at school? On the athletic field? Over the phone? Online? Don't eliminate the possibility that it could be going on at church.

Wherever it's taking place, talk to your daughter about how she can limit the bully's access. Explain to her that this is not a relationship she needs to "work out." This person is not a friend who has committed a "flub." Your daughter doesn't need to try to change her or figure out some way for them to become BFFs. The goal is to keep herself out of harm's way as much as possible. Don't sit near her at lunch. Don't try to join in her games at recess. This is not cowardly. This is a young woman avoiding someone who is toxic because she just doesn't want to be around her. This is one time you can tell your daughter to "fake it till she makes it." Work with her on not showing fear when she chooses to wait until the RMG is finished at the pencil sharpener before she goes up there. To practice, role-play if that works for you two. It's personal power she's showing: "I choose not to be anywhere close to you."

That's impossible to do in many instances, especially if they're in the same class or play for the same team. Your job is to help your daughter find ways to get her power back when she does have to be in close proximity to her tormentor. It is *not* a good idea to take her off the soccer team if she really loves the game or let her stay home from a birthday party because "she" is going to be there. Explain that she has the right to go where she wants to go and do what she wants to do, and if a bully is preventing that, you can help her take back that right.

Helping her see the difference between avoiding unnecessary contact with someone who treats her like a dog and asserting herself so she can do the things she really wants to do could take some time.

Mini-Women

"Fake It Till She Makes It"

"Once I was watching these two little boys for their mom and they tied me up while we were playing. I was stuck and it scared me half to death, but I acted like it was all part of the game. That wasn't any fun for them since I didn't freak out, so they untied me."

age 12

"I was walking home from school and these boys were following me and calling me names like Wide Load and Blubber. I really wanted to cry and scream at them to leave me alone, but I knew if I did that they would never stop. So I pretended like it didn't bother me and held my head up and kept walking. Then when I got inside my house I cried for, like, an hour."

age 10

You can try listing all the situations where she's faced with Mean Girl and together put them into their proper columns—*I Can Avoid Her and Be Happy* or *I Can't Avoid Her and Still Be Happy*. Don't do it for her. Just walk her through it. This is her first step in taking back her power.

Next explain that the bully is trying to scare her into thinking that she's nothing, nobody—but there isn't anything that bully can do to take away who she is. "She obviously doesn't even *know* who you are," you can tell her, "or she wouldn't even try this with you." Her power to be herself, then, is still safe. So—there is no reason to run away crying when the bully does her thing. Tell it to her straight: Yes, it hurts, but don't *show* the bully that it hurts. Running away in tears gives her a reason to pick on you some more. Straighten your shoulders and pretend it doesn't matter until you can get to a safe place, away from her. The worst thing you can do is tell or show her that she's getting to you. That's what she wants to do! Give her what she wants and she'll keep on. Take it away, and she's got nothin'.

When walking away is not an option—and it often isn't in her world—give your daughter responses she can use that don't turn her into someone she isn't. Our temptation as moms is to say, "Give back as good as she gives. If she insults you, insult her back." You might as well quote, "An eye for an eye and a tooth for a tooth." *Shutting* the bully up is the goal, not *riling* her up. These responses have been known to work quite nicely:

- **"Did you really just say that to me? Wow. I think you're better than that."** What's the bully going to say, "No, I am NOT better than that!"
- **"Is that supposed to bother me? Because it doesn't. I'm really fine without you liking me."** Any response a bully gives to that will be ludicrous and she knows it—or she'll find out. "No, you're not—you need me to like you," comes to mind. She wants this girl to like her so she treats her like trash? Huh.
- **"I'm really kind of bored with this."** Period. I can't even think of an answer even the meanest of bullies could give—because it isn't a question.

Speaking of questions, coach your daughter in not asking any she really wants answers to. That includes, "Why are you doing this to me?" "Why can't you just leave me alone?" and "How much longer are you going to do this?" That only fans the flames. The point is not to engage in conversation with the bully any more than she has to. Completely ignoring a bully doesn't usually work; she'll keep it up until she gets a reaction. Trying to work it out with her is worse. Avoiding her isn't always possible. But your daughter can always keep a confrontation short and, for the bully, pointless by refusing to discuss or try to work things out or take the bait for more taunting and ridicule. "I'm really over this" and walking (not running) away at the next possible opportunity are her best shot at getting back her power.

If your daughter has a hard time looking someone in the eye and saying what she needs under normal circumstances, the above is going to be incredibly hard for her. Rehearse at home. Then encourage her to gather supporters when she knows there's going to be an issue. If the bully and her pals won't let her go to her locker before school, she can ask a group of girls—they don't even have to be friends of hers if she's BFF-less at the moment—to go with her. If they surround her as she approaches her locker and stand there, ignoring the bullies, while she gets her books, and then accompany her on down the hall, you can bet that gang of meanies isn't going to start a rumble. If the bully works solo, there is no way. Remind your daughter that a bully is, deep down in there, afraid of something. A coward isn't going to fight a battle she knows she can't win. But caution your daughter: Don't turn the group who helps you into a bully gang of its own, sworn to get back at those Mean Girls once and for all. This is about being yourselves and refusing to give power to people who want to take that away.

Once your daughter gets the idea that she has personal power, she may get feisty and want to fight back. Remind her that she *is* better than that. She doesn't have to show that bully who's boss, because neither one of them is boss. It can be hard for her to discern the difference between power *over* and power *to*. The examples of DO SAY and DON'T SAY on pages 104 and 105 of *Girl Politics* can be extremely helpful, and are ready-made for rehearsing. Doing it is the best way to learn to do it right.

Explain to her that in the midst of all this she probably isn't going to change the bully, and, noble as that is, helping the bully isn't her mission right now. Her job is to let God heal her heart so she doesn't lose herself, and to be a strong example for her peers for how to live a Jesus life. What she does will make a huge difference in her in the best way possible—from the inside out. That way, no bully princess or anyone else who pressures her can determine what she does and says and how she lives.

What if what a bully says about your daughter has a little bit of truth in it? That may be the unkindest cut of all. Maybe she *is* lacking in some social skills. Perhaps she *does* have some habits that drive people nuts. She may even say to you, "They say I'm fat—but I already *know* I'm fat!" How is she going to take back the power to be herself when she doesn't even *like* herself—or at least who she thinks she is?

First, remind her that it's the *way* the bullies say it that makes it mean and wrong. Okay, so she has some things she might want to work on, but it's not okay for people to point them out in cruel ways. You're walking a maternal tightrope when you suggest that she *could* be cleaner and neater when she goes to school, or she *might* actually stop trying so hard to be funny. Let her think that *you* think her abusers are right and you'll both crash to the ground. Step carefully and you can show her that if she improves in those areas she'll be happier and more genuine—but don't allow her to think she needs to do that to avoid bullying. She's not the one committing the crime.

If nothing seems to work, and sometimes it doesn't, support your daughter in going to the adults who can alter the situation. She's probably going to balk. "My teacher won't listen—she tells us not to tattle!" "The other kids will think I'm a tattletale and then I won't have *any* friends!" Her arguments are valid, unless you show her the difference between *telling* and *tattling*. *Tattling* is done to get somebody else in trouble. *Telling* is done to get somebody *out* of trouble, including yourself. Work out with her who she should tell—coach, teacher, school counselor. Rehearse with her what she'll say—sticking to the facts and explaining the effect this is having on her. Plan what she'll do if she gets, "Oh, you girls and your drama. Can't you just get along?" Assure her that if no one listens and takes action, you will be there to back her up. Promise her that you will only intervene completely if —

- She's in physical danger.
- Her school experience is being affected.
- She's physically ill because of the way she's being treated.
- She feels so sad and hopeless she doesn't want to go to school or activities.

Assure her that the bully isn't going to make things worse for her if she tells and something is done. This isn't the mafia. There are people who can stop her. There is no shame if your tween tried to stop her and couldn't. There is great good in making sure somebody does. As for other kids — nobody's going to be disappointed that the bully is knocked from her throne. She's likely to hear a collective sigh of relief from the entire sixth grade.

The final step is the hardest one for girls to take, the one Jesus said, in no uncertain terms, we have to take.

> "I'm telling you to love your enemies. Let them bring out the best in you, not the worst. When someone gives you a hard time, respond with the energies of prayer, for then you are working out of your true selves, your God-created selves." (Matthew 5:44–45)

That is a recipe for an eye roll if I ever saw one. "Mo-om! She does all this dirty, rotten stuff to me and I'm supposed to love her? Could Jesus make this a little harder maybe?" Rush — and I do mean rush — to tell her that doesn't mean she has to hang out with the bully and try to be her friend while allowing her to continue to stomp all over her. Then you can walk her through what Jesus does mean:

Pray for her. Not, "Father, please let a bushel of basketballs fall on her head." And not, "God, thank you that I'm better than she is." Just, "God, please heal whatever's making her such an RMG."

Have compassion for her. Being mean never gives a person joy, so a bully is actually pretty miserable. Your daughter can be soft toward her in her heart, even though she can't trust her with her feelings.

Avoid telling everyone what a mean little brat she's being. She may be doing that to you, you can say, but as a Christian, you don't get to do that to her.

Forgive her. Not, "It's okay that you've made school a torture chamber for me." It's just a matter of not holding hate in her own heart and letting go of thoughts of making that RMG suffer. (While you're at it, you might do a little forgiving of her yourself, Mom. You know you need to . . .)

Helping when cyber bullying is involved

The most disappointing part of cyber bullying is that the Internet was designed to give everyone a chance to be heard, but it's so often used to criticize and humiliate, which shuts people down. As parents we can say, "All right—no electronic devices, just to be on the safe side," but that cuts our girls off from getting information they need or communicating in a fun way with their friends or doing positive works that reach more than their small circle of BFFs. It is so unfair for them to have to give up a valuable tool because someone else is abusing it—and them. The following are suggestions for how to both prevent cyber bullying and how to deal with it if it erupts.

The Internet is part of your household. You still get to decide who does what there. Have a designated computer area in the "command central," high-traffic part of your home. Family rooms and kitchens are the usual sites. Even if your tween has her own laptop, only allow her to use it in that central area. Her bedroom is not a good place for her computer, no matter how much she may wail.

Limit her time on the Internet and on her cell phone if she has one. Text messaging can easily get out of control—especially if you have "unlimited texting" on your plan. (The dad of a tween recently told me his daughter sent nine thousand text messages in one month. That's three hundred a *day*.) She can have input on those time limits, but hold firm (and while you're at it, would you teach her some cell phone etiquette)?

You may not be the most popular mom on the block for this, but provide an Internet filter (being aware that the older they get the more savvy they are about getting around the road blocks). Occasionally check her online history or skim through her emails. You don't have to be constantly POS (Parent Over Shoulder), and do assure her that you're not trying to invade her privacy. You just want to protect her. Just so *you* know, the number one risk factor for kids getting into trouble online is parental naïveté.[8] So stay educated and pay attention. Your daughter will be grateful for the safety, as long as she knows you aren't simply poking around in her business. Ah, it's another one of those tightropes.

Speaking of safety, go through the common-sense rules for kid safety on the Internet if you haven't already:

- Never give out personal information in chat rooms or on blogs.
- Don't share passwords, even with your BFFs.
- Don't give people you don't know or trust your cell phone number, instant messaging name, or email address, because they can use those things, pretending to be you.
- Use a screen name that doesn't give out anything about your age, gender, or location.
- Learn about your email program so you can create files and email filters, and route folders. This can help shield you from hateful emails.

If your daughter is the victim of cyber bullying, tell her not to reply to any kind of communication that's abusive or obscene. The first time it happens, ignore it and hang up or log off. If it happens again, even once, contact the service provider (Yahoo, Hotmail, Verizon, AT&T, etc.) and ask for a number to call to report abusive messaging. You (Mom) call it. You can even forward nasty emails to your service provider. If the abuse continues, save all the evidence — print out emails, save text messages, don't delete voicemail. You'll need it to take action.

Try to find out who's doing the bullying. In Outlook or Outlook Express, for example, you can right-click over an email to reveal details about where and from whom the email came. That puts you in a position to contact a parent or the service provider. If a bullying message was sent from a school computer, contact the school administration immediately. Keep reminding your tween that this is telling, not tattling. If cyber bullying is happening on a website, find out who hosts the site and report it. If physical threats are made online or by phone, call the police. I'm serious. Cyber bullying is against the law. Don't put up with it.

Helping your daughter if she bullies

I may be fooling myself to believe that any mother thinks this section applies to her daughter. Maybe it doesn't. It definitely doesn't *just* because she's popular and leads her posse. Not all "Cool Girls" are mean and controlling. But if your daughter shows any of the signs of bully-ship we talked about earlier, you owe it to her to at least look at what might be going on and how you can lead her closer to her true self and further from the path she's currently on. If your daughter is the bullied one, this section may be helpful to you as well—part of Jesus' instruction to have compassion on those who hurt us. My suggestions, however, are addressed to the mom whose daughter is acting like an RMG.

The first order of business is to confront her behavior. Your approach doesn't have to be "You're mean and I don't know how you got that way but I'm not having it." I'm not sure that's going to work anyway. A more effective go at it might be "I know you're not an awful person, but you have to stop treating people this way. We need to find out a way for you to feel good about your life that doesn't involve hurting somebody else." Keep working at it until she admits that what she's been doing is wrong. The consequences for her actions will be worthless unless she takes responsibility for them. Yeah, so "Go to your room and don't come out until you can say you're sorry and mean it," is pretty much out of the question. And for now, don't bother asking her why she does what she does, because she doesn't know yet.

Make sure she accepts the fact that she has no right to insult, intimidate, threaten, or abuse another human being. Period. No matter what her "reasons" are and no matter how much sense they make to her, it is NOT okay to bully. If you know her propensity toward meanness comes from her home life, promise her that you're going to change that. If that means admitting to doing some bullying of your own, do it. You won't lose her respect. If you've bullied her, she probably doesn't have much respect for you anyway, and now you have a chance to earn some.

Once she sees that the way she's been treating her peers is unacceptable, give her credit for facing what she's doing and wanting to change. That's your first chance to convince her that she herself isn't *bad*. She has to know that or there is no change in sight. And it's your first opportunity to tell her that now she can turn the power she's been using in the wrong way (because she is obviously a person with great personal power) into something that can change the world for the better. Knowing she doesn't have to creep meekly around for the rest of her life will lessen the blow of being toppled from her throne.

Your very next step, before anything else, is to urge her to go to God and pour it all out. Tell her she can ask God to forgive her and God will. Encourage her to ask God to help her to push the RMG ideas out of her head so she can be filled with love and compassion— and some real joy. If she gives you a blank look or doesn't seem to know where to start, offer to pray with her. Explain that she'll need to do that every day, whenever the urge to taunt somebody rises up in her. Be sure she has the time and private space to do that. Offer a candle or some quiet music, anything to help her set the world aside and focus on just God and her.

Only when she believes God is in this with her can she really begin to change. Now you can start to help her figure out why she's mean to people. Go through the false premises we talked about earlier and see if any of them fit. She won't be able to sort them out herself, nor can she sit for hours while you lecture her about them. Carve out some short sessions where the two of you can explore together. Spend most of that time listening to her, even if she says things that horrify you. ("I see that girl just being fat and ugly and it grosses me out and I can't leave it alone.") If you've already established that she's been wrong, wrong, wrong, there's no need to beat that dead horse. Stay focused on "What's really going on here?"

If after a few talks you realize you're not getting to the bottom of her behavior, don't throw up your hands and say, "I tried but she's just too stubborn." Seek professional help for her, and for your entire family if they form some of the basis for her false premise. There is no shame in bringing in someone who knows the child mind and has experience in helping girls change. If your daughter were suffering from diabetes or leukemia, wouldn't you take her to a specialist?

When she's ready—truly contrite and on her way to discovering what makes her time bomb tick—you can suggest these steps for *her* to take. They aren't things she has to check off to stay in your good graces and avoid punishment. They should only be done if she herself sees how important they are.

First, she can go to the girls she has hurt and ask their forgiveness, without expecting that they'll hug her and say it's okay. Whatever their response, just doing it will soften her inside.

Second, she can tell her bully-mates she isn't going to be mean to other girls anymore. That may mean losing them as friends, but keep telling her that the nicer she becomes, the more real friends she's going to have. Explain that people like to be around someone with personal power, as long as she uses it the Jesus way.

Third, she can get rid of anything in her life that triggers mean behavior on her part. If she gets mad when she plays sports, maybe she should back off playing for a while until she gets her anger under control. If she's only mean when she's around certain people, it's time to avoid them. Help her to fill up the empty spaces that may leave with new things that bring out the best in her—volunteer work, for instance (but not as a punishment—please!).

Fourth, she can carry a small mirror in her pocket. Every time she gets a strong urge to make fun of somebody or threaten them with social disgrace, she can pull out the mirror and look at the expression on her face. It brings to mind another one of Jesus' instructions: "It's easy to see a smudge on your neighbor's face and be oblivious to the ugly sneer on your own" (Matthew 7:3).

Finally, if she was a "Christian bully" who made the lives of the "unsaved" so miserable they'll probably steer clear of Christianity forever, she can apologize and offer to talk to them about how great

God is or answer any questions they have. She can even invite them to church. Just keep reminding her that girls who don't believe yet aren't carrying a contagious disease called "Non-Christian."

Helping your daughter stop being a bystander

Happily, this situation has fewer deep-seated issues at the bottom of it. A girl who doesn't step in to stop bullying isn't operating from a false premise. She's just trying to protect herself. She may even have heard from you: "Don't get involved in other people's drama." Most tween girls have a strong sense of justice, though. All your daughter needs is the message that there are no "innocent" bystanders, and a little direction, and she'll take off on a crusade that is worthy of her growing integrity. She'll not only help stamp out bullying in her class, her grade, and her school, but she'll learn how to fight injustice wherever it shows its ugliness in her life. I wouldn't doubt that she'll become an inspiration to you.

Start by rallying your daughter and her friends to declare war on bullying—but not on the bullies themselves. They'll respond well to getting the best of evil by doing good, by taking the power out of bullying with actions that are true and noble and right and pure. Again, there is no one more responsive to that call than a tween girl.

Help them develop a code of behavior for themselves. Before they can take a stand they have to embody what they believe. Their code of honor should state (in their own words) that they:

- refuse to put labels on people.
- won't laugh at put-down jokes.
- will not repeat rumors or listen to gossip.
- will not allow anyone else to control how they treat people and will be careful whom they follow as a leader.
- will make it their mission never to let anyone feel completely left out.
- will get to know people who are bullied, so they're less likely to allow others to be mean to them.
- will always tell other people that they think bullying is wrong —in a loud voice if necessary.

When the girls feel empowered by their code and have put it into practice, you can help them plan their attack—on bullying itself, not on the bully. Their plan might include:

- Apologizing to anyone they haven't helped in the past and assuring her they won't allow the bullying she's suffering to continue; seeing that a target has a friend, a bully will often stop.

- Accompanying a target as a group so she can go where she wants to go without interference from anyone; there is no need for a verbal statement—just shielding a bullied girl with love can put a bully off.

- Standing up to a bully-in-action as a group, calmly and politely, with something like, "This is wrong and you're so much better than this. We just don't want bullying in our school."

- Helping bullied girls stand up for themselves by doing role playing to build their confidence and give them practice in being assertive (activities in *Girl Politics* work well here). If she knows someone has her back, she can reclaim her power.

- Informing appropriate adults just to make them aware of the stand they're taking. Most grown-ups are supportive of peaceful, student-centered resolution.

- And finally, getting adult help immediately if things get physical or a mob forms; keep remembering the difference between tattling and telling.

Once they've helped one person, they may be ready to go the extra mile to make sure bullying doesn't happen again. Encourage that girl group to take their campaign global (well, you know, schoolwide). Help them write a pledge and ask permission that it be posted for students to sign, making it public that they won't tolerate bullying in the place where they should be able to feel safe and valued. This is the example used in *Girl Politics*:

As part of my community I will
Pledge to be part of the solution.
Eliminate taunting from my own behavior.
Encourage others to do the same.

Be more sensitive to other people's feelings.
Set an example of a caring individual.
Not let my words or actions hurt other people.
Stand up for those who are being mistreated.

With your help, tween girls can form an alliance for a world that is secure and accepting, where they can learn and grow and become all they were made to be. Isn't that the world we want for our precious mini-women?

Dealing with the inner bully

Finally, I don't know about you, but sometimes the meanest bully we have to contend with is ourselves. That inner bully was especially active when I was the mother of a tween girl. "You aren't doing this right," I would say to myself. "It's your fault she doesn't make straight A's—how's she going to get anywhere in this world on A's and B's?" "Look at her bedroom—I'm surprised you haven't been reported to the health department." "You are the worst mother! You cannot go to bed until you have cleaned her room, checked her homework, packed tomorrow's lunch. I don't care how tired you are." If anyone else had said those things to me, I would have told them to bite me. But I had trouble smacking down the voices coming from my own head.

If you have trouble with the inner bully, imagine what your daughter deals with. "I talk too much—I don't ever know what to say—I'm too tall—too short—so boring—so different—so chubby—so scrawny. I should be like my sister—my best friend—Miley Cyrus. But I can't—so I must be a loser!"

Without the filter that comes with maturity, she's more likely than you are to believe all that stuff that passes for truth in her mind. Even if she escapes bullying on the playground or in cyberspace, she probably won't remain entirely out of reach of the Mean Girl that is herself.

So how do we stop bullying ourselves? Here's one suggestion which you can also teach your daughter to do—or do it together.

In a quiet time and space, think of one way that you're mean to yourself. Do you keep on cranking out those bake sale cookies and

Mini-Women

"I'm trying to remind myself that I am a miracle, but when I look at myself, I ask, 'Where is the miracle in that?'"

Age 12

chauffeuring those children when you are about to drop from exhaustion? Do you look at yourself in the mirror and think thoughts you'd never say to your best friend (or your daughter), thoughts like, "You are so disgustingly fat it's a wonder anybody even wants to be around you." Do you belittle yourself even to the people who love you: "I am horrible at parenting." "I'm just too stupid at math to help him with his homework." "Why did I ever think I could be a PTO officer—I'm going to be horrible at this."

Now do one small thing to stop treating yourself the way an RMG treats her target. Write out a pledge to stop saying certain things to yourself. Set a limit on how much you can do in a day and prepare to let your family know what that limit is. Plan how you'll stop putting yourself down in front of your friends, maybe by asking them to call you on it when you start in about your weight or your lack of organization or your failure to be the perfect parent.

Save time to pray. I can't imagine that God wants us to take away our own power to be who he made us to be. I *can* imagine that he wants to hear how hard that is—and that we know he'll help. As the bullied David says at the end of our Psalm: "But as for me, I trust in you" (v. 23 NIV).

Bridging the Gap

Father, I think it's time to beg. _____ is dealing with the kind of cruelty no child of yours should experience, initiate, or witness. Please, bridge the gap between her need to cope with and heal the meanness in the world and what I am able to teach her. I do trust in you. Amen.

In Closing...

This is my favorite kind of email from tween girls—next, of course, to the ones that say, "You are my favorite author, Nancy Rue. Your books rock!"

- "My mom probably knows me better than I know myself."
- "Each night my amazing mom lets me rattle on about everything, and I mean everything, that happened that day."
- "I have a really good relationship with my mom and I can pretty much talk to her about anything and everything."
- "I love that when my mom talks to me, she doesn't talk down to me and treat me like a kid. She treats me like an adult."

That tells me that moms are doing so much "right." That you're raising your daughters with all the love that's in you and all the Holy Spirit that's in you—and it's working. It tells me that someday you will get an email like this one from my thirty-year-old daughter:

You are the best mom ever. The best thing you ever taught me was to listen to myself and trust myself, and you taught me that by listening to me and trusting me, and not judging me when I made mistakes or choices that aren't mistakes, but which differ from what your choices would be. You mastered the balance between being the mom, the authority, the guide, and then turning into the friend when it was appropriate. I love being your friend.

That was in response to an email I sent to her:

Thanks for being my friend as well as my daughter. No other woman in the world knows me exactly the way you do, and I think one of the most important desires we all have is to be known and understood. Perhaps that's why I'm working so hard on this book for moms. I could write faster and just get it done, but I want so much to make sure moms see that they can either be an exquisite influence in their daughter's lives, or reduce them to scars that they have to spend their adult-hoods trying to heal. I want them to know that someday their daughters can be the best friends they could ever have. That's what happened to me.

That was truly my intent in writing this book for you, the moms of mini-women. I didn't set out to give you a step-by-step, guaranteed plan to turn your daughter into your best friend, because there is none. I've only offered guidelines and suggestions born from the wisdom I've gathered in my years as mom, teacher, writer, and lover of all things tween. Most of it, however, comes from you. If you have learned only one thing from this book, I hope it is this: that you are the only one who truly knows how to raise your daughter.

So as you go on from here with that confidence—that *God*-confidence—just keep remembering these things:

- You have wisdom. God makes sure of that. Trust it.
- You know your child. As you allow her to grow more and more into her true self, you will know her even better. And best of all, you will learn from her.
- You know yourself. You know when you're parenting authenti-cally, because it sings.

That is all. The rest is in the details, and many of them are here, in this book, whenever you want to turn back to them. If you don't find what you need, you know how to reach me. We can talk together until we uncover the answers.

I lied—that is not quite all. I want to send you off with one more piece of advice. Fall in love with your daughter. It is a divine love that brings you closer to God.

And all the mothers of mini-women said . . .

"Amen."

Moms, please feel free to contact me!
nnrue@att.net
Nancy Rue
P.O. Box 217
Lebanon, TN 37088
www.nancyrue.com

Notes

Why Do I Need an Ultimate Guide?

1. I am paraphrasing Carol Gilligan, renowned psychologist and student of adolescent female behavior. I wish I could take credit for thinking of the pizza image myself.

2. Dr. James Garbarino, *See Jane Hit* (New York: Penguin Press, 2006), 5.

3. Dr. Daniel S. Acuff and Dr. Robert H. Reiher, *Kidnapped* (Dearborn Trade Publishing, 2005), 7. Acuff and Reiher are referring to a 2003 Kaiser Foundation Report.

4. Ibid., 143.

5. Dr. Mary Manz Simon, speaking at a seminar for booksellers at the 2006 International Christian Retail Sales convention on trends in children's products. Dr. Mary has become a trend marketer as a result of raising her own three children in this whole new world.

6. Janice Chaffin, "Can Technology Buy You Love?" Posted May 4, 2009. Norton Online Living Report, www.nortononlineliving.com. Accessed August 1, 2009.

7. Simon.

8. Garbarino, 22–23. Dr. Garbarino is citing a study done with 11,000 children by psychologists J. Lawrence Aber, J. L. Brown, and S. M. Jones and published as "Developmental Trajectories Toward Violence in Middle Childhood," *Developmental Psychology* 39, no. 2 (2003): 324–48.

9. "Stomp Out Cyberbullying!" Posted 2006. Café Aspira, www.cafeaspira.com. Accessed May 2009.

10. Ken Burger, "Looking at the World Differently." Posted September 17, 2009. Darkness To Light, www.darkness2light.org. Accessed September 20, 2009.

11. 2008 Harris Poll, as quoted by Laura Bishop of WAFG-FM radio in an interview with me in August 2008.

12. Melinda Wenner, "The Serious Need for Play." Posted February 2009. *Scientific American*, www.scientificamerican.com. Accessed February 12, 2010.
13. Simon.
14. Amy Green, "Finding My Religion," *Sojourners*, June 2008.
15. Michael Y. Sokolove, *Warrior Girls* (Simon and Schuster, 2008), 224.
16. Simon.
17. That's backed up by the aforementioned Harris Poll, in which 60 percent of the tweenage girls surveyed said they still rely on their parents more than they do on their peers, although peer pressure starts to play a larger role as they enter middle school.
18. Garbarino, 225.
19. Again, the Harris Poll concurs. Seventy percent say they turn to their faith for help with difficult issues.

Chapter 1: Will My Real Daughter Please Step Forward?

1. Neil Howe and William Strauss, *Millennials Rising: The Next Great Generation* (New York: Vintage Books, 2000), 20.
2. Ibid., 19.
3. Ibid., 164.
4. Dr. Mary Manz Simon, speaking at a seminar for booksellers at the 2006 International Christian Retail Sales convention on trends in children's products.
5. "Tweens Favor Inhalants to Get High." Posted March 13, 2008, CBS News Health, www.cbsnews.com.
6. Dr. Dan B. Allender, *How Children Raise Parents* (Colorado Springs: Waterbrook, 2003), 8.
7. Dr. Mary Manz Simon, *Trend-Savvy Parenting* (Carol Stream, Ill.: Tyndale, 2006), 3.

Chapter 2: Is She Herself, or Is She You?

1. True Colors™ I first learned about this concept at a Theatre and Education conference in 1993, but it has been expanded significantly since then. For more information, google The Source in You.
2. *The Book of Common Prayer* (Seabury Press, 1976), 302. The promise made by parents and godparents in the sacrament of holy baptism, when a child is presented to be baptized.

Chapter 3: Why Can't She Just Be Herself?

1. Emily Hancock, PhD, quoted by Elium and Elium in *Raising a Daughter* (Berkeley, Calif.: Celestial Arts, 2003), 52.

2. Allender, *How Children Raise Parents*, 25.
3. Sari Solden, *Women with Attention Deficit Disorder* (Ann Arbor, 1999), viii.
4. Ibid.
5. Elium and Elium, *Raising a Daughter*, 306.
6. Ibid., 308.
7. Ibid.

Chapter 4: What Does She See When She Looks in the Mirror?

1. "How the Industry Is Changing," *Seventeen* (May 2007), 149.
2. Janice Dickinson, quoted in "Role Models," *Seventeen* (May 2007), 149.
3. Elium and Elium, *Raising a Daughter*, 59–60.
4. Howe and Strauss, *Millennials Rising*, 19.
5. Elium and Elium, *Raising a Daughter*, 61.
6. Nancy Rue, *Beauty Lab* (Grand Rapids: Zonderkidz, 2007), 14–16.

Chapter 5: Passing the Beauty Care Baton

1. Dr. Mary Manz Simon, speaking at a seminar for booksellers at the 2006 International Christian Retail Sales convention on trends in children's products.
2. Ibid.
3. Rue, *Beauty Lab*, 17–18.
4. Ibid., 19.

Chapter 6: "But You're Beautiful on the Inside ..."

1. Rue, *Beauty Lab*, 86.
2. Dan Kimball, *The Emerging Church* (Grand Rapids: Zondervan, 2003), 136.
3. *The Book of Common Prayer*, 857.

Part 3: Who Are You, and What Have You Done with My Little Girl?

1. Paul Caminiti, at a "Tween Meeting" held at Zondervan Publishing, June 2006.
2. Lisa Marshall, "Early Bloomers," *Alternative Medicine* (September 2006), 60.
3. Ibid.

Chapter 7: The Biggest Deal Since Potty Training

1. Elium and Elium, *Raising a Daughter*, 67.
2. Quoted by Howe and Strauss in *Millennials Rising*, 190.

3. Tom Randall, "25 percent of teen girls have an STD, study reveals," *Nashville Tennessean*. Randall is quoting statistics from the Centers for Disease Control and Prevention.

4. "The Real Costs of Teen Pregnancy," Washington, D.C. National Campaign to Prevent Teen Pregnancy, September 2006.

5. Elium and Elium, *Raising a Daughter*, 319.

6. Nancy Rue, *Body Talk* (Grand Rapids: Zonderkidz, 2007), 125.

Chapter 8: The Care and Feeding of a Tween

1. Marilyn Lipsey, master barber at Salon YaYa, in Nashville, Tennessee, in a September 24, 2009 interview.

2. Gloria Beim, M.D., and Ruth Winter, M.S., *The Female Athlete's Body Book* (Contemporary Books, 2003), 217.

3. Sokolove, *Warrior Girls*, 189.

4. National Health and Nutrition Examination Survey, 2005.

5. Beim and Winter, 217.

6. Ibid., 218.

7. Sokolove, 226.

8. Ibid., 235.

9. "Americans Eat Out ...," *Business Wire*, June 14, 2006; backed up by research firm NPD Group, January 2009.

10. Howe and Strauss, *Millennials Rising*, 170.

11. Rue, *Body Talk*, 111.

12. Stephen Arterburn and Dr. Linda Mintle, *Lose It for Life* (Integrity Publishing, 2004).

13. Eugene Peterson, *Christ Plays in 10,000 Places* (Grand Rapids: Eerdmans, 2005), 215.

14. *Journal of Pediatrics* study, 2006.

15. 2008 CDC study, reported on the "Youth Violence" website, Summer 2009.

Chapter 9: The Gospel according to Friends

1. Elium and Elium, *Raising a Daughter*, 76.

2. Rue, *Girl Politics*, 110.

3. Dale McElhinney, doctor of psychology and therapist in private practice, in an August 2006 interview.

4. Garbarino, *See Jane Hit*, 108.

5. Barbara Coloroso, *The Bully, the Bullied, and the Bystander* (New York: HarperCollins, 2003).

Chapter 10: When It Gets Ugly

1. *Journal of Pediatrics* study, 2006.
2. 2008 CDC study, reported on the "Youth Violence" website, Summer 2009.
3. Elium and Elium, *Raising a Daughter*, 76.
4. Rue, *Girl Politics*, 110.
5. Dale McElhinney, doctor of psychology and therapist in private practice, in an August 2006 interview.
6. Garbarino, *See Jane Hit*, 108.
7. Barbara Coloroso, *The Bully, the Bullied, and the Bystander* (New York: Harper Collins, 2003).
8. Elizabeth Griffin, family therapist specializing in teen issues.
9. Rue, *Girl Politics*, 128.

Subject Index